Nightmare Made of Dreams

A Conservative Scholar Assesses Our Nation's Declining Taste for Self-Sufficiency

John R. Harris, Ph.D.

Nightmare Made of Dreams
John R. Harris

Cover photo and design by John Harris.

To Dr. James Newsom,
a rare true friend I discovered in the Ivory Tower...
who, as it happens, understands both history and politics
far better than I ever will. May such superiority
not cost him many a night's sleep!

Cum omnia quae excesserunt modum noceant, periculosissima
felicitatis intemperantia est. Movet cerebrum, in vanas mentes
imagines evocat, multum inter falsum ac verum mediae caliginis fundit.

"Although everything that exceeds the limits of moderation can harm,
the intemperance of good fortune is uniquely dangerous. It leads
reason astray, evokes fantasies in idle minds, and spills a layer of dense
fog upon the line dividing falsehood from truth."

Seneca, *De Providentia* 4.10

Other Books by John R. Harris Published Through Amazon Kindle

Educational:
The Traditional Mind in Greco-Roman Antiquity and Ancient Ireland (essays)
An Introductory Course in Greek and Latin Grammar and Vocabulary
(textbook)
Three Medieval Celtic Renditions of an Ancient Indo-European Myth
(translations)

Non-Fiction:
Climbing Backward Out of Caves (Christian apologetics)
Literary Decline and the Death of the Soul (literary criticism/philosophy)
We Even Saw Figures Tending Fires (faith/philosophy)

Baseball
Hitting Secrets From Baseball's Graveyard (history/instruction)
Landing Safeties (instruction)
Key to a Cold City (history)
Metal Ropes (instruction)

Fiction:
El Moreno, Vendetta Di Dio (novel)
Eventually, It All Gets Used (poetry)
A Sleepless Man Might Earn Two Wages (short stories)
Worse by Seven (novel)
Ivory Gutter Shining Bright (short stories)
Footprints in the Snow of the Moon (novel)

CONTENTS

Author's Preface

As I sit writing, only a week has passed since I definitively terminated the website of the moribund online quarterly *Praesidium*, the flagship publication of the Center for Literate Values. Both the journal and its organization were my "children": I edited one and founded the other. The book in your hands would not exist but for those labors of love, for over half of the essays appearing in the present collection were rescued from the good ship *Praesidium* before she went down. Her cargo included a great many years of my reflections. With allowances made for an early and minor adjustment in the organization's name, I had operated the Center (a 501[c]3 charity incorporated under educational and religious rubrics) for two decades.

There was indeed much for our staff to reflect upon in the first years of the new millennium—and all too few resources for broadcasting our insights, alas. As a professor of English, a father, a husband, and the partial caretaker of an invalid mother, I myself never seemed to have sufficient time for publicizing our endeavors... but, frankly, I don't think any amount of devotion would have kept our small fleet (including its flagship) off the rocks. Though I had begun the venture convinced that a critical mass of college educators, mostly in private schools, actually loved our cultural heritage and had not pledged themselves to subverting or eradicating it, we couldn't break even. Ever. Generating a faithful body of subscribers to the website and readers of the journal proved too stringent a measure of that "broad but quiet" support. Most professors, like most human beings, allow a substantial gap to open between what they believe in word and what they practice in deed. Subscribing takes a few dollars, and reading takes an hour now and then. Our fair-weather supporters always managed to find slightly better things to do with their money and time.

This is probably the epitaph of many a civilization: "The majority didn't want the temple's columns and architraves to come crashing down... but there was wine to taste and a dog to be groomed." I'm afraid, nowadays in my retirement—from academe, if not from writing—that I have about as much use for people's stated beliefs as I do for the pair of infrared binoculars I've never fully removed from their gift-wrapping. Even the well educated—perhaps especially they—will moan, "This new edict is outrageous! It's an insult to the principles of any free society! Things must change... somebody must be held accountable!" And having consigned all the blame to "things" and "somebody", they continue their downhill amble with, perhaps, the slightest alteration of course to see if the easier road they remember may be hiding just behind the new hedge.

Thanks to such moral and intellectual laziness, the typical American citizen doesn't strike me as a very likely heir to the future of secure freedom that our forefathers wished to bequeath to us. I write those words no longer even confident of just what a "typical American" might look like. Our decay is already so far along that we ourselves are apt to run to a mirror if asked about our identity. We need to double-check our race, gender, and age before confirming *who we are*. A shallow, arbitrary tribal range of allegiances has been thrust upon us, and too many of us too obediently select among the provided options. We are no longer souls in largely circumstantial bodies who seek our purpose in the supreme God of Goodness. We are Citizen X, white and privileged; Citizen Y, black and victimized; Citizen Z, Hispanic (now a racial designation, though indecipherable as such) and winner of the keys to most major US cities.

Plotting the future of a society so fragmented, incoherent, invertebrate, morally anemic, and intellectually torpid as ours isn't a great challenge. It's depressing... but it's not hard. I wouldn't have written that a few years ago, when many alternative routes still lay open to us and when, as editor of *Praesidium*, I liked nothing more than speculating about how we might reanimate ourselves. Even over the past month, during the work of gathering together my better essays from so much time spent pondering our collective destiny, I began in the naïve confidence that my chronological trail of reflections would end up describing some kind of forward progress. It didn't. Instead, I found that I had merely traveled in circles: I see certain things more clearly today, but I think they were visible enough two decades back. Let me explain.

As I reviewed my personal submissions to *Praesidium* from the twenty-first century's first decade, I discovered a robust, optimistic sort of "survivalism": or, as I would prefer to call it, an aspiration to self-sufficiency based upon growing one's own food. If only we could take more of our essential needs directly into our hands, removing numerous middlemen—the wholesaler, the retailer, the Bureau of Perfection field agent, the Office of Price Controls administrator—then we wouldn't have to be anybody's victim. We could take care of ourselves, and we could look out for our immediate neighbors. "Frontier virtue" wouldn't be a bad descriptor of my mindset. (The Latin word *praesidium*, by the way, means "outpost" or "garrison"—a post of guards on a frontier. I learned only a short while ago that its demotic Spanish morph means "jail" in Mexico, a shift suggesting the relationship that our major immigrant contingent has enjoyed over the centuries with the government intended to protect it.)

I still believe in independent food-growing—more than ever. The other thing I do in retirement (besides write, I mean) is plant orchards. At the moment, I have the modest beginnings of a survival-level pecan crop, a nice annual haul of apples, and a good supply of antioxidant-rich fruits like gojis and blueberries. Plants, I find, are altogether more cooperative than people. They can't tell you in so many words when you've made some bonehead blunder about soil selection or placement with respect to sunlight... but they send signals in their own cryptic language. They don't whine, and they don't go lazy. They fight silently until the battle for life is utterly lost—and if you successfully renew their chances, they perk up without lingering in a bid for sympathy or sulking in a coy attempt to guilt-trip.

I love my plants, though I may never live to see them prosper in a way that fills my own table. One day they may feed my son and his family from boughs stretching forty feet up in the air—but it may be a day (dare I say it?) when much of our nation fights starvation after an Electro-Magnetic Pulse has fried the power grid or after politically engineered race riots have rendered city streets unnavigable. When I wrote this book's initial long essay about self-sufficiency for our quarterly journal ("Freedom Grows on Trees"—still my favorite), I was thinking in terms of spiritual satisfaction and liberation from squalid marketplace employment rather than in terms of mere, bare survival. Over the years, my recurrence to the theme of working the good earth has, I find, allowed a certain exhilaration to leak away through the seams, until the final pieces in *Praesidium* (and in this anthology) almost appear reduced to the formula, "agriculture or death".

I'm sorry for that decay in my optimism... sorry for readers who may struggle through this decade of essays culled from the journal's corpse, but sorry also for myself—for my wilting spirit. Yet what I can promise everyone, including myself, is that I have never dressed up my writing on the subject of freedom to flatter a broader audience with "cheerleading". I accept the designation "conservative" because I believe our tried-and-true traditions to be worth conserving—because I believe them necessary to conserve if we are to follow our higher rather than our lower nature. I am not the sort of "neo-con" who chants, "Jobs, jobs, jobs! Better market, higher dividends, healthier 401k's! Go, team!" Even at my most optimistic in earlier days, I was deeply concerned (what teacher of literature would not be?) that our contemporary capitalist economy, based on multiplied markets in frivolity to feed multiplied cravings for gadgetry, undermined my notion of the noble, and even the manly (cf. Socrates' exclamation in the agora, "How many things there are of which I have no need!").

At its most homiletic level, then, this collection seeks not to convince you that all is going south very fast and that you need to mount a fifty-caliber machine gun at your bullet-proofed attic window... Heaven forbid! No, it seeks to win you to the charms of true freedom: of being your own boss, making your own mistakes, learning your own hard lessons, producing your own successes, and feeding—at last—your own family. I want you to see the glorious possibilities of such genuine, *conservative* freedom: an independence made all the more feasible by technological innovation, but ultimately reliant upon a hard-working relationship with sun, rain, and soil. I want to make the case to you that the true conservative actually *conserves*: that he clings zealously to what nature has given us and passes along reverently what culture has bequeathed to us.

Or do I? Well, at one time I did... and at certain moments, perhaps I still do. The truth is that I couldn't simply organize by chronology the essays I retrieved from the journal's wreckage, moving from earliest to latest; I couldn't, because my estimate of our social and cultural (not to mention political) trajectory kept circling my head like an ominous bird of prey. That's what I've been trying to express, in very (I fear) circular fashion. Absorbed by my speculations, I would for a few months admire a rift in the clouds... and then, for a few ensuing months, see a storm staring to crowd out the blue. I honestly don't know where "erchomenology" ("the science of things to come") leaves me as I contemplate the almost chaotic picture of our advancing technology vaulting over a people whose impulses seem ever more primitive. Half a dozen paragraphs ago, I claimed that plotting our future was all too easy now... but what will be the *specific* driver of our catastrophe, I wonder?

The penultimate essay of this collection suggests that a natural calamity of some sort—an EMP (yes, a fully natural solar storm can create one), a supervolcanic eruption, a collision with an asteroid—might force those of us who survive the initial shock to rediscover our connection with the land. There's that rift in the clouds again! Not a very uplifting exhortation to learn gardening, is it? But then, the specter of such necessity always seems to have peered over my earlier writing, too, if only in the less apocalyptic form of civil unrest. I suppose my gyrations are a little like the starry-eyed technologist's who tells us, "Get on board! Learn the new program! It's fun! It's so convenient! And anyway, it will inevitably take over the future, and those who don't master it will die."

Technology: that came to occupy the middle tier of my book's eventual tripartite division. The praises of the technically assisted pastoral life are Section One, and the dark forebodings about a hyper-urbanized slaughterhouse whose architecture we have insistently preferred to the barn's or the granary's fill Section Three. The intermediate section, I decided, was best occupied by more a adequate explanation of how I managed to ride the circle 180 degrees from Arcadia to Dystopia. Technology is the train that transports us to the "Auschwitz quadrant". To be sure, high tech can maximize the productivity of our manual labor and minimize the energy expended in our comfortable, if humble, residences and communities. I love useful technology, as I love my orchards—and as I love genuine free enterprise. But a kind of Charybdis keeps us circling around the vortex: a taste for artificial food artificially produced undermines the good food we grow with a clever touch of artifice. The mass-marketing of exotic "fake" diversions makes us view self-sufficiency as boring, and whatever pious acceptance of cycle lingers in us now appears caveman-dull. I won't deny that our shift to frivolous affluence has made American society the most prosperous in the world's history, from a GDP perspective. Are we not very lately, however—especially the self-styled conservatives among us who long preached this gospel of affluence—coming to understand how vulnerable such habits have made us to evil actors like the governing elite of Communist China?

This is the point where my brief preface should bundle itself into a tidy summary statement; and, if I were to accede to reverend literary convention, that summary would be "upbeat". I would write, "Taking all in all, we still have reason to believe that the sun will break through, if only we work hard..." and so forth. After all, why would anyone wish to labor through a book that does *not* finish in some kind of optimism or hope? In the interest of honesty, however, I prefer to leave the provision of hope to the spirits of those who may make the effort of reading on. *My* one hope is that the effort may not prove immense.

And if scarcely anyone does, in fact, read on because... well, because there are places to go, things to see, and "stuff" to do, then my adventure in publishing will simply continue the noble tradition of that great unread quarterly, *Praesidium*!

J.R.H.
Rome, Georgia
Fall, 2019

PART ONE

Freedom Would Have Grown on Trees

Freedom Grows on Trees: A Eudemonist Economics

Πόσων ἐγω χρείαν οὐκ ἔχω ~ "How many things there are of which I have no need!"
Socrates beholding the agora's merchandise (Diogenes Laertius 2.25)

This article was originally published in two successive issues of the online
*journal **Praesidium**: 8.1 and 8.2 (Winter 2008 and Spring 2008).*

I. The Tension Between Capitalism and Culture

I worry about the future. No doubt, every sane adult of average intelligence has always shared my concern… to a point. Yet I suspect that my anxiety—and that of my contemporaries (for we are generally a very worried bunch)—has something unique about it. Men have been farmers, hunters, herds, and fishers for most of human history: technically, since before historical records began. The cultivator would naturally worry about too much or too little rain. In many settings, starvation waited on the leeward shore of this unease. We do not nowadays fear starvation in the West. Between technological advances and socialized governments, we enjoy the luxury of biting our nails above a fine-mesh safety net. At the same time, we have never been farther—as individuals—from the food which actually enters our mouths. The frontier farmer whose crop goes bad might make shift in a variety of ways, from harvesting wild nuts to trapping prairie fowl to roasting locusts. (Hunger, as a very ancient saying has it, makes a good seasoning.) He continued to have a large measure of control over his survival even in the cruelest of times. If he possessed any sense at all, furthermore, he would have preserved whatever might be salted, pickled, or sealed from previous years of plenty. If he didn't manage to slither beneath the Grim Scythe, he could probably blame his lack of hard work and frugal planning for it in his last breath.

It's different with us. We who are virtually assured of survival—and survival, at that, in a state of relative luxury—cannot depend upon our strong hands and our moral stamina to get us through. On the contrary, we *pay* for our food and *grow* none of it (taking us, again, as typical individuals). More likely than not, the farmer or hunter in us will *inhibit* success to the extent that he clings to our consciousness. To put it bluntly, remuneration seems to have become inversely proportional in our Brave New World to physical exertion, sobriety, and husbandry: the silliest live the handsomest. The liveliest markets are in frivolities. The only jobs still requiring sweat suggest fragmentary caricatures of yesteryear's independent cultivator, hauler, or builder: tasks that might be performed by machines, and have been so—but that we lately discovered could be more cheaply assigned to human drudges. And the drudges collect their pay (with or without valid documentation of citizenship) and pile into the same supermarkets, shopping malls, and car dealerships as do we—their white-collar, fair-skinned handlers—to pay the going rate for staples and vanities, having no more proprietary a right to lettuces or shingled roofs than the more costly machine which declined to replace their labor....

We must not join their ranks, we tell ourselves, or allow our children to sink so low. We must struggle after the "better life" of fatter paychecks, secured by selling discounted drugs over the Internet or the latest cellular phones at Radio Shack or guaranteed tax advice at H&R Block. For some reason, we regard perspiring under an August sun as a betrayal of those intellectual gifts which entitled us to attend college, whereas none of the latter occupations is received as a slap in the face to our English or History Major. We have been well conditioned, like drudges of a higher order.

But I am not of this "we", much to my distress. I love to write, yet could never uncover a market for writers in my working lifetime. The prospect of hawking cell phones to pay the bills appalls me no less than if I were required to box the coffin-nails of literate culture on an assembly line—which is, in fact, my metaphorical estimate of electronic communication's current threat. I would truly, and substantially, prefer to grow and harvest fruit (as I do in the most modest of ways on my tiny patch of property). The endeavor would be far less gainful financially, but far more congenial to that independence of spirit which the literate life awakened in me from an early age. I do not wish to utter absurdities, to make a frivolous display of myself, or to extol playthings that strike me as subtly pernicious in order to put food in my mouth. Feed my family I must; but to draw a salary in return for behavior sometimes nothing short of morally loathsome strikes me as doing such violence to the conscience that one would be dishonest not to call it servitude.

I—and those like me (for there are more than a few, though we are not the great "we", apparently)—am a slave; or, at best, my economic existence is a constant battle against becoming a slave. I have heard all my life that we of the progressive West enjoy a "strong economy". In my middle years, however, I increasingly find myself wondering why the strength of an economy should be defined by dividends paid to investors or the degree of ascent in the Gross National Product's vector. Should not *human happiness* serve as at least one ground of assessment? And if a man who must fawn before fools or peddle snake oil throughout the week is less happy than a man who digs his own carrots and potatoes, in what sense may our economy correctly be called a triumph over yesteryear's?

In this essay's title, I borrow the word employed by Aristotle— eudemonist—when he made his case for the *goodness* of material happiness. I am enough of a Stoic to balk at his argument; but here, in matters economic, the criterion of happiness seems much more appropriate to me. Granted, the ultimate measure of a human being is moral rather than economic: it lies in his or her success at ignoring specific conditions to serve a purpose beyond the will of the flesh. Yet the flesh is instrumental in these high aspirations (which may well be the innocuous gist of Aristotle's case). It must eat and sleep in order to build and lift a Jacob's ladder for the spirit. There must, after all, be a *sufficiency of material things.*

As a student of the humanities and a devoted servitor of the literate life's higher rewards, I shall contend in what follows that our pursuit of winning our daily bread, right here and right now, has heeded the flesh too narrowly. Our habitual "work life" has *not* been well designed by recent practice to accomplish the ends of spiritual enrichment, individual awakening, enlisted creativity, and other worthy destinations valorized by the great traditions of classical duty and Christian abnegation. We have turned our collective back on a noble past. As a capitalist economy dedicated to marketing or exploiting ever newer products and drawing consumers ever farther (therefore) from a contentment with the status quo, our system is resonantly *not conservative* in any meaningful sense. Indeed, I maintain that inasmuch as contemporary capitalism feeds the progressive impatience with the present, it is every bit as destabilizing to happiness as the self-contradictory Marxian quest for a world devoid of envy, laziness, despair, and spirituality. Though the two systems radically disagree about human nature, they are alike in eschewing fixity—a similarity which suffices to make both inimical to the cause of humane culture.

II. The Failure of Free Trade to Bestow Freedom

I hasten to add that the notion of capitalism's disjuncture from conservatism is nothing new. Among a very select circle of intellectuals in the mid-twentieth century, it was indeed something of a commonplace. Richard Weaver, author of *Ideas Have Consequences*, observed in another setting that "capitalism cannot be conservative in the true sense as long as its reliance is upon industrialism, whose very nature it is to unsettle any establishment and initiate the endless innovation of technological 'progress'."[1] The lucidity of this remark is of the order of "two plus two equals four": a system that depends upon the rapid obsolescence of purchases to bring consumers back to the store for "new and improved" versions could not be more definitively anti-conservative. The sublime Russell Kirk raised this objection, essentially, in response to Clinton Rossiter's highly tendentious *Conservatism in America* (1955): "A conservative order is not the creation of the free entrepreneur...."[2] Businessmen sell things, and they sell more things and things of greater variety when the consuming public has more and greater "needs". The solicitation of such yens and itches is not the work of a Socrates, a Diogenes, a Seneca, a Marcus Aurelius, an Augustine, or a Francis—or, for that matter, of a Confucius or a Gautama Buddha. Profit margins are uncomfortable closets for cultural treasures and timeless wisdom.

Yet in Kirk's reflections, one may already see an unfortunate paradox beginning to knot the corridors of a labyrinth. The conservation of a precious cultural bequest must not be equated with blind atavism, for the life of our forefathers—if we go back very far indeed, into the shadows of prehistory—possessed no culture worthy of the name. Our heritage of humane institutions and uplifting creations, then, is at least somewhat dependent upon a degree of technical innovation capable of freeing up time for leisurely endeavor. The survivor of a plane crash does not reconstruct his shattered guitar without first assembling some sort of shelter and retrieving or gathering a minimum of food. We can imagine very early examples of our species toiling away at cave paintings of bison or mastodons whose accuracy and finesse a bright kindergartner could surpass today. Surely we may therefore say that we have come a long way—and surely we *must* say so before we claim that what remains in our cultural tracks is worthy of bundling into the present.

Kirk seems to stress such progress in the critical seventh chapter of *A Program for Conservatives*. His explicit theme here is the absurdity of a blunt, sweeping egalitarianism. "Man was not created for equality," he writes, "but for the struggle upward from brute nature toward the world that is not terrestrial. The principle of justice, in consequence, is not enslavement to a uniform condition, but liberation from arbitrary restraints upon his right to be himself."[3] Nature is not self-evidently good in this view as it is in the romantic liberalism descended from Jean-Jacques Rousseau. Savages are not noble. They are exceptionally clever animals whose life nonetheless ends without having fulfilled a higher purpose. Cultivation of the spirit must awaken them to a higher calling just as cultivation of the land will at last free them from having to scavenge every day for bare survival. Some will contribute more than others to the great awakening. The essence of culture is precisely that it makes of these unequal contributions a common legacy. "Ability," concludes Kirk, "is the factor which enables men to lift themselves from savagery to civilization, and which helps to distinguish the endeavors of men from the routine existence of insects."[4] Though the emphasis in this passage differs from mine, falling upon the individual's need for spiritual elbow-room rather than upon the community's profit from such generosity, the positions are two sides of the same coin. A single brilliant innovation can turn an entire tribe or ethnos into an elite. As long as the collective recognizes and indulges individual sources of brilliance, it may paradoxically be said to honor a grand tradition rather than to stagnate or degenerate. Its conserving efforts are focused not just on knowledge of what fruits to eat or what herbs to use in cures—an attachment often more superstitious than cultural—but on the technique of inquiry which allowed such discoveries to be made.

I called this dependency of cultural conservatism upon technical innovation an *unfortunate* paradox because the forces which create a grand tradition, alas, can also undo it simply by operating in their established, conserved manner. Western culture has been engineered by at least two such dubious vectors, both vaulting from the consequences of alphabetic literacy. One is individualism. Reading and writing (especially writing, for reading usually begins as and stays an oral exercise over many comfortable generations) draw people in upon themselves, upon their inner voices and private spaces. The worth of the individual human being is first widely conceded in literate cultures, where that individual first becomes assertive.

Yet the enfranchisement of so many autonomous units can also exert a fatal drag upon society's energy when their various assertions become plangent and petulant for lack of proper tempering. That is, individualism has a tendency to sour into narcissism as its creative vigor solves ever finer, less pressing needs, and we are left with a throng of spoiled brats.

The second worrisome impetus inspired by literacy is, of course, scientific inquiry. The alphabet is itself a highly analytical and abstract tool, dividing words into component sounds and then representing like sounds with an arbitrary cipher. Minds immersed in literacy engage in dissecting and reconstituting sensory experiences with a rapid dexterity that soon grows unwitting. The literate mind comes to "read" its physical environment quite fluidly, parsing disparate phenomena readily into a limited and shared pool of hidden causes. It gives us technology at a rate never approached in any other sort of human society—and hence, eventually, the laziness of heavy dependency upon technology, and also the tasteless infatuation with anything new. "Pure" science becomes "applied" science with the same dismaying acceleration as we observe in the individualist's slide into vain egotism. These movements which have bestowed upon our culture the inestimable knowledge of what first to cultivate and how best to cultivate it always have the potential to plow the garden topsy-turvy just as its plants are bearing their richest fruit.

The central problem, then, for a conservative economy—an economy that would hold onto the best of the past rather than routinely render yesteryear's trappings obsolete—is how to abstain from such suicide. How does an inventive, progressive culture preserve those elements essential to cultural identity rather than tinkering with or marginalizing them until they vanish? The urgency of this question, I should stress, will be recognized only by those of conservative tastes and convictions, for the contemporary form of liberalism has discarded all overt submission to the classical or universal. ("Universalist" is indeed a word of reproach in academic circles, the reasons for its opprobrium assumed to be self-evident.) Today's liberal is a materialist, and hence believes that happiness can be found only in one's circumstances. To the extent that circumstances are manipulated to produce more happiness— more chickens in the pot, more indoor plumbing, more health care, lower-priced football tickets—an economy achieves superiority. Nothing deserves to be retained *per se*: everything is susceptible to complete overhaul, and awaits only the right technological advance to visit the scrap yard for meltdown. Of course, such carnal wants as those for food, shelter, good health, and spectacle-class amusements are invariable and hence universal, after a fashion. Biology is allowed to decree universality among progressives: it is the materialist's version of destiny. Here the liberal may even locate a few shreds of lingering spirituality: any resuscitation of the inner beast repressed by bourgeois hypocrisy, from a sublime hike up a mountainside to a tawdry program of sexual experimentation, may qualify as an epiphany. On those rare occasions when the liberal admits that contemplating the sunrise from a peak really is sublime, and *not* a mere response to the call of the wild, he or she risks walking a few steps along a trail once dear to humane cultural conservatism—and now largely abandoned, to be sure, by "conservatives" who plead the economy as an excuse for their barbarity, their *progressive* energy.

Yet the conservative's paradox, I reiterate, is much the more imposing. Historically, we cannot escape the sad fact that self-styled conservatives have permitted their affinity for individual rights and robust creativity to ally itself with laissez-fairest, "anything goes" capitalist ventures. In reading over the works of the late Oriana Fallaci, I lately happened upon a perfect example of mid-twentieth-century hubris emanating from a figure who most certainly identified himself with the political Right. The scene was Saigon, shortly before the Tet Offensive. Fallaci was treated to an extended interview with venture-capitalist millionaire Barry Zorthion, who told her (while chauffeuring her on a tour of the area in his private pontoon-plane) about his grand plans for Southeast Asia. They did not include preserving much of anything: they projected, in fact, a rabid zeal for changing everything.

> Mr. Zorthian is a 54-year-old of Armenian origin, with a great nose, a great paunch, a great faith in this war, and an unshakable conviction that "the United States should teach civilization to these poor wretches who have never heard anyone mention democracy and technological progress." In other words, Mr. Zorthian maintains that America is doing Vietnam an immense favor, not only from a military but also from an economic point of view. "Once the war is won," he says, "Vietnam will become rich like Japan, modern like Japan, respected like Japan—because we'll teach her to harvest her resources on an industrial basis. Factories, skyscrapers, and highways will spring up everywhere, and the Mekong will be humming like Florida." The suspicion that the Delta's peasantry may not want it to hum like Florida—that they may want only to live in peace among their hand-planted, hand-harvested rice—doesn't so much as cross his mind.[5]

I shall refrain from drawing parallels with foreign policy of our own time—they are accessible enough in Zorthian's dual hymn to democracy and high-tech capitalism that the reader may make connections as desired. I will stress only that this largely self-appointed emissary of "Western values" (as they are understood by such people) not only registers triumph in Florida's having been "developed": he is eager to inflict similar transformations upon parts of the world about whose culture he knows nothing nor can imagine any lesson being worth the effort of study. His "go-getter" Yankee spirit, when exported to go get profits beyond his native shores, can discern in ancient religions and social customs no more than childish obstacles. Whatever his independence may be said to "conserve" (in a tightly pinched meaning) of traditional rugged individualism, his attitude and actions could not be more transparently anti-conservative in every profound sense. Face it: if the new order of which he dreams were motivated more strongly by a desire to bring electricity and hygiene to the peasantry, we would be witnessing the resurrection of FDR's Tennessee Valley Authority under Eastern eyes. The Soviet Union's criminal devastation of Lake Baikal is perhaps even more akin—for dams shift regional balances in nature yet leave their region fairly natural. Zorthian's vision is so progressive that relics of nature would seem somewhat humiliating within it, signs of wasted space.

As for theory rather than practice, nominally conservative economists were authoring a doctrine of free trade throughout the mid-century. There was something of the primal barter at the logic's foundation. Two men want to make an exchange, they dicker, and finally they cut a deal. Why create a bunch of abstracted, bureaucratically enforced rules in order to placate other people far away from the interests of these two? If one party happens to speak a different language and live on the other side of a river declared to be the national boundary... well, a man should still be a man: his autonomy to trade a horse or swap grain for bacon is still really no one's business but his own, if we imagine life on the frontier. This, indeed, was the *old* way, a way that had worked for millennia before the first map was ever drawn.

Naturally, my homespun images are a very poor crash course in the libertarian doctrine of Milton Friedman. I hope that my highly simplistic presentation of issues beyond my ability to explain fully, however, betrays a certain sympathy. People should live free. The conservative, especially, with his belief in a metaphysical purpose to human life, should insist not just upon our right to be frugal, but also upon our right to choose risky options, to make bad choices producing instructive failures, and generally to grow as a moral being. In the broadest sense, perhaps the idea behind free trade is not merely to be allowed to learn that cheaper shoes from overseas fall apart sooner: perhaps there is an implied civic calling to save one's fellow citizens from living in a fool's paradise of artificial protections aimed at postponing hard realities; for the shoes from overseas may *not* fall apart—we may need to stop making shoes and start making satellites.

The free-trader, in this view, is supposed to be a mature globalist, not a ruthless adventurer. In the words of Friedman's distinguished contemporary, Henry Hazlitt, "The art of economics consists in looking not merely at the immediate but at the longer effects of any act or policy; it consists in tracing the consequences of that policy not merely for one group but for all groups."[6] Paying "real world" value for goods and services is facing up to the "longer effects". It forces the diehard traditionalist to admit with traditional resignation that, while there may be nothing new under the sun, neither does anything under the sun last forever.

Who would have guessed half a century ago that indexing prices to the international market would come to be less the mark of dry common sense than—once again—of giddy progressivism? Yet so it has happened. With respect both to the individual barterer and the entire society seeking to avoid self-delusion, free trade has forged heavy shackles. Its original architects (going back to the sainted Adam Smith) could not foresee that huge multinational corporations would exploit grossly unequal economic and social conditions around the globe to grind out the cheapest possible product. Half a century ago, specifically, American workers were having to learn the hard lesson that their destiny lay in becoming highly skilled—that unskilled manual labor could be found elsewhere in abundance and at a discount. Free trade thus ushered us, certain sectors kicking and screaming, into a golden age of technological innovation. This *floruit* lasted a generation or two… and then the rest of the world began to produce technicians and engineers as competent as our own, but available for far less pay. As we have watched "outsourcing" blaze its somber trail with the impeccable logic of greater profits, we have seen—just as logically—the lead in the race after more refined technology slip beyond our borders, as well. The best-case scenario is that, as other nations grow more prosperous, the cost of living will rise on their shores, their social welfare programs will multiply as ours have done, and the American worker— at last willing to accept far less, like a starving laborer after a failed strike— will appear attractive once more. Our standard of living, in other words, will meet somewhere in its downward spiral the ascending standard of the Third World. Economically, we shall have created the Planet of High-Tech Lackeys.

The worst-case scenario, by the way, is that societies ruled by megalomaniac oligarchs will acquire the dangerous technologies which we have thus far kept on a creditably tight leash. Gaffes of the Chernobyl variety will inevitably turn entire cities and provinces into morgues; but beyond that, the oligarchs—whether enflamed by eschatological zealotry or simply unmoved by the prospect of killing millions—will launch doomsday weapons which we will no longer have the ability to defuse or fend off. In short, this "cold market logic" could well be embarking us upon a voyage to annihilation.

That, you must agree, doesn't seem a very "conserving" sort of endeavor. Friends of the free market may object that, if the bartering frontiersman tires of buying cheap Christmas toys from China, he may always crank up his own company back home and appeal to similarly disaffected countrymen. In most particular cases, this is a practical impossibility. Take the toy industry: we have found (as if we had any right to be surprised) that a wholly unprincipled Chinese regime exports products under respected American brand names which are neither well made nor safe to handle. An opportunity for native manufacturers to rise from the ashes? Alas, no: for the brand names, despite their highly publicized embarrassments, are *just too big*. It's no longer a question of a garage-enterprise competing with a local factory: the Internet has dispensed with all locality. The presence of a company like Mattel, say, on the Net simply gobbles up the virtuous competition. There is no quaint and curious new store front on Main Street, no favorable report from a friend, no small ad in the back of Sunday's newspaper: utter oblivion, rather.

The Net was heralded by neo-conservatives like George Gilder as a kind of libertarian utopia where every vendor could display his wares, untaxed and unharassed, to the whole world. With the curious overreaching into cultural matters so typical of progressive prophets, Gilder proclaimed in 1995 that "the Internet has already made of this era a golden age of letters."[7] Yet the technology of universal publishing and publicizing turned out to be an impassible logjam. Contradicting Gilder's cornucopia of diversity and free expression, the Net, by exploiting the very finite time which most people have to spend peering at a very small window of images, has queued up all the competition for miles and then allowed only the first two or three contestants a screening. Our barterer may have the prettiest little milch-cow in five counties... but there's no fair where he may display her. His neighbors aren't even sitting on the front porch any more: they're in a dark room hunched over a monitor, perhaps Googling "heifers".

As if to accelerate the collapse of our independent small producers into a nineteenth-century mass of minimally skilled laborers servicing the edges of twenty-first century digitalized markets, free trade has even been used lately to justify the complete dissolution of national borders, permitting the unskilled masses of other countries to flood our own workplace. If this is conservatism, then one is hard-pressed to distinguish it from Soviet paternalism. In both cases, a tiny elite—political in the USSR, economic *but increasingly political* in the USA—assumes the "burden" of providing the basic needs (and, *chez nous*, a few frivolous wants) to a passive throng that lifts, hoes, and scrubs when and where it is told to. We are to believe that these masses are actually happier now that their physical survival is guaranteed, and that they are happier still because the rich are "soaked" in taxes to fund the cook's ration of weight-loss pills or to subsidize the gardener's switch to high-definition TV. That is, the masses envy the millionaire less because, after the tax man cometh, the millionaire's bank account looks infinitesimally more like theirs. Richard Layard, a British MP and professor emeritus of Economics, explains trough assignments on this behavioristic animal farm with appalling bluntness and the chilling *superbia* of a born-and-bred social messiah:

> If a person works harder and earns more, he may himself gain by increasing his income compared with other people. But the other people lose because their income now falls relative to his. He does not care that he is polluting other people in this way, so we must provide him with an automatic incentive to do so [i.e., to care]. Taxation provides exactly this incentive.[8]

Dwight Lee, whose brief essay brought this passage to my attention, places "polluting" in italics—as well he should; for it is most remarkable that elitists like Layard fancy themselves to be cultivating turnips or adjusting an artificial lake's size to duck migrations when they write of tinkering with human lives through mandatory taxation. The reader may recall my claim that contemporary liberals, being devout materialists, cannot view happiness as other than an arrangement of circumstantial factors. Layard does not recoil from the tendency of his fellow beings to envy the wealthy, let alone exhort them to build happiness's foundation on more spiritual ground: he determines, instead, how best to channel envy so that no one has too great a measure of it, quite as clinically as one might station sugar-water for laboratory mice in a Skinner Box. Yet Lee documents that both Layard and Cornell University economist Robert Frank view their proposed heavy taxation as encouraging the *hoi polloi* to spend more time with their families, and perhaps even to "develop the preferences of university professors... [for] more 'elevated' activities."[9]

We have come full circle again. Socialist theoreticians and lawmakers are concerned about "family values" and art museums, while free-traders who claim conservative colors are busily engineering a swarm of docile masses beholden to its self-taxing masters for education, health benefits, and cues about taste and morals. What, I ask, is the difference between the socialist Big Brother and the capitalist Dutch Uncle? Multi-billionaire adventurer Bill Gates has lately expressed an interest in creating European-style educational tracks, the better to separate worker-bees and queens in the hive of humanity which he claims—by divine right of net worth—to know how to prepare for tomorrow's world. Multibillionaire CEO Warren Buffitt has lately insisted that he and his financial peers—a microscopic group, to be sure—pay far too little of their earnings to the sacred cause of central government's good works. To consider these men somehow antithetical to the snobbery of "nanny totalitarianism" on the Left is absurd. In them, rather, we see that "harmony with the opposition" which the electorate is supposed to desire so piously of its representatives. The Gateses and Buffitts would have us all well groomed, fat, and content—not the least bit volatile or brooding, without the least need of Heaven—in the caressing hands of some global mass-distribution plan. A few drops of manna for all... with the servers, of course (for we are never to forget that our rulers *serve* us), deploying bowl and ladle as they see fit.

No, this is *not* any imprint or facsimile of that cultural legacy which the conservative was to conserve. On the contrary, it is a cluster of symptoms hinting at pathological egotism—the "benign tyrant", the "bully who didn't mean it". The ruthless entrepreneur is embarrassed one day to wake up and find himself incalculably rich as the corpses of slain adversaries surround him. Jules Romains precisely sketched such "social consciousness" in the unsavory person of Sammécaud, an oil magnate who seduces the wives of aristocratic colleagues because he finds them "purebred" and secretly subsidizes a Syndicalist newspaper. Musing to himself, Sammécaud reflects:

It's so chic to concern oneself about the people's plight without
being forced to do so by circumstances or self-interest—while
risking one's interests, even, and without believing in any ideology.
The secular, gratuitous generosity of the superior race ("race"
understood as "essence", a mysterious something, a spontaneous

volunteering of the elite). Ultimately, these poor buggers owe us their access to civilization, to whatever little well-being they have. And that little is already a lot.[10]

Sammécaud discovers a "fake spirituality" of sacrifice—fake because he himself is the god who deigns to bend over. His "service" is the game of an imaginative nihilist, and it besmirches the hubristic player while demeaning his pawns. If the classical view was correct in asserting that human beings only find happiness in seeking after transcendent, eternal truths—that the unexamined life is not worth living—then we have forgotten which way is up, for playful giants are not gods. If Aristotle himself, who insisted that food, health, and shelter could not be excluded from happiness, was correct in explaining their contribution as merely instrumental, then we are fattening our loins for a slaughterhouse of the soul.

III. Farming and True Freedom of Speech

Stipulate, then, that unimpeded marketplace activity is not a blueprint for preserving that creative introspection, nurtured by literate culture, which tends to yield true, deep happiness (as opposed to those balmy affects deemed the signs of happiness by questionnaires). A vigorous day trading at the market may make us well-to-do, or a year of such days leave us positively wealthy... but it may also, eventually, enslave us. For a master is enslaved along with his slaves: the wheeler-dealer in any of his more sophisticated guises and locations is chained to his business interests in a way that corrupts his little bit of leisure (about that much, Professors Frank and Layard are correct). Even the billionaire-philanthropist must discover that being one of the welfare state's messiahs is an Atlas-like burden. To escape the horrible fact of one's own tyrannical power, one is apt to be mugging constantly for cameras and servilely courting a kind word from the popular press. The satisfactions of the palace cannot be much more durable than the spectacles of the Colosseum if supplemented by no inner magnetism to an unconditional, immaterial goodness.

Richard Weaver was fond of alluding to the forsaken nobility of medieval Christendom, and Wendell Berry loved to mingle the Gospels with earthy oral-traditional wisdom like that of the Sioux sachem Black Elk. We all know that the Right was able to galvanize its political base in the latter twentieth century by appealing directly to Christian fundamentalism; yet Weaver and Berry would clearly have been uncomfortable with any formula that might equate material affluence with God's blessing and reserve moral censure only for specific behaviors like abortion and homosexuality. I believe they were correct to insist that the fulfilled citizen must prosecute every stage of his daily existence in a conserving frame of mind—the *parsimonia* which Cicero extols in his *Tusculan Disputations*, the Socratic joy in needing so very little which rings resonantly through classical philosophy and persists in Augustus, Boethius, and medieval monasticism. The "happy American" must be something more than a person whose mate is of the opposite sex, who slightly undercuts the competition at "year-end clearance sales", who watches multimedia productions in a large church on Sundays, and who celebrates Christmas the way he would a child's birthday. If he is only this, he does not really understand happiness. He is merely the product and the purveyor of mass-mentality, accepting material comfort as a self-evident good, rather too sensitive to public approval to be enlisted among the devoted knights-errant of moral duty.

I have found few references in Weaver to José Ortega y Gasset, and none in Berry; but I have no doubt that both thinkers were familiar with *The Revolt of the Masses*.[11] Weaver's sixth chapter in *Ideas Have Consequences* is even entitled, "The Spoiled-Child Psychology" (very probably an allusion to Ortega y Gasset's *señorito satisfecho*). Like the Spaniard, too, Weaver charges modern technology—especially the "Great Stereopticon" of instant info-entertainment provided by pandering communications media—with reducing our masses to this state. Yet the accelerated pace of city-living is implicated in the degeneration from numerous other angles:

No one can be excused for moral degradation, but we are tempted to say of the urban dweller, as of the ancient heathen, that he never had an opportunity for salvation. He has been exposed so unremittingly to this false interpretation of life that, though we may deplore the silliness of his demands, we can hardly wonder at it. He has been reared in the notion that progress is automatic, and hence he is not prepared to understand impediments; and he has not unnaturally translated the right to pursue happiness into a right to have happiness, like the right to vote or protest. If all this had been couched in terms of spiritual insight, the case would be different; but when he is taught that happiness is obtainable in a world limited to surfaces, he is being prepared for that disillusionment and resentment which lay behind the mass psychosis of fascism.[12]

Parallel passages could readily be found in Ortega y Gasset's great book.[13] The difference lies in the emphasis: Weaver pits the urban against the rural and carnal whim against spiritual longing. He is constantly pulling back on the reins, harkening after a precious legacy squandered. The Spaniard, in contrast, will imply as his essays feel their way along that fascism might be averted if Europe's nations would bond together in a progressive venture. The former is more conservative, the latter more liberal. Weaver was disappointed in contemporary Christianity: Ortega y Gasset apparently concluded Christianity to be a relic of the naïve past, incapable of a contemporary form.

This distinction is worth stressing, because Europe turns out to have followed Ortega y Gasset's recommended course once it weathered the overt fascism of Hitler and Mussolini—with the result that it is now a loose collective whose manners are tightly monitored by *gloriosi* like the Right Honorable Richard Layard. Far better would have been a rediscovery that envy is a sin: that all creatures must die in the flesh, that all things must decay to dust, and that only a fool would therefore stake his happiness upon never sickening and always acquiring more pelf. To the Stoic philosopher Epictetus (for such insights are by no means confined to Christianity), the deduction was as simple as A, B, C: "The good should be such that one might be firm upon it and trust it.—Yes, it should.—Can one be firm upon the unsteady?—No.—But surely pleasure of the senses is not steady, is it?—No.—Out with it, then, and clear it from our scales!"[14] The masses have only the fleeting image of pleasures and luxuries, fulfilled briefly or in part from time to time, upon which to found their sense of achievement. That manipulators like Layard are so aware of the image's vacuity as to create a finely engineering calculus of misperception—to design, indeed, an entire social order from well-orchestrated illusions—testifies to the new Europe's ruinous cynicism in choosing intoxicants over the sobriety of real striving.

For to strive is to integrate oneself into the natural cycle begun with birth but not ended with death: it is to *exchange* oneself for something not oneself, yet enduring after one (to speak in earthly terms) as an expression of what one has chosen to serve—perhaps literally to die for. Such is the perspective of Wendell Berry's elegant essay, "Discipline and Hope". Berry, alas, refers not to Europeans but to his own countrymen when he writes,

> Because of the prevalence of economics [i.e., profitable, faddish "conveniences"] and the philosophy of laborsaving, it has become almost a heresy to speak of hard work, especially manual work, as an inescapable human necessity. To speak of such work as good and ennobling, a source of pleasure and joy, is almost to declare oneself a pervert. Such work, and any aptitude or taste for it, are supposedly mere relics of our rural and primitive past—a past from which it is the business of modern science and technology to save us.[15]

The "specialist", that arch-villain of Ortega y Gasset's, is again very visible in Berry's assessment. Particularly aggrieved by the predations of strip-mining in Kentucky, Berry was incurably astonished that human beings could create such hellish landscapes for the sake of such temporary gains. Only someone fitted with the blinders of an obsessively narrow ambition could so ignore an exploitation that outraged both the human spirit and plain common sense. Berry, you see, like Weaver and other Southern Agrarians (a vague movement inspired by the publication of *I'll Take My Stand* in 1930), was as quick to observe that people cannot live very long in wastefulness as to lament that no one could enjoy living in wastelands. The heart hath plenty of reasons, *pace* Pascal, which reason understands full well.

To conserve is hence not only a spiritually enriching duty, in this view, but also a practically necessary one. The specialist or "economist" cannot see this because he measures success by the quarter-year. Perhaps the unnamed Ortega y Gasset could not see it clearly because a clinical positivism had not scalded Europe's physical appearance, for the most part, but only made her consumers hungry for American gadgetry. Uniting specialists in a common adventure, however—in harvesting the ocean bottom or mining the Moon—will do nothing to restore the missing spirituality of life that reconciles man to his lot and makes enduring happiness accessible. On the contrary, it will feed the illusion of the far horizon's heavenly amplitude. It will slate new Lake Baikals for execution by progressive, Soviet-style bureaucrats with inflexible timetables for "productivity".

If the key for both Weaver and Berry was spirituality, then the key to *economic spirituality*—to feeding one's children and paying one's bills in a fashion pleasant rather than odious to intellect and soul—was the land. The good, rich earth: source of perpetual rebirth from death, sacrificial mother to the human race, inspiration of human creativity's most powerful images and melodies. Berry actually revived the fine art of plowing behind a draft animal: as if to emphasize that labor itself is as important for the spirit as food for the body, he embraced grinding toil with zeal. My own objection to such devotional acts, rewarding though they surely are to the individual, is that they invite caricature of an entire range of positions on critical economic issues. We will not convince most Americans to become Amish farmers—nor should we try, in fact. The technological genie is out of the bottle. If we were willing to surrender the lead in the arms-and-energy race to our hungry pursuers, we should have to live in the world—and very possibly die an untimely death in it—that would result. Allowing the current Chinese regime to dictate the course of the twenty-first century would be a crime against humanity that we would scarcely have time to regret.

The alternative to the great hive which Chinese communism seeks to make of the human race, however, is not—cannot be—another hive, set in motion by the lure of profit and the goad of envy rather than by a soldier's machine-gun. That alternative, rather, is a society of self-sufficient individuals. To be truly independent in a high-tech economy is no easy matter, and the hardest value of the equation to supply is food. Farming one's own small plot of land has come to look appallingly low-tech. It is greeted both with a certain derisive social stigma and with the practical difficulty of demanding too much time; for you can't farm in the city, and to the city you must go if you would pay your other bills after growing your own vegetables. Yet the high-tech job awaiting us at the end of a painful daily commute through smoggy traffic jams is less likely the design of a satellite system to avert hostile missiles than the design of a new cellular phone which starts the hot water running in the tub back home. What contemporary man needs for his happiness—and maybe even his sanity—is the economic ability to refuse work on this cell phone, to refuse the employment of throwing pizzas together at a "drive-thru" window, and to refuse the occasional third option of living on the dole. He needs to be able to participate in contemporary life without being enlisted into the West's growing army of wage-slaving clowns, acrobats, and snake-oil salesmen. He needs, with all his learning and humanity and optimism, to be able to *conserve* a sense of honor.

Land can give him this honor, because it can provide him with a) a place to find shelter, and b) a source of food staples. He may or may not find conscionable employment as an architect or copy-editor within a few weeks of refusing to market pills for "sexual enhancement" or to sell used cars in Spanish. If a satisfactory option is slow in coming, however, he and his family will not starve—not, that is, *if he can deploy technology in farming his half-acre of suburban property*. A few tomato plants on the patio, or even a back-yard garden of the conventional kind, won't do the trick; but if he knows or learns how to maximize his yield with innovative strategies, then he will be a provider in the word's true, direct sense while also being nobody's toady or pimp.

So privileged a position, unfortunately, is enjoyed by ever fewer in our entertainment-economy. Land is the key to our recovering our personal dignity—the power of announcing at a lucrative but morally squalid place of employ, "I won't do it—I quit."

IV. A Series of Hypothetical Contrasts

Heretofore, I have argued that a genuine concern for happiness has been all but exiled from contemporary discussions of economics. I have been especially critical of *soi-disant* conservative theories in this regard, precisely because I believe that the secret to human happiness, considered as an empirical phenomenon indexed to a certain material state, must contain substantial elements of *conserving*. Coherence with the past, a fairly secure anticipation of the future, a perceived harmony between one's personal values and those of one's neighbors... surely these are circumstances attendant upon the satisfaction in life expressed by sane, responsible adults of any era. Today's liberal, in my view, has therefore disqualified himself from addressing the great question at issue. Since contemporary liberalism is so heavily invested in change, as if people were mere morsels in a stew whose proportion and seasoning could be adjusted until the perfect recipe finally produces just the right savor, I have looked in the other direction for answers.

They have not been forthcoming. Indeed, the neo-conservative of today shows little interest in conserving anything of the cultural or the spiritual—or even, perhaps, of the social. Here, too, change reigns supreme, usually in the holy name of free trade. Institutions must make way when they stand in the path of financial gain. Even religion and family are typically defended with reference to statistics that correlate church-going and marriage to income and longevity. Such reasoning certainly implies that Bible-reading would have to go if, for instance, a new survey suggested memorization of the Beatitudes to accompany a reduced ability to scale the corporate ladder. In the same way, Main Street's boutiques have lately been boarded over or paved under because shoes and soccer balls can be made more cheaply in India than in Omaha.

Both to recapitulate and to clarify further, I should like to proceed from this point by positing a series of images. I shall ask the reader to picture typical people living in various cultures. The method is no doubt unscientific in numerous ways; but then, happiness is neither a bank account nor a ration of grog and beef. It is something, rather, that those of us who study *belles letters* and past civilizations should be less shy about identifying, for our qualitative sensors should be more apt in this investigation than the clinician's weights and measures. All the same, I hope that I shall not offend grievously against objectivity. The portraits that I advance are highly generalized, but not at all distorted as generalizations.

Imagine, first of all, human society in its simplest state: that of the hunter-gatherer who lives in semi-temporary camps of two or three dozen people, migrating within a fairly fixed range as nuts, tubers, fruits, and game within easy walk of a given site are depleted. This manner of living, to be sure, is "simple" only in regard of its minimal technology. In other ways, it can be quite sophisticated. Popular representations of it often err in both directions: we are invited either to see Adam and Eve delighting in Eden or a clan of "cavemen" eking out a brutish existence. A few objective remarks will serve our purpose here. Of primary importance is the fact that hunting-and-gathering is not arduous toil. The men who track down prey do not race antelope or wrestle bears: they are infinitely more likely to snare small animals and to address larger ones with poisoned darts, patiently shadowing them for hours, perhaps, until the dose takes full effect. The women who dig roots and grope after berries do not spend hour upon hour doubled over or balanced on their toes: they have no quota of bags to fill, no specified number of fields to harvest. Though life depends upon the success of such food-gathering expeditions, we seek almost in vain for any instance of a malnourished people straining under great burdens or against massive obstacles with every fiber of their frail bodies. To call their life a leisurely one would not, in a sense, be inaccurate. The chores of gathering, especially, can be combined with socializing. (Hunting demands less noise and rewards spreading out.) In a long-standing culture where knowledge of healthy and unhealthy plants, safe and unsafe approaches to predators, secure and unreliable shelters, etc., has accumulated over the centuries, the hunter-gatherer existence may well be viewed as robust, free, peaceful, and even mentally challenging—in short, as a regimen not incompatible with *happiness*.

I would stress that the medical technology upon which we found our era's superiority to all others with such overweening confidence would not have been sorely missed in hunter-gatherer communities during a typical month, or maybe even a typical year. Granted that broken bones poorly set would permanently reduce an individual's contribution, and probably his or her lifespan: yet what I have written above should suggest that activities involving a high risk of fracture or internal injury must have been rare. Members of such societies tend to know how to budget efforts and avoid dangers.[16] That having been granted, our "superiority" dwindles to an acquired skill at making up deficiencies in our diet and daily exercise artificially and an advanced technology of fighting infections with injected antibodies. Here again, our pride is somewhat presumptuous. Concerning diet and exercise, the hunter-gatherer could no doubt teach our best clinicians a thing or two. As for infections, we are especially prone to them despite our keen awareness of hygiene because we constantly expose ourselves to strangers in our footloose, densely populated lifestyle. The tribesman-counterpart of our frequent-flyer executive passed most of his days among the same thirty people and their progeny. His vulnerability would become apparent only if some representative of our world were to intrude upon his, importing a host of new bacteria and viruses along with the best of intentions.

Yet there's no denying that such a life, at its less fortunate moments, could be very hard indeed. The vagaries of a fitful climate often brought about such moments. If the USual foods could not be harvested within the tribe's usual range—or not in sufficient amount to sustain the group—then starvation might virtually annihilate the small society. Severe weather conditions might also render habitations inadequate: grass huts might blow away, and wigwams of hide might not keep extreme cold at bay. Settlements were an answer to such afflictions. A permanent home, of course, could be more soundly made; and the limits which it would impose upon one's wide-ranging habits would introduce no problem if the production of food stuffs could be intensified artificially within a small area. Grains, nuts, and perhaps some tubers could also be stored in anticipation of a lean year. The more mobile hunter-gatherer would not have been able to transport any such depository from campsite to campsite. Furthermore, as agricultural technique emerged in response to long-term risks, hunting would be similarly transformed into the herding of domesticated antelope and swine. Human society began to sink deep roots.

For Rousseau and his heirs, this was not a happy development. Among other things, it was the birth of private property. Communitarians always keenly feel the loss of the share-and-share-alike ethos without conceding (apparently without noticing) the tragic fragility attached to that habit of existence—its constant exposure to aberrations in the natural cycle, to incursions of stronger tribes, and so forth. They are more aware of the setbacks which the wandering lifestyle imposes upon nascent individualism: such a "liability" simply leaves them unmoved. Perhaps associating the hunter-gatherer existence with a perpetuation of childhood joys, they cannot see the more independent human being's evolving sense of self and other, with all of its many moral and spiritual implications, as a significant advance. To them, the farmer bartering potatoes for cheese is but one step removed (and in this supposition, they are right enough) from an entrepreneur charging prices for goods in his inventory. If a hoarder was ever detected in the days of wandering tribes, he must have been stiffly reprimanded by a council of elders. Now he tallies up his sheep as his neighbor's herd dies of thirst, foreseeing an opportunity to corner the market in wool and mutton.

Let us be fair: there is a modicum of truth in such nostalgia over the child's lost innocence. When people graduate to greater autonomy—when, in a word, they become adults—we find certain ones rising to the occasion and certain ones degenerating. That religion itself should shift from a placatory reverence for natural forces at this evolutionary phase to embrace a budding sense of conscience, responsibility, and soul is clearly no accident. Contemplating the child's initiation into such potentially fatal complexities is not without sadness, yet this sadness belongs to a fuller life, a higher reality. Far sadder still would be the child-of-forty-years, a stunted plant which will never bear fruit. If one accepts that human beings achieve their most human level when they achieve a measure of self-awareness, then the farmer's life must be rated happier than the wanderer's. No doubt, it is a very different kind of happiness, less spontaneous and less trusting, and so perhaps less intense. But it is also a *subsequent* happiness, and that which does not graduate to its next natural stage is less successful even though it could be said to have found a kind of eternal youth. Death itself is eternal youth: the unplanted seed never dies because it has never decayed to yield new life... but it has also never lived.

Such mysticism may seem ill-suited to the agriculturalist's life (though I think those of this persuasion must neither have read Hesiod nor have studied varieties of monasticism). A popular misconception holds that farmers are "rubes", "rednecks", and "hayseeds" who toil like mules and are just literate enough to sign their "x" on a deed. The truth is that, like hunting and gathering, farming is usually more pleasurable than the unremittant drudgery of the factory or the chain-gang. The farmer labors mightily for stretches of time during the day and over certain seasons during the year. Yet he does not race a clock, being generally endowed with the luxury of taking breaks as desired; and he knows long months, as Hesiod writes, when there is little more to do than linger near a stove and repair tools.

> Those mid-winter months, foul days fit to rip an ox's hide off his back—
>> Watch out for them, and the frosts which make of the ground
>>> A hard bed as North Wind howls outside,
>> That visitor from Thrace 's wild-horse mountains across the wide sea
>>> Huffing and thrashing until the forests groan.[17]

If the rural dweller does not profit from such enforced rest by reading, he is nevertheless turned in upon himself with an intensity largely unknown to the urban laborer. Indeed, we easily forget how many deep thinkers of the past were living close to the land in their periods of greatest literary activity (Cicero, Virgil, Sallust... Jefferson, Madison, Thoreau) and how many urban scribblers were somewhat constrained by their fear of censorship or dependency upon volatile patronage (Horace, Statius, Suetonius... Descartes, Pascal, Fénelon). The farm is not the cradle of literacy: that distinction belongs to the city, with its need of accurate record-keeping amid the flux of materials and the crush of the crowd; but the farm turns out to excel at sustaining the best literate habits of thought—self-examination, freedom of inquiry, and assessment of ideas against observed results. The eccentric

Tycho Brahe erected massive star-gazing equipment on his estate, and the eccentric Michel de Montaigne penned essays from a sequestered turret in rustic retirement. The courtly masters of Renaissance Italian epic, Arioso and Tasso, wore themselves out with clerical work for ungenerous patrons, in contrast; while the genius of Edgar Allan Poe took leave of this world in a Baltimore gutter.

I am perhaps selecting my examples with prejudice so as to demonstrate, at the very least, that agriculture is not inconsistent with cultivation of the spirit. I submit, at any rate, that we should not assume hives of urban intellectuals such as universities, symphony orchestras, art galleries, and research laboratories to be the ultimate destination of the humane life. More of that anon. Let us develop the simpler end of the contrast first: the hunter-gatherer and the unskilled urban laborer. I understand, of course, that the thousands of human cogs supplied to vast assembly lines in the nineteenth century's second half came from farms, not from savannas. With regard to cultural rather than historical opposition, however, the proper yin to the day-laborer's yang must clearly be the bushman and not the cultivator. Whatever skills the blue-collar worker brought from the farm were not generally in demand: he was hired, rather, to swing a mallet or an axe.[18] He lived from day to day, bringing home just enough to keep his family alive; and after a month or a year of working in one locality, he would be roaming the streets looking for new employment. He might quite literally transport meager belongings and family from one tent city to another as the railroads progressed; or he might transfer his residence from one hovel to another as a job loading barges was replaced by a job digging tunnels. His way of life, if not explicitly migratory, had the shallowest of roots, and of superfluity stockpiled for leaner years he could show not a bite or a dime.

To imagine this urban gypsy's enjoying a single advantage over his nomadic progenitors on the open plain is a formidable challenge. His tenement housing (if he had such) was usually more secure than a hut of reeds or sods—but it was poorly ventilated, prone to catch fire, and impossible to heat or cool with any help from the moist earth sealed far below under concrete and tar. His illnesses sometimes were treatable with drugs that were sometimes affordable—but he was more apt to take sick on a diet of diminished fruits and vegetables and in constant close proximity to hundreds or thousands of other urban dwellers. His clothes were probably not as adequate as the wanderer's hides and skins. His children often went barefoot on filthy brick streets, while the nomad's brood plodded a softer earth not steadily washed with horse manure and emptied chamber pots. The air breathed by the former was poisoned by coal dust and the sulfurous exhalations of nearby factories, seldom warmed by sunlight visiting between high-rise barracks and sooty veils; for the latter, air and sun were free and abundant, a daily charity from the heavens.

Quite frankly, I should suppose the life of the nineteenth-century urban laborer to have been more distant from happiness than any previous existence not lived directly under the thumb of an insane, bloodthirsty despot. Even as he died, the ailing wanderer could at least lie his bones down and watch the stars come out (perhaps made safe from large predators by kinsmen who had lofted him high into a tree). The dying laborer had a squalid cot, four cold brick walls, and a tiny window opening upon more gray facades to cheer his last moments. Whatever family hovered near him was probably terrified or dazed before the prospect of an uncertain future; his more extended relations had usually been left far behind in the old country or scattered throughout the New World by the four winds.

In passing, I cannot resist remarking one of the many absurdities awash in current discussions of labor, lifestyle, and happiness. The temporary laborer admitted from Latin America (or illegally shuttled across our southern border) indeed resembles the typical nineteenth-century immigrant from Ireland or Eastern Europe, as we are often reminded, in the following ways: he is unskilled except in agricultural techniques for which there is no demand, his English is imperfect or non-existent, he is scarcely literate even in his native tongue, he has left his extended family and the external supports of his belief system far behind, and he has enjoyed little exposure to state-of-the art conveniences like microwaves and CD-players (or even, perhaps, to televisions and air-conditioned automobiles). We are invited to believe that this person is "bettering" his lot by plunging into our blue-collar work force— invited, especially, by those of liberal political inclinations who believe devoutly in the forward progress of human society. Yet to define progress as the acquisition of microwaves and CD-players sounds very like the overture to a defense mounted by right-wing advocates for bourgeois capitalism. If my observations above about comparative happiness are not hopelessly flawed, then we might just as well expect that the undocumented roofer, gardener, or meat-packer will end up more miserable than he was at his point of origin. To the extent that this is not so, the explanation, I think, must surely be that political corruption and oppression back in his homeland did not permit him to farm a small plot of land in peace; and in that case, his problem becomes an officialdom swollen to intolerable heights of arrogance—*not* a deficiency of affluence.

Our own political commentators may justify the human deluge over our border with throw-away lines about the discomforts of bathing in a stream or living without Internet. We should strive, however, to imagine a pair of scales wherein one dish is occupied by an overweight contractor munching chips before a wide-screen TV on his day off, the other dish by a slender *campesino* leaning on his shovel to admire his irrigated chili peppers as chickens cluck in the background.... Which of these two scenes possesses more *human* value? If there is something missing from both of them, which is likely to be more receptive to a greater degree of thoughtfulness or reverend mystery? That the Left should vote for the former, in all of its complacent high-tech nullity, must be a shocking surprise (shocking, that is, to those previously seduced by leftist rhetoric). That elements of the Religious Right may end up preferring the humble villager (as they should) hints at what a very incautious bargain these *naïfs* have made in hitching their wagon to the consumerist cult of ever newer gadgetry.

Of course, both liberal and self-styled conservative would probably claim that the real comparison should be drawn between farm life and the middle-class lifestyle of skilled employment. No one wants to roof houses for thirty years. Just as Irish and Polish immigrants graduated from swinging a pick in mines or a sledge along the railroads to running small shops or doing fine brick work, so the objective of the Mexican fruit-picker is to open a restaurant and eventually send his children to college. Even though today's blue-collar laborer already enjoys immensely better conditions than his counterpart one hundred years ago, his real happiness awaits him in the future—in circumstances which he himself may not live to see fulfilled, but whose approach will suffice to delight his heart as he glimpses a new world opening before his sons and daughters. The liberal finds in this visionary happiness the vindication of progress which is the soul of his or her philosophy, while the neo-conservative finds in the vast upward thrusting of economic and social ambitions a self-renewing energy to drive the mechanism of consumption. If their motives do not exactly converge in this picture of rising material affluence (and I would suggest that they do, far more than the liberal likes to believe), then they nonetheless share the same behavioral outcomes for society. We witness the convergence, in fact, more clearly every day in these times as we watch our nation's political landscape endure major upheaval.

And here, precisely, is the most critical juncture of this essay's quest after economic happiness. Is the farmer's happiness a match for the burgher's? Let us at once remove corrupt police, oppressive landlords, and other such factors from the equation on the farmer's side: we are not envisioning an ill-starred Mexican peasant, but a successful planter who feeds his family with a bit left to spare. Likewise, let us imagine that our roofer now owns a small business, with a fleet of pick-up trucks bearing his name on their door panels in constant cruise about town. Who would question that the latter is the "better off" of the two? He has invested his substantial profits in stocks and bonds, he has moved into his "dream home", his children will attend not just any college but rather one of their choice... he has achieved an estimable degree of *control* over his life.

Or has he? I wish to examine that assumption very closely, for I find it dubious under the surface at several points. In the first place, we can scarcely suppose that any human being feels a mission in life to shingle houses. Let us harbor no romantic illusions about our man's success: he started out in the business because it produced a paycheck, and his persistence and hard work have merely produced bigger paychecks. One supposes that hammering on shingles all the livelong day offers few spiritual rewards, and one readily imagines that those who do the hammering may even loathe their work at times. But the shingler is a shingler: he cannot switch his skills to painting murals or designing bridges. He is stuck—more or less for life—in a trade which happened to make money for him, and money is all he will ever really have to show for "success" in that trade. Is that such a bad thing? Can he not use his money to take guitar lessons or travel the old country or collect sports memorabilia? The liberal/neo-conservative vision asks us to accept that our man will have enough energy left over during his brief vacations and his silver years to supplement a life of indifferent, perhaps repellent drudgery with spiritual awakening.

The farmer, on the other hand, lives every day of his life shoulder-to-shoulder with certain basic truths of life. He follows birth, growth, and decline; he studies what his dependents need from the process to secure their own survival; and he exchanges hard labor, not for another's vain displays, but for personal necessity. To rephrase the last of these insights, he understands the spiritual value of work—the purifying quality of honest labor applied to honest ends about which Wendell Berry wrote so lyrically. If the exchange rate of sweat for inner peace is not exactly a "basic fact of life", it is closer to the foundation than the investment banker and the stockbroker care to admit. I shall argue that its absence from our present habit of life is indeed the fatal flaw in our system.

For such peace, in terms of historical breadth, is very soon lost after the move to the city: life in town is about making a wage, not about bringing in a harvest. Growing food can never be ignoble unless one finds life itself ignoble; and in that case, one may always choose to starve and shuffle off this mortal coil. Nothing in the city, however, directly produces food. At most, food is processed or distributed here—food from the country. Already, even among butchers and grocers, chores are performed directly *for pay*, which may or may not be spent upon sufficient and healthy sustenance; and the work, being often heavy and repetitive (lifting, cutting, sorting—over and over and over), is less bestializing than mechanizing: i.e., it reduces man, not to a dumb beast straining in the traces, but to a mindless appendage taking its cues from conveyor belts and automatic doors.

Such service *cannot* be a setting for human happiness, I maintain. Yet so contagious are its dismal effects that they tend to reach out into the country like tentacles, poisoning even the farmer's domestic economy. Farmers begin to grow, not what their family needs, but what city-dwellers want. When enough city-dwellers want country-grown products with enough persistence, they pay top dollar, and the richer farmers buy up the holdings of the poorer ones. Since the poorest usually have the misfortune to be tenants, as in Mexico —or as in Ireland during the Potato Famine or in England during the Enclosure period—the humble cultivator profits not a whit from having soil at his fingertips. He may not even survive: he may starve, as perhaps two million did in Ireland (counting those who died of cholera on their way to the New World). In tragic venues surrounding Connacht, one scholar writes,

> ... food would be transported out of the district where a poor harvest had occurred. Usually it would go to a town or city, for the city-dwellers also needed sustenance. The country people would sell their food to pay their rent and to buy food later at an elevated price. The district's residents, therefore, would see lorries or barges carrying their food away, even though they themselves were in dire need. It is scarcely surprising that there were often attacks mounted on these lorries and barges.[19]

Tenant farmers in western Ireland dropped like sheep at the slaughter during about half a decade, not because their potatoes were blighted, but because everything they grew besides potatoes was carted away to generate profit in the city. Similar circumstances, less homicidal but just as unnatural, exist in northern Mexico today.

I digress from my argument precisely to stress that the servile farmer, in constant need of government subsidies and tax breaks just to survive, is indeed unnatural—a reflexive creation, as it were, of our rural population's mass-exodus to the high-tech city's artificial environment. I return now to the main point: that the true farmer holds his fate in his hands quite literally. He can grow his own food, and he can repair or extend his own house. He is the model of nuclear independence. The burgher must proffer money for food and shelter—and I mean not just the green-grocer or the meat-packer, but also the publisher, the lawyer, the advertiser, and the professor. Such people are commonly viewed as having reached the pinnacle of civilized life. There is a strain upon their existence, however, which remains latent in the best of times, and which must sooner or later, as one generation succeeds another, assert itself: *they all provide services to the public, and public taste must eventually prove a tyrant*. Richard Weaver, enamored as he virtuously was with the self-sacrifice of medieval chivalry, viewed the lapse of such noble sentiment as cracking the door open for the marketer:

> ... the disappearance of the heroic ideal is always accompanied by the growth of commercialism. There is a cause-and-effect relation here, for the man of commerce is by the nature of things a relativist; his mind is constantly on the fluctuating values of the market place, and there is no surer way for him to fail than to dogmatize and moralize about things.[20]

Weaver's noble naïveté is itself on display, I suspect, in this pedigree. More likely, it is the growth of commercialism which strangles the heroic ideal, for the burgher need not start out venal and cynical. Many have been known, indeed, to perish in high principle rather than adjust to the "demands of the market". The mid-nineteenth century witnessed the glorious triumph of the middle class—and the pillorying of a few hold-out free spirits who did not bend a knee to mass taste. Baudelaire was successfully prosecuted for obscenity because (among other reasons) his poem "Delphine et Hippolyte" dared to address the subject of lesbian love. Were he a resident poet on the English faculty of a state-funded university today, the same poem would earn him summary dismissal *because its treatment of the subject is censorious*!

If a poet must thus adjust his credo, professionals with a Yellow Pages listing must be rigidly faithful to the whim of the day. A lawyer who refused cases on moral grounds (who chased from his door, say, a husband wishing to reduce his child-support or a retailer plotting to exploit a contract's fine print) would soon be unable to pay his office's rent. A landlord who refused to raise rent above the prevailing mean would soon find his property being defaced by disrespectful tenants, though a few deserving poor would also bless his name. Everyone who sells a service incurs at least the potential risk of having to play the prostitute. Our freedom to say what we believe in the city is severely circumscribed by the necessity of eating and finding shelter; for if we choose to play the prophet instead of the prostitute, who will pay for our supper?[21]

One may credibly maintain that the Renaissance poet or artist enjoyed more such freedom than we do, in fact. He had only to win over one well-healed patron: we must win over the masses—we must find a "market". Liberal intellectuals want the government to stand in for Lorenzo de Medici, assuring creative free-spirits of a regular honorarium. Yet where do the representatives of popular government derive their tastes, if not from the people? The bare truth is not only that most people lack taste, but that the general taste must inevitably grow worse if commercial capitalism has free rein. Upon what do people spend money, once they have accounted for the necessities (and recall that we are now scrutinizing the successful bourgeois)? They opt for convenience. Our technology excels at spewing out new conveniences with a volcanic kind of energy, so these affluent expenditures are self-accelerating: the more cellular telephones are bought, the more investment will be drawn into developing cell phones that render previous versions obsolete. The public's taste makes a decisive shift toward embracing the new *per se*—and worship of trend has always been a defining factor in poor taste, since its focus is on ostentatious display rather than on engagement of intellectual faculties.

To be sure, such acquisitive "feeding frenzies" generate new jobs. More trends, and the acceleration of existing trends, translates into more demand, which means more producers and more hucksters. More and more workers will be able to receive pay doing frivolous, even degrading acts in order to buy food; and, if the degradation grows too palpable, perhaps they will have enough money left over to buy enough frivolity themselves that they will not be left alone in a quiet room at week's end contemplating the utter futility of their existence.

I am back on the humble worker's gritty doorstep again, a destination which has a hidden magnetism. We are observing an epochal economic shift, in fact, wherein the white-collar executive is watching his shirt change color. As machines do more and more of our complex labor, human workers are finding that more and more job openings are for the "human machine" once again—the low-level, repetitive task which once characterized sweatshops, which machines faintly lifted from our shoulders for a while, but which now may be done *more cheaply* by two hungry hands than by sophisticated equipment. The engineer and the accountant are unemployed, their work "outsourced" to countries whose newly educated are "happy" just to get off the assembly line; and our manual laborers are seeing either a similar exit of their jobs to hungrier shores or a furtive awarding of those jobs to foreign nationals imported under the law's radar. Perhaps the best chance today at a high-paying domestic position is the software company whose creations will at last render even work-for-room-and-board engineers and accountants redundant. (Employees of tax services already do little more than "key" numbers where "prompted" on a screen.) Of course, the day when computer programs create new computer programs cannot be far away.

On that day, we shall witness the sickly birth of the world's first fully "service" economy, the Age of the Servant. Some, perhaps many, will be waiting tables and emptying garbage cans. A modestly more prosperous group will be driving trucks and pointing the drills and nozzles of heavy equipment in the right direction—but this, too, will be essentially a custodial duty. The more prosperous still—the one group which will yet enjoy a long shot at striking it rich—will be peddling various stimulants chemical and electronic, legally and illegally, online and in the street. Stimulants, sleeping pills, fantasy games, the alternative realities we call "movies"... and let us not forget pornography, the prostitute's passport to a relatively healthy prosperity... such are the growth industries of the future. People will participate in them because they have to eat—and eating means food, and food means pay, and pay means awakening and exacerbating every latent whim in a mass public whose ashes may yet be fanned into a flame.

But what if we grew our own food?

V. The Suburban Farmer

I will at once reassure the reader that I have not taken leave of my senses and do not propose the evacuation of our cities to repopulate the countryside. The farming of the past must remain in the past, for all but a few determined eccentrics like Wendell Berry. Whenever we hatch a plan for improving the future (and here I speak of a "return to happiness", not the much more suspect "progress"), we must not ask of our neighbors what we ourselves would or could not do; or, if we happen to be Wendell Berry, we must ask rather less of them, understanding that some spirits are but faintly willing and some flesh very weak indeed.

Taking full account of human inertia, then—of our instinctive *resistance* to change when its vector does not carry us toward greater convenience (what *is* progress in current culture but a shift toward less work and pain?)—I can envision several entirely feasible means of bringing agriculture to our residential suburbs. Technology would assist us in many of these efforts; some are mere common sense, however, with minimal "upgrading", the equivalent of cultivating a backyard garden a little more seriously. Bear in mind that the motive for my proposals is terrestrial happiness: I seek to expound nothing less than how a contemporary human being might best supply his or her basic material needs without loss of self-respect, subservience to a vile regimen of collective intemperance, and the moral exhaustion attendant upon living only for surfaces.

• Conventional Methods: Let us start with the family garden. Tomatoes, potatoes, cucumbers, beans, peas, and other staples of a healthy diet can be grown in some variety just about everywhere, and with relatively little effort. (I find that, other than regular watering, most of my ministrations only torment my plants.) Major problems can develop, however. Some residences may have precious little real estate to spare for a garden, especially closer to downtown areas. Families with young children and pets will also find their produce under constant attack. Then, too, the weather is undependable in some regions; and natural competitors for the fruits of one's labor like birds, moles, and squirrels can also be immensely annoying. I am led, therefore, to propose my first major adaptation.

• The Greenhouse Roof: Most residences represent a major investment in attic insulation. We are warned by experts that the cool air we churn out artificially inside our domestic domain during the summer and the warm air during the winter literally travels through the ceiling, incurring the social and political costs of higher energy demands as well as personal costs to our checkbook. Now that glass can be manufactured which resists hail at least as well as wood shingles do, why do we waste these 2,000 square feet or so of solar energy—why do we actually expend energy to repel energy? If our residence's roof were a greenhouse, our living quarters could be just as well insulated throughout the year. (I am less confident, frankly, that this would be so in summertime down South: but greenhouses can be ventilated, and leafy plants absorb a good bit of heat.) The greenhouse would be impervious to birds, baseballs, and burrowing pests. Its contents could grow year-round. It would be a very pleasant retreat for adults after a hard day—both more sedative and less wasteful than, say, a sprawl in a hot-tub. Its light chores would occupy children who are currently burning their eyes out on PlayStation as they cultivate nothing but a criminal ignorance of how the natural world works. Hardier plants—roots and tubers, for instance—could still be grown in the back yard, but the more delicate species would find safe haven up in the roof.

• Nut Trees for Protein: Unfortunately, trees that bear nuts take a long time to grow—but landscapers and surface-sensitive, manicure-minded "yuppies" have waged an unreasonable war against this crucial variety of plant for decades now during which many a pecan orchard might have risen loftily. If one can endure the nuisance of having "rubbish" fall all over the lawn at certain times of year, then the nut is manna from heaven. It is that rarest of finds, a plant-produced source of protein. Nuts also survive in storage a very long while, unlike more familiar protein-intense foods. Most of us consume them in holiday deserts, or perhaps lightly as condiments on certain dishes; but they have lately been found to have numerous health benefits quite in addition to their deposits of protein, even as conventional protein-powerhouses like cheese and red meat have acquired a spotted reputation.

• Livestock for Milk: Nevertheless, milk and cheese remain the time-honored means of surviving handily and healthily for poor folks. Slaughtering animals for their meat has always been a dubious proposition: the harvest of steaks may be rich, but their source is gone for good once the axe falls. (Studies have indicated that the Hindu prohibition against killing cattle has probably allowed a great many families to survive on milk that would have starved on steak over the centuries.) The milk cow (or goat, for that matter) consumes a repository of the sun's energy not accessible to us mammals—grass—and turns it into easily ingested protein, renewable throughout the animal's lifetime. The milk cow is the mythical glass that never drains.

With none of my proposals have I encountered such weak-kneed, wide-eyed, pusillanimous incredulity as I have in arguing for a neighborhood milk cow. Our urbanized nation seems to believe collectively that udders squeezed by our own hands would produce a noisome liquid excrement sure to poison all who might consume it, and that the animal itself would bury lawn and driveway under its "chips" until flies were breeding on our necks and acrid stench inducing swoons in our womenfolk. A clear plastic jug at the grocery store, sealed and stamped by richly remunerated federal and state officials, is required to exorcise the malodorous demons issuing from the cow's bowels like Greeks from the Trojan Horse. The word "squeamish" hardly begins to capture the extent of a rather contemptible naïveté frequent even among those who style themselves environmentalists.

Of course, cows *do* expel fecal material. It makes excellent fertilizer: gardeners routinely pay several dollars a bag for it. The animal's stall would certainly have to be cleaned regularly and the "harvest" spread and watered into the ground. The flies and vermin drawn to such an operation, however, are no more formidable when the "pet" has hooves than when it has paws—and Americans often lodge the litter boxes of their precious cats in the kitchen! The unsavory chores involved in maintaining a clean premises would do our spoiled children a world of good; while the process of sterilizing the gathered milk, though usually redundant in cases where a single animal is being housed, could be accomplished expeditiously with simple technology, and would likewise teach valuable "hands-on" lessons of the sort that our mammoth education system seems so hard put to supply. That Third World nations are notoriously inept at taking hygienic precautions with their livestock and poultry (viz. the impending threat of Avian Influenza) is a cautionary tale, to be sure; but to assume that our government is providing for our welfare in such matters better than we ourselves could do is not only a disappointing response in a free society—it is inaccurate in specific cases, and likely to become ever more so as our public resources grow more strained.

I might add that cows and goats, in cropping the ample lawns to which Middle American suburbia is so partial, would spare us the misery of lawnmowers and grass-blowers—"conveniences" which not only guzzle gas unconscionably, but also pollute at a far higher rate per gallon than any vehicle on the road. I do not know of any study of the probable toxic emissions inhaled by the wretches condemned to lives of pushing this gadgetry around day after day, all year long. Apparently, we are so eager not to deprive them of their labor that we cannot be bothered to entertain the notion of their health's being irreversibly damaged.

I envision a cow being grazed up and down every residential block. The milk provided would probably suffice for as many as a dozen families—or perhaps two cows could be stabled. When I consider how many billions of dollars we invest in pets annually, I cannot imagine that a slight shift to more functional varieties of animal wandering about inside our picket fences would call for much of a sacrifice.

• Piscine Protein: Another protein source occurs to me, but I confess that the subject soon carries me out of my depth. Victorian novelist Standish O'Grady wrote a thrilling novella titled *Between Sea and Land* wherein a young man becomes trapped in a network of dark caves and can sustain life only by virtue of the fish that a family of seals shares with him. Eventually, the castaway feels himself declining and knows that he must work harder to escape: the diet of fish does not sufficiently restore his energy. Whether there is a nutritional basis to this fictional peripety, I do not know. Fish may offer rather less protein than red meat does—but it is healthier in other respects, and I am not suggesting baked carp as an exclusive source of protein, in any case.

My ignorance is more profound in matters logistical. Having never raised fish, I do not know if they could be brought to maturity in a domestic aquarium quickly enough a give them a steady place on the menu. Certainly we all find an aquarium a very relaxing prospect, however. To pipe in a little oxygen and feed the tank's scaly occupants with scraps would not pose much expense. I assume that the *piscina* would be an indoor set-up, since an open pool outdoors would draw insects and vermin and also create a hazard for small children. Even a modest residence could easily afford the cubic footage needed to graze a prospering school of fish, I should think; and the problems involving cost-effective population density, vulnerability of the fish to small changes in the tank's temperature, the product's appeal to human palates, and so forth could probably be resolved by selecting carefully among various breeds.

I insist that these strategies for feeding one's household, and others like them which have not occurred to me but must be evident to practiced gardeners, do not demand of us a major alteration of our lifestyle. On the contrary, they demand that we *resist the highly artificial lifestyle which has been thrust upon us by narrow economic interests.* Nothing could be more natural than plucking a snack off a tree, and nothing is more embedded in the history of human experimentation than coaxing fruits from the earth in slightly engineered circumstances.

The hesitation in which our misgivings torpidly hold us is very like the mesmerism in which the automobile keeps us courting our own ruin. Consider the evidence. For centuries, human settlements have mingled residential functions with commercial functions. People ate meals behind their shop and slept above it, as they indeed continue to do in whatever towns around the globe have not been turned inside-out by highways. To all appearances, this is the *natural* way for humans to socialize at a higher level where private property exists and commodities are exchanged.[22] In our own nation, the compartmentalized city, wherein one must navigate traffic to transport children to school, reach a place of employ, or make even the simplest purchases, is scarcely half a century old. Yet we already find the image of corner grocery stores and neighborhood repair shops so outlandish as to be fatally stigmatized. The picture makes too much sense—it is too childishly easy! If it were not fraught with hidden difficulties and dangers, we would already be modeling it in our daily lives. Besides, it is also *archaic* (for even we Americans are not such ignoramuses as to be wholly unaware that we indeed used to live this way). Answers for complex problems never involve turning the clock back: the very idea blasphemes against the sacred cult of Progress.

Yet the multi-functional neighborhood and the agriculture-intensive residence would solve many of our major social and economic (not to mention spiritual) problems in the same manner—and one must confess that it is a pretty obvious manner, and also more than a little beholden to past lessons.

• Traffic would be reduced. Growing food would give at least one of the two adults heading a household a good reason to stay home. Clearly, the greater number of people remaining in their residences throughout the day would represent more potential customers for the café or the bookstore across the street. As life in the suburbs became diverse, residents with the option of staying or leaving each morning would choose to stay: their home street would now seem an *enjoyable* place. Expenditures of fuel would perhaps be halved (much to the dismay of those whose joy depends upon our national oil dependency), less tax money would be spent on paying traffic cops and maintaining roads, hospitals would be less strained, insurance rates would drop, and the one American in about five or six thousand who dies every year in car wrecks would have to find another ferry across the River Styx.

• Crime would plummet. With residents staying in their neighborhoods, fewer homes would be abandoned all day long to pose tempting targets for burglars. A man would never be wandering the streets out of work if he owned property, for he would always have the work—the noble work—of tending his crops and livestock. (I shall say more anon about my casting the urban exile here as a man.) Young people, who tend to commit crimes incidentally as they cruise streets far from any adult capable of putting a name to their faces, would have chores to do. Chores done, they would also have recreational locations to *walk* to a few blocks away. Perhaps most important, the "apprenticeship of subservience" (reminiscent of the hazing administered by college fraternities) which eats deep into our nation's soul—which inspires the bromide that delivering pizzas from a buggy with an illumined sausage on its roof is the proper path to success—would be undermined; for young men want most of all not to be lackeys, and a planter stands on his own two feet without bowing or scraping. It would be impossible to calculate how much criminal behavior in our time—specifically, how much gang-related drug-dealing—originates in a refusal among young males to "step and fetch it" for a few bucks a week... but the figure must be a sizable one.

Is agriculture really a solution—or is it, perhaps, a potential magnifier of the problem? I have utterly no doubt that some readers will instantly have formed in their minds the thought, "These greenhouse roofs will be mere hothouses for marijuana!" My answer is that Americans will stop wanting to anesthetize themselves when their lives stop becoming so painfully absurd and petty that a frontal view of them is intolerable.

• Public health will vastly improve. Besides a fall-off in annual traffic fatalities, the resuscitated neighborhood where residents actually buy and sell products and services and grow their own food will obviously elicit more pedestrian circulation and favor a better average diet. Among the plain facts in support of my proposals is the nutritional and hygienic superiority of food straight off the vine to food canned for months or else picked green and shipped (all too often) in contaminated containers. Frankly, fresh fruit and vegetables also taste better. Children are more likely to eat them. By default, food of the "fast" and "junk" variety, with its whopping doses of sugar and trans-fatty acids, will occupy a reduced portion of the daily diet. Adults will also live under less stress day to day. Relieved of fighting heavy traffic, secure in the knowledge that an abusive boss cannot suddenly cut them off from all sustenance, and attached to the pacifying rhythms of the natural cycle, they will be less prone to cardiac disease, insomnia, and perhaps some kinds of cancer. They will *enjoy* life more: that, remember, was our point of departure.

• Our young people, who have arrived at an extremely worrisome state, will perhaps be reclaimed for humanity's higher endeavors. I shall not write the essay-in-itself which poises to spring from this assertion. Readers may draw their own conclusions, or rate mine on their own scale. I simply observe that a child raised to be intimately familiar with true necessity, natural cycle, a disdain for gaudy frivolity, and a high regard for thrift is much more apt to govern his actions soberly as an adult than a child rigged with an iPod, a cell phone, a GPS, a laptop, and whatever other gear for whose possession a seductively pandering "culture" primes him with yearning. I will add, quite editorially and without claim to objectivity, that those who discern something distinctly Christian in the workings of our present system seem to me a far greater mystery than the god of goodness.

It should be added that the agriculture-intensive residence, quite apart from policies about traffic flow, would be an inestimable boon to struggling Third World nations. Apologists for unbridled capitalism and free trade typically point to images of squalid huts in Southeast Asia, wholly without indoor plumbing and overrun by chickens and pigs, as examples of the living standard from which we must rescue the planet. They seem to suppose that the toxic yellow clouds which satellite photos reveal to have settled permanently over "progressive" population centers like Hong Kong are a small price to pay for a carpeted apartment with a toilet and air-conditioning. Yet the truth is that small farmers, whether in Vietnam or Chihuahua or Nigeria, suffer primarily because of abusive tenantry systems and because of ignorance about hygiene and helpful technology. There is no need to throw out the baby with the bathwater. Such populations would eat better, have a more secure future, enjoy more autonomy, and feed fewer of the problems that threaten entire regions and continents—they would be, in short, *happier*—if they could just stay put and be introduced to a few advantageous techniques. The progressives who masquerade as conservatives, however, would prefer to transform them into heavy consumers of oil, junk food, and electronic entertainment; for massive infusions of uncritical, disoriented, easily seduced customers are the cannon fodder of bull markets.

I conclude this vision of the independent urban farmer with a modest Philippic, whose tone will seem more political than it should. Except perhaps in an attic-turned-greenhouse, crops cannot be raised without land—and even the glass attic perches on a piece of real estate. The citizen must not be charged for the right to live and grow food on his own property. Otherwise, we might as well break his hoe and spade and send him back to the pizza parlor. Specifically, government has no moral right to levy a property tax if the assertions of the Declaration of Independence are yet held as valid. *Individual citizens own their land.* They do not lease it from state or federal (let alone local) authorities, or hold it upon royal sufferance of same. For the traditional citizen—whose virtues I should like us to recover—land is both home and food. We do not rent the food that we feed to our children: we do not tuck them into bed at night calmly resigned to the thought that a SWAT team may show up at the witching hour and eject us all from our borrowed residence. Yet when I informally surveyed a group of about fifty college freshmen recently, almost all of them agreed with the statement, "Property ultimately belongs to the government: private ownership is a privilege which may be revoked in times of crisis." Most of the young people in my geographical area, furthermore, would style themselves *conservative.* In their enthusiasm to give centralized government a *carte blanche* to pursue malefactors, they seem quite willing to relinquish their "inalienable rights" upon a bureaucrat's whim.

If the property tax is not declared unconstitutional, one may easily foresee the day when a man who owns his residence free and clear and raises on his suburban plot much of the food his family needs will nevertheless have to sell up *because he cannot pay his annual fine.* The situation, I submit, is intolerable. The tyrant's reasoning seems to be that property-owners tend to have families, and that property taxes go largely to the funding of schools: ergo, let the former pay for the latter. Yet surely the state as a collective has a profound interest both in allowing families to survive financially and in striving to educate all children adequately. Where collectivism is justified, our rulers mete out individual levies; where the individual's intimate household duties are concerned, they assert the preemptive interest of the vast social unit. If local government is convinced that parents should bear upon their backs the majority of a titanic public school budget, then it should withdraw from the schooling business entirely and allow parents to fund schools of their own choice out of their own pockets. That failing, such revenues must be raised as sales taxes, paid by all.[23]

Richard Weaver denominated ownership of private property "the last metaphysical right", emphasizing that the land over which one has sweated and bled to build a house and grow food is something very like one's body, and perhaps even more like one's soul.

Private right defending noble preference is what we wish to make possible by insisting that not all shall be dependents of the state. Thoreau, finding his freedom at Walden Pond, could speak boldly against government without suffering economic excommunication.[24]

The political Left, which is so fond of lionizing whistle-blowers and free spirits, should be able to recognize the value of feeding oneself from one's land even after strings have been pulled to dismiss one from a sensitive, influential position. Since the New Right seems unmoved by such issues, perhaps a nostalgic liberalism should step into the gap. It was classical liberalism, after all, which cried foul when Irish landlords elevated the rent on any tenant who improved his shanty with hard labor and initiative. One such enterprising peasant on the Aran Islands found a plank which had washed ashore and hauled it home to make a door of it. The bailiff sniffed out the affair, and the poor wretch was sentenced to one hundred days of hauling stones to create Lord Charley's precious enclosures.[25] A third of a year... approximately the same sentence served by the average American taxpayer annually in order to fund the services which he is deemed too stupid to provide for himself—and, of course, to salary the lords who administer said services.

Work and Gender: The Unhappy Man

When I talk to people about the issues discussed in this treatise, I detect little disagreement with the assertion that we are a spendthrift society, that the cost of necessities is outpacing the average wage, that consumerism is turning our culture increasingly coarse, and that the urban sprawl created by our oil-based habit of life is distasteful and oppressive. The one claim about which I am most likely to be challenged is the most critical to my case: that large numbers of people are sincerely, profoundly unhappy doing the labors essential in a high-tech service economy. I have compared these labors to prostitution. Everything will eventually become marketing, I warned, and the market's target will eventually be only Ortega y Gasset's "mass man", whose needs are visceral rather than spiritual and whose responses are reflexive rather than reflective. The seller "shows some thigh", spills more perfume, circles seductively and purrs—even the computer programmer is equipping a given site to do more of this sort of thing with greater effectiveness. And the programmer, I have also opined, must at last devise programs that program: the destiny of market-driven technology is to erase human beings entirely from all productive ranks of the labor force—to reassign them from the *ratio* to the *libido*. Then we have only Pandars and their Cressids.

Yet women, especially, often reject my formulation. Perhaps this is because they have been denied general admittance to the salaried workforce for so long that they are still enjoying the freedom it offers relative to the narrow duties of wife and mother. I doubt it, however. Few female college students who cross my path grew up in a household where the mother did not have a paying job. I suspect that the rift between male and female perceptions starts at a much deeper point. It seems to me that women are more social, less keenly aware of the wall that separates Self and Other. They are more receptive to persuasion and compromise, less apt to view a concession as cowardly or traitorous. A fine little book in whose publication I once collaborated attributed the fork in this ethical road to childbirth, women having been raised in the knowledge that they might one day carry life *in them*, men having been raised to know that their body could never possibly nourish another's. Call this Freud stood on his ear if you will: it is an assessment with much to recommend it. The author summarizes:

> As a result of this detached perspective, men tend to see things more abstractly than women and to be more suspicious than women of mixed motives and combined purposes. They tend to think in Platonic ideals, and to act in Stoical defiance of compromise.[26]

Howard Schwartz has approached the same issue from a more straightforwardly psychoanalytic direction. He believes (if I follow his complex argument) that young men today are insecure in their manhood because they grow up seeing their mothers occupying the father's traditional role of provider and head of the household.[27] Though these two views may appear opposed, both concur that 1) men and women evaluate their experience differently, 2) the woman's values are typically less trenchant than the man's, and 3) the woman is playing a more active role today in supporting the household. For the former advocate, I should quickly add, sees women as filling more jobs and at a higher level precisely because so much work now consists of recruiting a clientele rather than lifting barrels.

I suspect that we have here the origin of a dissonance in our society whose painful strains we have not yet begun to distangle from the many other sources of cacophony around us. That is, we have not noticed that men, particularly, are unhappy. They will often ascribe the professional bottleneck which they feel closing in around them as the devilry of women: women unwilling to stay home and tend to their family, women without a family robbing a "family man" of his livelihood, women obsessed with promotion by hook or by crook not concerning themselves about the product's quality, etc. Such resentment, I now believe, arises fundamentally from two consecutive conditions: 1) jobs in our service-dominated economy increasingly involve persuasion and compromise, and 2) women are simply better at such jobs. Even without the epochal entry of the New Woman into the workforce, I think men would have found themselves confronted more and more with jobs that grated on their nature. If it is indeed true that the space between magnanimous concession and pusillanimous surrender is much more slender for a man, then most men are probably less suited to placating angry customers, winning over prospective clients, creating broadly pleasant settings, and so forth. Furthermore, men who excel at such work despite their aversion to it probably grow far more cynical—more jaundiced by daily survival's sordid league with hypocrisy—than their female counterparts; for the female would be less likely to perceive her accommodations as doing violence to high principle. She would emerge relatively *happy*, because she would not carry home with her the heavy burden of having been two-faced.

Stunningly, I find that historical overviews of gender roles in the workplace never seem to take much account of *how seldom sociability was required of the man* when he was the exclusive breadwinner. The hunter was a silent loner compared to his chattering womenfolk, left behind to dig roots and pick berries; the farmer had only his horse and his ox to talk to most of the day while his wife called after the children and borrowed sugar from a neighbor down the road. The stevedore, the bricklayer, the carpenter—all went about their tasks with a kind of introversion. Had they paused too long to chat, they would probably have been reprimanded or dismissed. Yet as townships of the same era (say, the sixteenth century) were beginning to burgeon with small shops, women were already prominent. The baker's wife served the public while the baker tended the oven, and the wine merchant's wife filled glasses while her mate rolled another barrel up from the cellar.

Only since about World War II—just as the advanced technology of cars and televisions and telephones was transforming Western culture in so many other ways—have men found the more reticent occupations known to them for centuries drying up and blowing away. The image of the "hard-selling" male huckster, barking out prices of used cars or wheeling and dealing with brokers over two phones, is a potent one in the popular mind. Yet the fact remains that this figure is more myth than reality, as if males were reassuring themselves through his cartoon-like antics that they, too, had a role in the brave new world. How on earth does a grown man truly become excited to the point of shouting about the prices of automobiles? He must be either obsessively greedy (and greed, like fear, is an unmanly passion) or else playing out a game—a literal role, complete with script. As a schoolboy will play the fool for laughs, so the grown man will leap and howl like an ape in the knowledge that *he* is not his part, and in the devout hope that his audience will understand the "joke". My own suspicion is that most men would be thoroughly embarrassed if they supposed other men to be taking their "act" at face value. The car salesman, like the charismatic preacher and the Dionysian sports announcer, relies upon his fellow males to appreciate the exigencies of his role—to understand the genre—if he values his manhood.

If men could stay home and labor with their hands to produce food for their children, how many would prefer to hustle around the car lot for commissions all day? Certainly I have elicited from far more men than women in my questioning of college freshmen an affirmative that self-employment is a significant personal objective. Indeed, women frequently register an *aversion* to "flying solo": they seem to prize the interaction of an intricate office hierarchy, or at least to dread the loneliness of being thrown upon their own devices. The ideal situation, then, appears to be that the woman of the house should sally forth to trade words behind a desk while the man of the house is milking the cow and digging spuds. We are warned by some that this reverses the traditional paradigm—but I have stressed that such "traditions" have increasingly contradicted their more reverend versions. "Man as provider" is an icon positing a competitive, almost adversarial relation to the environment. The bourgeois rendition of this drama on a dollars-and-cents stage immediately raised questions about the clerk's or shopkeeper's virility, as I have just explained; but at least the womenfolk back home continued to enjoy numerous social outlets. An unstable balance seems finally to have been upset in our time. Having considered why the man lost his poise, let us examine what happened to the woman at the same time.

By 1950, children no longer stayed home for their schooling; cars emptied out neighborhoods every morning; radio and television kept indoors most of those few residents who had not abandoned the suburbs for the day; air-conditioning made the den cooler than the porch even in summertime; and growing corporations transferred their employees from city to city, disrupting ties with old friends and extended family. On top of all that, women now did less work at home than ever, their washing and cleaning chores greatly alleviated by machines… but the social vacuum into which these very sociable beings were forced, I contend, was the deciding factor. Women wanted to work—but they wanted to work *in company*.

Would the man be content to bring food quite literally to the table if his wife were bringing far more paychecks to the bank account? Basing my response, once again, only on a great many informal interviews and personal observations, I should say that men worry less about their earnings than about what women may think of those earnings. That is, men tend to feel that women look down upon them for drawing humble salaries—and in this, alas, their fears are far from groundless.[28] The vulgar relegation of all our labors to a money standard is in many ways a consequence of the American male's trying to please the New Woman while competing with her. (There can be little question that the coarsening of our popular culture has overlapped the influx of females into the workforce.) The woman seems to read a large salary as proof that a person can successfully negotiate society's many roadblocks and hurdles—a quality which she much admires. Frustrated by this standard, men are more apt than women to respond to it by pulling out all moral stops, for they cannot grasp how a facility with social challenges would be the game's ultimate end rather than money. After all, money buys food—it *provides*—while flattering various interests is vile sycophancy. As Thomas More's outspoken Raphael Hythloday puts it in the first book of *Utopia*, "A man of courage is more likely to steal than to cringe."[29] Well, then, if it's paychecks the woman wants… by God, the man is going to bring her the biggest checks she ever saw!

That money causes divorces has become a cliché. Yet I believe it would be more accurate to say that a basic misunderstanding between the sexes about the nature of work is what fractures marriages. I am convinced that few women would complain when seeing their husbands haul basket-loads of succulent vegetables in from the garden, and few men when seeing their wives go off to a day of high-intensity "relationships". Men would be doing *their* work, and women *theirs*. The children of our urban farmer, I hasten to add, would be surrounded by grandparents, extended family, and trustworthy neighbors, as they were for centuries before we started changing residences every three years. Aging relatives themselves would be more likely to spend their last days among those who care about them rather than in an antiseptic cell, for at least one household adult would usually linger nearby around the clock. How can we suppose that things could never be this way again when they were precisely this way for yesterdays time out of mind?

Yet the single most visible benefit of self-sufficient food-growing remains political. Happy people must be free people—free, that is, in the Burkean sense of having enough autonomy to sustain their life's enriching web of associations.[30] The Stoic would say that everyone always has autonomy—that one can always decide to starve rather than labor as a slave, or to be executed rather than adore a tyrant. Stoics, however, tend not to be family men: whatever web holds them is thin, simple, and easily rent. For those of us who want to keep our mates and our children relatively healthy and secure, we must be free to give them what they need *and also* to speak out against folly, vice, and corruption or to refuse service to arrogant boars and unprincipled schemers. We must have the freedom to say "no" without saddling our loved ones with dire consequences.

Western culture has probably reached a more critical juncture than it has known since Christendom and a millennium of literate culture took refuge from Goths, Vikings, and Muslim holy-warriors on a few rocky, windswept islands. Within a decade or so, we shall learn (those of us who know what we are watching) whether an oligarchy will assign our work, our tastes, our candidates, and our amusements to us for the ensuing century—or whether, instead, we shall willingly embrace the "poverty" attendant upon a self-sufficiency in all that matters. The emerging oligarchic elite already has us crinkling our noses at the word "isolationist". The truth is, however, that the independent citizen of a democratic republic is and chooses to be *isolated* in the formation of his value judgments. He makes up his own mind, and then he proceeds to seek or to form a community of fellow believers. In his inviolable residence, surrounded by cultivated patches that sustain him, the independent grower needn't fret unduly about China's calling in our debt, about the Middle East's refusing to sell us more oil, about an immigrant population's rejecting English in the public forum, about the central government's shrugging off its Social Security promises. He will be impossible to finesse into Hobson's Choice when his "leaders" announce with feigned regret that it's either the Devil or the Deep Blue Sea. He and his independent neighbors will understand the true meaning of "neighborhood". They will comprehend that no one need ever eat with the Devil who cannot be lured to Hell's table. For this citizen will always be able to stock his own table, with no thanks to anyone but God and his own two hands.

No wonder the oligarchs dread him!

NOTES

1 Cited in George H. Nash, *The Conservative Intellectual Movement in America Since 1945* (New York: Basic Books, 1976), 204.

2 *Ibid.*, 198.

3 Russell Kirk, *A Program for Conservatives* (Chicago: Regnery, 1954), 176.

4 *Ibid.*, 177.

5 Oriana Fallaci, *Niente, e Così Sia* (Milan : Rizzoli, 2002), 85. Reprinted from 1969. The translation from Italian is mine.

6 Henry Hazlitt, *Economics in One Lesson* (New York: McFadden, 1961), 13.

7 From p. 209 in George Gilder, "Breaking the Box," *The Information Revolution*, vol. 67 of *The Reference Shelf*, ed. Donald Altshiller (New York and Dublin: H. W. Wilson, 1995), 202-210.

8 Richard Layard, *Happiness: Lessons from a New Science* (New York: Penguin, 2005), 228.

9 P. 43 of Dwight R. Lee, "Happiness and Liberty," *The Intercollegiate Review* 42.2 (Fall 2007): 41-48.

10 My translation from Jules Romains's novel *Les Superbes*, p. 829 of *Les Hommes de Bonne Volonté*, vol. 1 (Paris: Robert Laffont, 1988 [reprinted from 1958]).

11 Cf. Richard Weaver, *Ideas Have Consequences* (Chicago: U of Chicago P, 1948), 130; and Nash (*op. cit.*, 38) claims that the Spanish theorist was a major influence on Weaver's doctoral dissertation.

12 *Ibid.*, 113-114.

13 Besides the already suggested eleventh chapter of Part One, "La época del señorito satisfecho", the ensuing chapter of *La Rebelión de las Masas*, "La barbarie del especialismo", stresses the role of the technician in narrowing cultural vision—a perspective even more central in Wendell Berry's argument shortly to follow.

14 My translation from the discourse recorded by Arrian "On the Beginning of Philosophy," 2.11.20-21.

15 Wendell Berry, p. 117 of "Discipline and Hope" in *A Continuous Harmony: Essays Cultural and Agricultural* (New York: Harcourt Brace Jovanovich, 1972), 86-168.

16 Even dental health, after generations of trial and error with diet, is often better in traditional societies than we might suppose. Tag O'Buckley, an itinerant tailor whose story-telling prowess was known to Frank O'Connor and others, claimed during an interview recorded in 1942 that "the white flour did more harm than good" when it was introduced among the Irish peasantry at the end of the nineteenth century. "I remember the good strong teeth that the old people had in their day. That was when they had yellow meal [*mín bhuí*] and porridge. They were all solid, strong, and lively, with excellent health. Afterward, when they began with the flour, their teeth started decaying and falling out." (My translation of *Seanchas an Táilliúra* [Dublin and Cork: Mercier, 1978], 45). The dental health of Mississippian Native Americans similarly deteriorated once hunting and gathering shifted decisively toward corn agriculture.

17 My translation of *Works and Days*, 504-508.

18 Cf. Wendell Berry: "Most settlers who farmed in America farmed in Europe. The farm population in this country therefore embodies a knowledge and a set of attitudes and interests that have been literally thousands of years in the making. This mentality is, or was, a great resource upon which we might have built a truly indigenous agriculture, fully adequate to the needs and demands of American regions. Ancient as it is, it is destroyed in a generation in every family that is forced off the farm into the city—or in less than a generation, for the farm mentality can survive only in sustained vital contact with the land." *Ibid.*, 101-102, in "Discipline and Hope," 86-168.

19 From p. 159 of Niall Ó Ciosáin, "Dia, Bia, agus Sasanna: An Mistéalach agus Íomh an Gorta," in *Gnéithe den Gorta*, ed. Cathal Póirtéir (Baile Átha Cliath [Dublin]: Coiscéim, 1995): 151-163. The translation from Irish is mine.

20 Richard M. Weaver, *Ideas Have Consequences* (Chicago: U of Chicago P, 1948), 32.

21 That this selling of one's talents to the highest bidder has tarnished even the jewel in Western intellectualism's crown, science, is apparent to anyone familiar with patterns of research at universities. Academic departments now covet grants to fund their operation, and the richest grants naturally reward programs of study that promise practical solutions to widely publicized problems (automobile pollution, the spread of AIDS) or specific confirmation of popular social theories (the equality of all races in every regard, the identity of biological factors in the behavior of both sexes).

22 On all issues involving the sacrifice of sensible residential construction to car traffic, I would direct the reader to Andres Duany, Elizabeth Plater-Zyberk, and Jeff Speck, *Suburban Nation: The Rise of Sprawl and the Decline of the American Dream* (New York: North Point Press, 2000). Awareness of this folly, however, is about as old as the folly itself. I recently stumbled upon Jane Jacobs, *The Death and Life of Great American Cities* (New York:

Random House, 1961), which commemorates the virtues of the multi-functional neighborhood with irresistible lucidity.

23 A sales tax, by the way, would ensure that cultivators of plants grown illegally for distribution on the black market would not escape scot-free: they would pay a fixed percentage of their ill-gotten gain to the state every time they themselves made a legal purchase. Such types currently enjoy a tax-free income until and unless the slow arm of the law finally catches up with them.

24 *Op. cit.*, 136.

25 The incident is described in Pádraig Ua Cnáimhsí, *Idir an Dá Ghaoth* (Baile Átha Cliath [Dublin]: Sáirséal, 1997), 151.

26 Peter Singleton, *Return to Chivalry* (Tyler , TX: Arcturus, 2001), 29.

27 See Howard S. Schwartz, *The Revolt of the Primitive* (Piscataway , NJ : Transaction, 2003).

28 The delightful conservative commentator, Betsy Hart, exemplified this mentality in several of her columns before her regrettable divorce. I recall particularly a paean to her then-husband for earning money at a rate which jeopardized his health, a feat which she viewed as making him a manly provider.

29 More's cryptic little book was always taught to me as a proto-Marxian tract, yet the truth is that Utopia's emphasis on a quasi-urban, universally practiced agriculture is nothing more than a sensible rejection of the gimmick-and-frivolity market's cultural relativism and moral subversion, as I have argued here. The single point on which More "got it wrong" is that very point which induced my partisan instructors to enroll him in the Party: his apparent condemnation (through Utopian practice) of private ownership. In fact, Marx's naïveté was probably less than More's inasmuch as he at least assumed that the proletariat had already been pried loose from the land. What he failed to see (among numerous other things) was that the poor *needed back on the land, and needed to own their fields.*

30 Edmund Burke, of course, emphasized the role of community in forming identity and constrained his understanding of freedom within ties of custom, tradition, and circumstance. My point is precisely that individual choices made in the context of one's duties to immediate dependents requiring specific assistance are the surest measure of one's freedom. That Burke would approve my disdain of the contemporary "community" of venal interests is further implied by how similarly to "isolationist" (see the next paragraph) the word "nativist" has been stigmatized—a silly verbal concoction full of assumptions that Burke would have deplored. True communities are created by oil no more than by ideology.

Livable Spaces: A Radical Alternative to False Conservatism

*This article first appeared as two parts in successive issues of the online journal **Praesidium**: 11.1 and 11.2 (Winter and Spring 2011).*

I. Ship in Distress: Captain Overboard

Say that a ship is sinking, far from any port. The crewmen are divided about what to do, and so fearful of imminent death that the captain's word has no authority with them. Or say that the crew and captain have already abandoned ship (as in Conrad's *Lord Jim*), and that only a hundred or so passengers who have no particular knowledge of seamanship remain. Half of these insist on bailing and working the bilge pumps. The other half insist with equal urgency on jettisoning everything portable. The two sides are furious with each other; for the bailers need every able-bodied person to bail, while the would-be stevedores need everyone to life and carry. The plan of either side possesses a certain amount of logic. Weight, after all is pulling the ship down, and both water and cargo contribute weight. Yet whatever the passengers collectively decide to do (and consensus is nowhere in sight), some few of them should devote themselves exclusively to *stanching the leak*. Unless the original problem is addressed, no amount of reducing the problem's consequences will allow the ship to reach safe harbor.

This is approximately the condition of American politics today, in my opinion. One side is virtually taking apart the ship of state in an effort to "save" her. The other has a more effective plan for reducing the immediate crisis, but no apparent plan at all for solving the long-term problem—no inkling, indeed (to judge from its most vocal exponents), of just what the problem is.

II. The Death of Socrates

If I have previously devoted far more space to describing the "conservatives" at the bilge pumps (i.e., they who do not wish to throw the economy's very scaffolding overboard), it is because I consider their option the only one worthy of criticism. Human nature doesn't change. At gunpoint, it may briefly go underground. Those who expect it to change in response to lofty exhortation, if they have reached the age of consent, can only be called fools; while those who intend to fill mass graves until it changes surely have the damnation of high heaven and the loathing contempt of all decent people. To argue with fools is folly: to talk policy with butchers is to dine with the devil on foul carrion.

With whom, then, may we remonstrate about our ghastly urban sprawl, our brutally coarse "pop culture", and our insipidly servile "careers" if not those mature enough to grasp that nobody works for nothing and that no one willingly pays for wine to drink grape juice? Free enterprise allows people to live in squalor if they work, or to lose their employment if they loll about on the job. It is a hard taskmaster; but the alternative is to steal from those who persevere in order that free passes may be supplied to those who on no account lend a hand. Communities seldom permit their dysfunctional flotsam and jetsam to starve: common humanity demands that the indigent, even if indolent, be provided for somehow. Yet the idle must not be rewarded with mansions, chefs, and butlers. This would fly in the face of justice: it would indeed outrage sanity.

So much for the flag-waving hymn to virtue and industry which the "our way of life" exponents typically recite at campaign rallies and over air waves. What worries me about this position is—if I were to condense much into one word—Socrates. In his *Memorabilia*, Xenophon (who remembered Socrates from frequent personal contact) recalls when the philosopher once questioned the young Euthydemus about fair government. The naïve lad was of the opinion that those who had more than they needed should surrender the excess to those who had less than they needed (*Mem.* 4.2.38). Socrates leaves his interlocutor nonplussed by asking if there are not powerful despots who have committed atrocities for want of sufficient resources. Euthydemus must surely know, as well, that the man before him is the antithesis of the "needy" megalomaniac: that Socrates goes unshod in winter, has but a single cloak, and never accepts payment for his tutelage. The lesson is clear from either direction: human need can be indefinitely scaled down in a person of character or indefinitely magnified in a person of no discipline.

Socrates' state, of course, is the human ideal: not to live in the biggest house on the block or to extort a subsidy from that house's occupant through the tax code, but to have a sufficiency of all material necessities while being so free of wasteful addictions and covetous passions that one is not a salaried slave. Which of these would you imagine to be the happier, more exemplary, more civic-minded, and more spiritual human being, *ceteris paribus*: the senior partner in a law firm who inhabits a 5000-square-foot domicile in a gated community, or the owner of a small business who has settled into 2000 square feet in a suburb full of cracked sidewalks and ancient oaks? The CEO who endows charities and candidates with tens of thousands of dollars a year, or the dad who coaches a Little League team and volunteers to serve as a Cub Scout denmaster? The single mom who makes company president at 40, or the mother who home-schools her own and several other neighborhood children?

Such questions, to be sure, are loaded. In reality, most of us inhabit a picture somewhere between those imagined by Norman Rockwell and Jacques Lyotard (e.g., the low-octane attorney whose digs are humble and whose children hang the moon for him). To the extent that my crude profiles capture reality, however—and they have a certain value as generalizations—we may surely admit that whatever moral fault line separates "either" from "or" in these cases does *not* put Republicans on one side and Democrats on the other. In the popular mind, the billionaire CEO must beyond any question be a conservative (or a Republican: the popular mind seldom grasps the distinction, thanks largely to the propaganda of political hacks: Charles Gasparino's *Bought and Paid For* would be a useful corrective on this score). Yet what about the female company president? Is she not a feminist success story? The home-schooling mom is apparently a feminist's nightmare... but is not this woman's frugal lifestyle and her dedication to the neighborhood quintessentially suited to the liberal vision of a virtuous lower middle class struggling against fat-cat conspiracies?

More to the point (since I have already confessed my uninterest in the left-wing extreme make-over), conservatism itself, as styled by those who piously invoke its high authority, is riven through and through by such images. The CEO, whether male or female, young or old, white or black, is achieving the American Dream of dazzling wealth through long investment of skillful, persistent labor—but he or she is also changing residences every four years, pulling children out of school, and straining marriages beyond their limit of endurance. The small businessman, for that matter—another private-sector conservative success story—has likely ruined his own marriage, along with his health and his fatherly aspirations, in the losing struggle to save what he has built; and the forces driving him to fifteen-hour days and alcohol are partly stirred by big government, but primarily by private-sector monstrosities like the Internet and the corporate giants' outsourcing of labor. What is the recommended "conservative" course of action for him now? Return to college and study computers, twenty years too late to catch the wave?

We would like Socrates to be our neighbor: we would like, if we are pure of heart, to *be* Socrates ourselves. Who would not want a next-door neighbor proficient at pulling troubled youths aside and talking some sense into them? What residential area does not profit from older people with enough time, energy, and benevolence to stroll the sidewalks, direct lost traffic, briefly exchange an encouraging word with the orphan or the widow, toss a few pitches to children on the playground... but, alas, this world is now dead. It is so, not because Socratic individuals may no longer exist, but because the environment in which they must exist has been devastated. More than one of the activities just described would have our kindly moralist sitting in the back of a squad car within minutes, under close scrutiny as a child-molester or prowling vagrant. Virtually all of them would subject the "perpetrator"—especially an older person—to constant risk of assault, robbery, and even murder. Children have guns. Residential streets in the "wrong part" of town are patrolled by gangs and avoided by cops. Windows are barred and boarded. Playgrounds are fairs for drugs and prostitution. Alejandro Martí, whose son was lately kidnapped and murdered by inhuman thugs, remarked in an overpowering address to the Mexican Congress last year that parents used to release their children into streets and parks without fear. No longer: not in Mexico City, or Atlanta, or Sioux Falls.

So what creates this "siege scenario" of pedophiles, punks, prostitutes, and pirates? Is it big government? On the contrary, the member nations of the former Soviet-bloc countries were very tidy in this regard, as are fundamentalist Muslim nations today. The suspension or cancellation of individual rights by autocratic authority and the Procrustean punishment of violators is a recipe for very quiet streets. Yet Mr. Martí is correct: our streets here in the West were also safe a mere thirty or forty years ago. No doubt, if local governments had ten times more cops on residential beats, order might be somewhat restored; but this, too, is a big-government solution (at the local level). I do not recall, frankly, ever having seen a squad car in the neighborhood from end to end of which I habitually rode my bicycle fifty years ago.

Conservative commentators sooner or later cite the rising incidence of unwed mothers and of teenaged mothers (two distinct but related graphs) as a cause for unemployment, high crime, and degenerating neighborhoods. They are right to do so—yet they are again pumping water without patching the leak. Among the major forces driving the sexual revolution were two generated by the free market: the proliferation of automobiles and the mushrooming of "trash" TV. Of course, the waves of assault followed about the same timeline. Automobiles spread out communities and also allowed young people instant, easy mobility: teenagers could suddenly go places and commit follies without any fear of being recognized and reported to their parents. (One day a socialist will have the bright idea of indexing, not just single-motherhood, but also the growth of gangs to the rising abundance of cars.) Television was actually quite conservative throughout the Fifties and most of the Sixties. As its fare increasingly escaped the jaws of de-toothed censors, however—and especially with the arrival of UHF channels and then cable—the volume of dissolute behavior placed at every child's fingertips multiplied like a killer virus

It should be noted that such trends are seldom as natural—as proximate to the wholesome and proverbial "growing pain"—as their champions contend. Cars would never have managed to take over our landscape and our lives to the present extent had not the federal government favored the interstate highway system and the airlines over railroads (much the most efficient of haulers) after World War II. Cable networks, too (and, to a mounting degree, the Internet), are primarily the feeding ground of very big corporate fish who generally manage to make regulations drive small fry into their maw.

A free market uninhibited by strictures that protect the community's health from its excesses eventually creates a captive cesspool. Those who prosper acquire more and more power, by fair means or foul, with their prosperity; and the quickest path to the greatest prosperity is the forbidden, the gaudy, the vulgar.

Free enterprise has killed Socrates from another direction, as well: not just by degrading the stoa to a jungle, but also by making Socrates himself choose between life as a white-collar bureaucrat and a dumpster-diver. You say he should move to a safer neighborhood? Moves cost money. In the age of the automobile, nothing is within walking distance, and mass-transit is a gas-guzzling debacle; in Kansas City or Peoria or Des Moines, one *must* have wheels. The car itself is a huge expense. Gasoline is a further expense, rising all the time. Insurance demands its sacrifice of thousands. Having thus accoutered himself to reach a job every morning, Socrates finds his ruminations preoccupied with traffic for about two hours a day. Now time itself must be added to the costs which eliminate leisurely walks through the neighborhood: that is, once possessed of a safer house and street, when would the philosopher have hours of liberty to discuss the good life with his neighbors? If his rush-hour commutes have not stultified him, furthermore, by requiring the utter absorption of his consciousness into the rhythms of a machine, then his job itself—following stocks on the Internet or processing forms for faceless, numbered applicants—will beat the word "why" right out of his soul.

I would say the following in all candor and simplicity to the lions of the supposed, self-styled conservative scene. Where is the *savor* of this life—the beauty, the reverence, the grandeur? The intellectual and spiritual depth? Is Socrates' best hope—his only hope—a fatter paycheck that allows him to flee the prevailing squalor and eventually find a golfing or drinking buddy who loves to shoot the breeze? Is this the kind of snapshot we wish to offer into evidence that shoes are superior to sandals?

III. A Tale of Two Cities

My wife and I drove our fifteen-year-old son this past summer to Indianapolis for what is known as a baseball "showcase". (Scouts no longer condescend to drive dusty backroads to rural sandlots: baseball now pulses with so much money that would-be mountains must come to Mohammed.) None of us had ever seen this part of the nation: I had visited Chicago in the mid-Eighties, but via plane and without intermediate touchdowns. It turns out that every American town and small city, from Texarkana to Hope to West Memphis to Cape Girardeau to Effingham to Terre Haute, looks the same from an interstate highway. The green signs preceding exits advertise food, gas, and motels in different logos sometimes; but, once having taken the exit, you descend into the same spaghetti of impatient traffic navigating in and out of eateries, filling stations, and cheaply stuccoed horseshoe chateaux (with rooms as low as $69 a night). I don't know if a teenaged Rush Limbaugh or Karl Rove would—with excited naïveté—have viewed lunch at the Cracker Barrel or El Chico as tantamount to a cultural odyssey into backwoods Appalachia or to a hacienda on the high sierra. My strong suspicion, however, is that they would not have. Had they not by nature shared my own dread of the mawkish and the mass-produced, such men would never have been driven to insulate themselves with wealth from the nauseabund reign of tawdry artifice over Main Street, USA. When one plays lumberjack or cowboy with one's toddler, off-the-cuff impersonation is great fun; but at Flapjack Heaven or Rudy's Wild West Steakhouse, the peeling decor that squints at wooded Arcadia or wide-open spaces draws no smile as one sets about imbibing enough endorphins to face six more hours of road.

How many Americans keep body and soul together by scurrying about in bistros like these—waiting tables, tending registers, flipping omelets? Even gas stations are now fast-food outlets, some with Serve Yourself hot-dog buffets and smoothie bars. Truckers deliver, stock boys shelve, attendants ring it up, and motorists hit the road again with guts as restless as a troubled conscience, hoping to get home before their shift at the mall begins or to reach Toledo before Cindy's second daughter leaves for college. Eat, and drive, and dream while trying to stay awake... home... a bed of one's own, without strangers on the wall's other side....

In places like Indianapolis (i.e., in most mid-American cities), little burghs have grown together by running out tendrils of such fast-food alleys and strip malls. A developer creates a new subdivision just beyond the reach of this hamlet's taxes, another plans similar escapes from the opposing direction... and very suddenly, as it seems—often in less than a decade—ten such whistle stops collide in the same way that asteroids are said to form planets. A body of visionaries (consisting of ambitious lawyers and developers who forever keep the middle class on the run from heavy urbanization) throw a traffic loop around the whole mess, declare it a single municipality, and hike taxes to improve the quality of life through new schools, civic centers, freeways, parks, parkways... multiplying someone's riches with every stroke of the pen. Free enterprise in bed with populist-flavored paternalism: no one-night stand, but an illicit liaison that survives most marriages. And its offspring are all monstrosities.

If the sun had not shined pitilessly on central Indiana during most of our stay, I doubt that I would ever have found the varied venues on our schedule—this stadium or that high school or So-and-So College. Only thanks to shadow could I always sort out east from west and north from south, like a castaway in a jungle. Every map I could find was already hopelessly outdated, lifelong residents were themselves puzzled by my requests—and, no, I do not own a GPS. Since most of the city was never conceived as part of a greater unit, streets doubled back on themselves or changed names without warning. A central parkway which promised to get us expeditiously from A to B turned out to have no exits where we needed them, as if the sprawl alongside them had been meadow and forest during their construction. This road abruptly became one-way; that one inexplicably vanished after a mandatory turn; there the locals were prudently running a red light which never changed; and over there, of all things, a sign warned of stray deer! Is this an American city on its way to greater things... or is it not, rather, a typical American city—a labyrinth of chaotic construction traveled quickly only by human rats who have worn ruts to favorite spots?

In my estimation, certainly, Indianapolis is the latter—and I would stress the word "typical". We have encountered very similar frustrations in trying to find tournaments buried under the pullulating sediments of Shreveport (transformed by offshore casinos) and Dallas (awash in Mexican refugees). Maps rendered useless, GPS devices (as I hear) scarcely more helpful, unnamed or mislabeled streets to nowhere, single streets of many names, crisscrossing streets and highways without any means of transit from these to those for five miles, roads that glibly reverse their original direction, pastures or forests or oil derricks in the midst of metropolitan bedlam, residents who speed from apartment to job but couldn't direct you to a major landmark for ready money... this is the rule rather than the exception in America. Indianapolis is Middleville, USA.

Urbanites joke wryly about the bedlam as they would about the summer heat—except that even the heat is now being laid at the doorstep of global warming. Americans confront the horrors of their cities, that is, with more resignation than they do the weather. They must know at some level—even the dullest of them—that men and women have not always lived this way. Yet they accept their common misery as a fact of life from now on: the cost of admittance into a wonderworld of pizzarias, drive-thrus, malls, sports arenas, airports, car lots, and strip clubs. What worries me is the thought that many may really consider this a fair exchange—that human taste and intelligence have already grown so debased that we "live for" shopping sprees and eating binges. If we have indeed been reduced to such a tribe of gaping, belching kine (and a trip to Houston's Minute Maid Park last year very nearly forced me to that conclusion), then our indefinite imprisonment in these hell-holes really does present itself to the mind with all the grim gravity of Fate.

But Señor Martí and I (if no one else) can recall another world of not so very long ago. Speaking only for myself, I can remember the Austin of my childhood, a city which passes for old in Texas and which we would visit two or three times a year to see my grandparents. In his infinite wisdom, my grandfather warned that the University should move its campus to Lake Travis rather than trying to expand into the city center. It did the latter throughout the Sixties, sending shirtless-and-shoeless waifs into every quarter of the downtown area, creating incessant traffic congestion, nourishing Third World-caliber blocks of hovels with high rents, imbuing every shady avenue with disorderly conduct and drug traffic, releasing a fleet of stench-ridden rattletrap buses upon the whole metropolis to haul surly students to and from their classroom indoctrinations... the Austin I once knew, as of 1968, was as dead as Socrates.

But when I was a child, towering pecan trees kept old sidewalks permanently cool. Century-old residences of granite or limestone were maintained by elderly people who wouldn't hesitate to wave from behind a mesh screen, their windows and front doors wide open. Jackdaws cackled more loudly than cars could grumble, and the University Tower (from which Charles Whitman would gun down three dozen victims to ring in the new age) could be heard chiming the hour far more often than an ambulance would hit its siren. Yet Breckenridge Hospital was scarcely a mile away from my grandmother's 1870-vintage premises, whose second-storey rooms she rented out as apartments to "respectable" state workers. (She would pay off the house eventually from those years of collected rent, my grandfather having been forced to change careers abruptly after a crooked politician ousted him from his teaching employ for daring to contend in a small town's school-superintendent election.) There was no plumbing for washing machines of any kind in the old manse—but no great need for it, either. My grandmother and her celibate tenants thought nothing of rinsing dishes in the sink after supper or wringing out underwear in the bath tub. For larger jobs, there was a washateria two blocks down the hill, toward the high school and Pease Park; and by the laundromat sat an H.E.B. grocery store, from which I would later, as a teenager, transport many a brown bag home on foot.

In the other direction (due east), the Capitol was a mere three blocks away: an easy, pleasant stroll. Within those three blocks, one would have passed another antiquated structure with "Austin School of Beauty" emblazoned over its facade; and then—an indispensable pilgrimage on every childhood visit—the Toy Palace. I recall at least two restaurants farther up Guadalupe Street, as well. In my grandfather's company as a boy of five or six, I would sometimes walk all the way to the Capitol grounds and beyond, up Congress Avenue. Lamme's Candies sat at the corner. Mexican farmers would sometimes, in mid-summer, be parked along the sidewalk selling cantaloupe out of the back of their trucks. There was a jeweler's, a family-owned department store, and a movie theater, as well. My mother marched all of us kids to this last to see *Babes in Toyland* one afternoon. For some reason, I recollect this as one of the happiest days of my childhood, simply because the real setting was no less idyllic than the film's.

All that is gone now—long gone. My question is not why people must grow old and die, by why places in their prime must be razed to the ground and replaced by inhuman racket, rush, and ugliness. The businesses I have mentioned made a nice go of it: they were not fatally flawed with some internal deficiency. What has torn American cities asunder, in a manner which I think both a national disgrace and a profound symptom of the cancer rotting our whole society, is the diabolical allegiance of free enterprise *and* paternalistic, top-down government. H.E.B. and the Toy Palace went under long before anyone ever heard of the microwave of the Internet. The University's explosion drove them to the bottom in a tsunami of tax hikes and shattered residential blocks. People in real estate and banking who had Town

Hall's ear (or perhaps some other part of its sickly anatomy) within easy reach knew precisely where the wave would move and what damage it would do. Property values skyrocketed. Construction companies and their tentacles (mostly leading back to the banks again) feasted off of fat new contracts. Century-old homes were demolished to make room for high-rise office buildings. (My grandparents' house, sold immediately after their death, survived only because it wore the Historical Commission's medallion—and survived only partially, at that.) The high-rises rose so high, grasping after the premium rent of downtown spaces, that they threw the Capitol itself into their shadows. (A few legislators fought to impose height limitations: they lost.) Traffic multiplied exponentially. New highways had to be constructed for its expeditious rush to and from the city center. More taxes, more federal grant money, more construction boom-time. Even if a small business had been able to cling to its premises, none of its clientele would have wanted to battle the ant swarm of downtown congestion only to park—expensively—five blocks away after a half-hour's search for one space. I believe that Lamme's Candies survived, miraculously, through a strategy combining the Internet and a multiplied "live customer" base of state-bureaucrat types on break. Attorneys and politicos are not supposed to return from lunch stoned: being revved up on sugar, however, is entirely acceptable,

My liberal friends in Austin sometimes put me out of patience with their response to the city's meltdown (my translation of "build-up") even as they vex me with their "babes in Toyland" reaction to other crises. Most of them, by way of solution, can think of little more than riding bikes to work—which, of course, few actually do. Austin is usually hot, and biking can be hard labor. The darker truth, to me, is that they really don't mind working in air-conditioned government offices or law firms on the twenty-eighth floor, making stops at the Starbuck's by the parking lot. After all, as students, they had railed and clamored *against* the bourgeois life which allowed an apartment house, a toy store, and a "beauty school" to turn a humble profit among blocks of quiet, clean residences. Toward the end of my grandmother's life, they very nearly drove her into the red as their phalanxes supplanted the mannerly celibate state employees of the Fifties. Since she paid all her tenants' utilities, this incomparably gentle-souled landlady could ill afford to subsidize girlfriends and boyfriends who sneaked in (violating the lease agreement, but often not at once detectable) after the new guest had taken a month to settle down. The live-and-love-free crowd turned out also to be very hard on furniture. Though my grandmother had supplied all her apartments with tasteful antiques, squatters were not deterred from tossing mattresses on the floor and resting lukewarm beers on end tables. Their "natural" style very nearly trashed the neighborhood before the banks had time to buy it up and plow it under.

I am uninterested, then, in listening to a "social revolutionary" talk about anything. I have wasted too much of my life harkening to the hypocritical bombast of those who crush little people on their way to freeing the Common

Man. Where, though, are the voices of the Right? When a proposed Wal-Mart threatens to transform a neighborhood in the fashion I have just described and a citizens' group mounts resistance, on which side are the golden voices of Talk Radio? When a metropolis ineffectually struggles with traffic congestion by attempting the umpteenth resurrection of the mass-transit option, what alternatives do self-styled conservative mouthpieces offer to this invincibly flawed strategy? What is their conserving vision of a community where people can walk pleasant streets in health and safety? Simply to behold the mixed response of this group to such atrocious private/public sector conspiracies as using imminent domain to create posh new resorts must inspire indignation in any of us who rates lucre well below justice or decency.

In the second half of this essay, I shall suggest a mechanism for political centrifugy, without which any attempt to restore a human rhythm to our kidnapped tastes, values, and cultures must be futile. I shall argue for how communities might be able once again to push their shared vision of a certain quality of life to the head of the pack—well to the front of various private-sector "visions" radiating dollar signs, well ahead of their covert-bedfellow public-sector "visions" awash in hopes of mass manipulation. I know that the ever-derisory "neo-conservative" advocate will characterize—or rather caricature—people like me who value a quasi-rural simplicity in urban settings as technophobic Luddites. Yet one such of my critics, beyond guffawing in print over the notion that anyone would prefer stability to a mountain of ready cash, could adduce no further evidence of his cause's superiority than that he himself enjoys frequent travel, craves lively parties, and finds himself bored in more sedate circumstances.

I am angered when I think of my grandmother's home (for so she considered every inch of the living space under her roof) being vandalized by ideology-soaked leftist brats; but I confess that I grow far angrier when I ponder an entire city's being transformed into a pulsating playground for trust-fund princelings with money to burn and appetites to feed. Such people may inherit a great deal of power, but genuine progress requires that they be parted from their ability to shape our living space as best amuses them. This would be an honest conservative's progress: i.e., keeping good things substantially the same as the world's essential degenerative forces seek to gnaw at them.

IV. Regulation and Taxation Dictate Social Policy

In the first part of this essay, I lamented that neighborhoods in most American cities—and even in most large towns—no longer reflect a human scale of activity, but are rather built to accommodate machines. Widened streets and segregated functions (especially residence and commerce) have eradicated sidewalks and friendly corner shops in order to meet the needs and minimize the risks of our cars. Because businesses are concentrated in specified areas, tall buildings must be constructed to exploit costly space; or in younger, more westerly cities where space abounds, an endless sprawl results. Furthermore, because residential sections have grown so distant from these areas, other tall buildings—offering apartments with staggering price tags—have arisen a few blocks from business megaliths in confined eastern spaces. Here and likewise farther west, speedy, regular mass transit receives major emphasis, as well: metro trains and commuter flights, in particular. Trains require unhampered track space, which further divides and degrades inner-city neighborhoods—factors rendering escape to the far-flung suburbs yet more attractive. Airports, of course, cannot safely be surrounded by residential areas even if anyone should choose to live within the radius of their steady racket. Hence the city's sprawl oozes still farther, and the car becomes less dispensable than ever.

I contend that this situation would only represent progress if we completely eliminated human comfort and happiness from our calculation. From a machine's point of view, we do indeed appear to be creating more and more spaces for wheels to turn and pistons to pound with ever greater ease... but why should we be so solicitous about the satisfaction of steel hulks? Would not a better measure of progress be the number of miles a city-dweller might walk in safety and peace (dare we even throw *pleasure* into the equation)? What about indexing our level of civilization to the number of people we address directly, eye to eye, in the course of a day without expectation of monetary exchange or material profit? Or perhaps to the number of children we can name in the residences adjacent to our own?

If any of these latter is a true measure of human success in civilized circumstances (and only an uncivilized brute or a robot could doubt that all are so0, then our contemporary megalopolis is, in fact, retrogressing. I am well aware—painfully and indignantly aware—that some among us, perhaps many, don't give a fig about the lost world of our grandparents; that they would regard shaded sidewalks and neighborhood diners as a recipe for deadly tedium, and that they would kick and scream if deprived of their cocktails in first class served by blonde models, their business lunches in *cordon bleu* restaurants covered by expense accounts, and their nights on the throbbing, luminous town in the company of professional escorts. I think the vapid, push-button brats of "technopoly" should certainly have the "darkness visible" of their Big Apples and Big Easies as long as their patronage suffices to pay for the operation of such costly fantasies. I cannot, however, see a speck of justification for their visiting misery upon the rest of us in order to protract their naughty childhood.

For contrary to popular impression, preserving human settlements does not require a vast legislative umbrella of artificial nurture, like the habitat of an endangered species. The high-tech megalopolis, rather, is that setting which feeds on the artificial intrusions of big government and big business. Urban life on a human scale has existed for thousands of years: it has perfectly overlapped, until very recently, the decision of humans to live in towns. (Yes, I am having my ironic joke—but how absurd it is, on the other hand, for progressives to imagine that we would soon perish unless smothered in "convenience"!) If 500 refugees were stuck for months on an island after the ditching of a jumbo jet—if, for some reason, they concluded that they would pass the rest of their lives in this isolation—the order established within a year would feature a degree of safety, helpfulness, and general neighborliness which would shame our most "advanced" capitals of progress today.

So the state of contemporary cities cannot be explained to most sane adults by the sheer joy of living in them. In what respects are these near-chaotic places the malignant manifestation of a public-private sector pathology rather than the robust prow of Progress's advancing ship? Allow me to begin by remarking a few untreated infections latent in modern economic and political life:

- Legal regulations imposed upon the work environment (OSHA standards, wheelchair access, fire exits, etc.) ALWAYS favor big business. Such laws initiate a chain-reaction of at least three stages that allows larger enterprises to thrive, and I suspect a fourth stage is often involved. 1) The corporation funds whatever expense is necessary to come fully into compliance with a new code while its smaller competition struggles to meet stricter standards. 2) Many smaller businesses simply shut down, since they can no longer turn a profit under the growing legal burden of operational strictures. 3) Big companies, having survived the regulative strain thanks to their greater resources, can now raise retail prices because much of the smaller competition that used to undercut them has evaporated. Informed by this paradoxically happy ordeal, said companies may also 4) donate heavily to political candidates championing the cause of further government intrusion; for the process can be repeated with the same benefits as long as such companies are somewhat better financed than their remaining competitors.

- In a closely related matter, the "seal of approval" supplied by various accrediting agencies (some of them private-sector "for profit" entities) seldom significantly protects the buyer from anything, while collectively the process further undermines a system that allows buyers a diverse marketplace. Safety ratings, for instance, often function similarly to an arm of government oppression. Larger businesses can afford lawyers, self-study officers, quality control checks, and other luxuries involved not only in bringing them into required compliance with government standards (as above) but also in acquiring the additional fluff and frills of gold-medal certification. (In other words, advertising assumes a disguise of clinical evaluation.) As a career teacher, I would say without hesitation that the licensures and accreditations so coveted by institutions from kindergarten to college have a net *negative* impact on the educational product; for they consume valuable resources in generating reams of paperwork, and the "quality standards" of the licensing bodies are often outrageously subjective (if not rigidly ideological).

Or say that a man with carpentry skills makes rockers from a workshop in his back yard. This industrious artisan would probably be ruined if a certain 300-pound customer decided to sue him for injuries incurred when a rocker collapsed under his enormous weight. In contrast, the furniture-manufacturer with five factories in China will infallibly affix a small-print sticker beneath the rocker warning of limited liability beyond a precise weight limit. Another sticker will clarion that this assembly-line clone is approved by The American Society of ****. Meanwhile, the hard-working carpenter is taking out a second mortgage to pay his court fees.

•   The previous anecdote leads directly to another cancer in the American body-politic: trial lawyers. In a sane, responsible society, the public would renounce its "right" to preposterous suits if it wished free enterprise to thrive in small communities at an individual level. After all, industry and creativity are natural to man: the invention and exploitation of verbal formulas with hidden meanings is quintessentially artificial. Common sense dictates that a producer's legal liability should be strictly limited to cases where a high risk of life or limb attends *normal and competent* use (i.e., children who fall from swings, cooks who cut themselves on knives, and boxers who break wrists on punching bags would have no legal recourse). The unholy brotherhood of attorneys, however, has long ago slipped a noose around common sense's neck.

How likely is change in the legal profession to occur when it requires action on the part of the very professional class which most profits from the status quo? Yet the public would be well served simply to recognize that trial lawyers as a group constitute a big business whose stifling effect on economic opportunity and creativity far exceeds the conspiracy-theorist's wildest fears of oil companies.

As for the romantic notion that these same lawyers routinely haul wicked corporations into court to answer for their misdeeds, large businesses (each with its own fleet of attorneys, naturally) can often forestall such suits with a letter or two. Extremely large corporations may indeed find themselves shielded by the very government agencies intended to police them. Case in point: the recent pursuit of foreign-owned Toyota by U.S. government prosecutors even as government-underwritten General Motors began to enjoy a host of new contracts for vehicles rejected by the private-sector consumer. To say that government-fixed-and-enforced safety standards invite a rash of bribed inspectors would be excessively harsh at this time in this country (though throughout most of the world, the relationship often blossoms precisely into a "shakedown"). Yet the presence of "a good lawyer" on its payroll usually equips any organization with the "stealth" technology needed to fly under Big Brother's paternal radar. My own struggles to bring The Center for Literate Values to a 501(3)3 status, opening the door the donations enjoyed by "recognized" charities, would have been immensely easier had I simply known to avoid certain phrases and to repeat others during the application process. Under the circumstances, if someone were to say to me that our system actually represents a much more complex, lucrative, and subversive shakedown than the Third World cop's who tears up tickets for a fiver, I would not have the heart to call him a cynic.

• ANY form of taxation other than a universal sales tax can easily be manipulated by special interests. Licensing fees, though justifiable when they help to maintain facilities used only by a small segment of the population, can potentially screen "undesirables" from certain activities (e.g., the very exclusive confraternity of undertakers, whose life's work—with the help of government—is to make dying too costly to endure). Property taxes effectively keep people at a certain income-level from entering certain parts of town. More than that, the property tax has played a major role in keeping American families on the move, much to the delight of developers and real estate agents. As taxes within the city limits rise, homeowners exit to the suburbs— which, inevitably, are roped into the more highly taxed circle within a few years. Improvements upon existing homes are also promptly punished by the local tax assessor, thus providing yet another motive to move. (I am reminded of nineteenth-century tenant-farming in Ireland, when your landlord would immediately raise your rent if you built a door for your hut.)

Naturally, that most infamous and onerous tax of all—the income tax—punishes hard workers even before they dare to buy property. Certainly the fear of stumbling into a higher tax bracket must motivate anyone of average intelligence to weigh carefully whether he really ought to expand his business or invest his money where it is likely to earn big dividends. If government were to bribe citizens to remain indigent, would the result look very different from a graduated income tax?

Most of the moralizing offered on behalf of the taxes named above ("Someone needs to pay for society's upkeep—let the ones who have profited most from living here pay the most!") would be fully satisfied by a sales tax. If necessities such as food and medicine (*necessary* food and medicine) were excluded from the levy, then the high-roller would pay every time he purchased a Cadillac instead of a Ford, every time he vacationed in the Bahamas instead of Gatlinburg, and every time he bought Champagne instead of Budweiser. Those who should be shopping at Wal-Mart rather than spending themselves into debt at Tiffany's would have further incentive to learn a little thrift—for this tax is essentially one on luxury. The wealthy Scrooge who prefers to live like a pauper would (unless his mind were touched) have invested his hoard in sound enterprises, which would proceed to prosper even more with his patronage and produce further jobs for laborers. Society's illegally resident element and its criminal class would also ante up at every trip to the movies or the barber shop. All would chip in. And because the funding of local, state, and federal government would come almost entirely from this source, citizens would be constantly and acutely aware of just how much government was costing them.

The very resistance of the universal sales tax to devious manipulation is, of course, the main obstacle it faces. How will the powerful elite control the rest of us when they cannot set one class against another and hide their squandering folly within a mist of complex bookkeeping? Of course, our tax code is a raging example of devious artifice. If such a design reflects the triumph of rationality in the progressive world, then Suleiman the Magnificent's harem was a model for simple marital bliss.

•   Probably the most direct way of influencing significantly a neighborhood's appearance through taxation comes from intrusion at the very highest level—and the influence is pernicious, I hasten to add, exactly because the central authorities sit hundreds or thousands of miles away from the affected community. Our system, for instance, allows the federal government to collect tax revenue from law-abiding residents throughout the nation and then *re-introduce that money with strings attached* into its original setting. The construction of interstate highways perhaps applies this kind of manipulation in more daylight than any other such project. Municipal leaders want federal money pouring into their district (and maybe into the pockets of their friends or relatives in construction and real estate… who knows?); so they lobby actively to bring these highways straight through their cities, usually plowing under or otherwise ruining the oldest neighborhoods, in the process. Federal and state money is indeed usually available for any kind of mass transit, whereas no such money at all awaits the rare planner who wishes to keep cities tightly knit rather than continuing to scatter and sequester their functions. Big-government patronage of mass transit, always a favorite of self-styled "green" politicians, simply aids and abets urban sprawl by making daily migrations of workers all the easier.

To reiterate my main point, if such regulations and taxes as those just mentioned were obliterated from the books, our local communities—without further stimulus than that—would at once begin to conform themselves again to more human (and humane) patterns. Many contemporary Americans would shrink from this proposition with the cry, "But how would we survive without oversight, bothersome and intrusive though it is? Take it away, and robber barons will run roughshod all over our towns!" In fact, the historical robber barons of the late nineteenth century were ruthless businessmen who monopolized market power and bought political influence. That is, their *modus operandi* was closely analogous to that of Warren Buffet, George Soros, Teresa Heinz, and other champions of paternalistic government today. If you bought your clothes from your neighbor the tailor, and an assembly-line apparel factory suddenly moved into town, would your neighbor go hungry? Probably not: his product could be individualized to suit each client's size, he would surely correct any flaw or repair any damage without a customer's having to "go through channels", the quality of his work would surpass the cost-cutting mass producer's, and he would extend credit in cases where he knew trust was justified.

What has put people like this out of business in our time is less a market-flood of merchandise assembled by slave labor in China and Mexico, I suspect, than incidental fees and hassles such as the following incurred by any would-be tailor: purchase of a vendor's license, filing for an Employer Identification Number, purchase of place of business if home workshop is deemed to violate zoning laws, taxes on place of business, local sales tax on all articles sold (not to be confused with a universal sales tax), payment of franchise tax, upgrading of work and sales locations to satisfy safety code, payment of OSHA fines, engaging attorney to handle "nuisance" lawsuits… at some point, people would rather punch a clock at the factory. And the factory's owner knows it—which is why he is always a covert friend to the bureaucracy that buries small entrepreneurs.

V. Sole Owner and Operator: Happiest Man in the World

To be sure, communities cannot be left completely unguarded by regulations and ordinances, any more than their streets will be safe without a police force. I do not suggest that we embrace a libertarianism that would flirt with anarchy. If a homeowner were allowed to graze cattle in his back yard, neighbors might buy milk from him or not, as they chose; but no neighbor would exercise any choice over whether or not a dense fly population settled upon the area, and flies spread bacteria—they import diseases. Hence such zoning laws as would force this man's livestock beyond the city limits are common-sense. They are not top-down mandates from invisible powers whose innumerable hangers-on very likely stand to profit from some arcane restriction: instead, they are the will of the majority that actually lives in the neighborhood. Thus Zia Giuseppina can make a diner out of her front room if she wishes and serve pasta from her kitchen to anyone who walks through the door; but the moment that she collects more garbage than her trash cans can hold—or is found to have trash cans that won't resist stray dogs—she will receive a fine and a court order to clean things up. This much makes sense. It is not inimical to individual enterprise: it gives the individual entrepreneur, rather, a safe and healthy community from which to draw clients—people who are not frightened away by filthy, dangerous streets.

Of course, the zoning of certain areas as exclusively residential and others as commercial was originally intended to maintain health and safety, for the fear was that racing, wheeling auto traffic would harrow spots where children rode their bicycles if the two functions were mixed. This fear fails to withstand scrutiny, however. If every neighborhood contained small shops as well as residences, then the typical patrons of any particular shop would be pedestrian. Why get in your car and drive ten miles for a haircut when a fellow two blocks down can satisfy you? In any case, nothing prevents neighborhoods from creating car parks where those from outside the immediate community must leave their vehicles and walk (or be conveyed, for a small fee, by golf carts). Technology makes such an operation more feasible than ever: a scaled-down, affordable, and downright pleasant form of "mass transit" might even be created to serve larger neighborhoods. This arrangement, then, need no more be conceived of as Luddite than as anarchic. In the case of both technology and regulation, the major criterion of selection would simply be *what makes sense to the locals*. Commands from on high would be sent back to the clouds.

I shall return to the subject of regulation in the final section. For now, I wish to emphasize how happily a creative individual could live in the "reduced circumstances" I have described. Let us admit, first of all, that circumstances would indeed be reduced in the accepted sense of producing less profit. A local entrepreneur who serves a largely neighborhood clientele would make less money—probably far less—than his counterpart in the downtown office of a multinational corporation. Let us leave entirely to one side the matter of how very limited is the number of jobs in any such downtown office (where "lean and mean" has been the catch-phrase for years): let us grant, for argument's sake, that our hypothetical laborer might have either gig. If he stays in the neighborhood, he will enjoy certain intangibles that are intimately related to the happiness of successfully socialized adults. He will not fight traffic two hours a day, he will remain among friends and acquaintances, he will be close to his family, and he will have a far richer involvement in his work (such that he can make his own hours, doubling his output or cutting it in half).

How does this man find true happiness, though, on an income perhaps one fourth or fifth of what the office offers? Besides the spiritual rewards of being closer to the significant people in his life and taking pride in the work of his own hands, he is substantially diminishing his cost of living. He may well sell one of his cars: the savings on gasoline will certainly be enormous, and also on auto insurance. No need to pay for day care: he is at or near home when the kids return from school. His health improves as his stress level declines: fewer visits to the doctor. The taxes which he is now *not* paying—

whose disappearance would greatly contribute to the possibility of this scenario—are now on the "credit" side of his ledger. He need not sell his house for a more expensive but less taxed one in remote suburbia as his family grows: he may simply add a room (or pay or barter with a neighbor to have it added) without fear of that wandering ogre, the tax assessor. Enough savings are implicit in his new way of life that he may very well end up breaking even.

The case is occasionally made these days that the image of the independent, self-sufficient individual is a male one ("phallocentric", as academics say in their polysyllabic species of crudity)—that it repels more than attracts females. I could send the hostility of this charge back where it came from by arguing that the recent ascendancy of women in our economy is indeed a major cause of growth in intrusive centralized government. Inasmuch as women are usually more social than men, they would presumably feel less oppressed—and might even feel exhilarated—by a work setting of intricately layered bureaucracy. If this is so, then many women might regard a return to stable, self-contained neighborhoods as being cast back into the oubliette of kitchen and nursery. (On this score, my voice and the academic feminist's would sound agreement.) The destiny of the stay-at-home mom would loom heavily over the New Woman's head.

Yet I find such fears exaggerated. My personal experience suggests that energetic women often draw at least as much pleasure as men from creating and sustaining a small business, and the localized and tax-liberated environment I envision would multiply their opportunities to engage in such enterprises. In fact, men would have far more opportunities to share in household duties such as child-rearing. No doubt, the bureaucratic setting does offer the petty-despot personality greater latitude for making the world just a bit more miserable... and who's to say if this most loathsome of character-types is gender-neutral? I certainly have no opinion on the subject! At most, perhaps female bosses who have only lately enjoyed the chance to climb onto a little throne are making their edicts heard more loudly than they will do after settling into the role.

Meanwhile, the revitalized neighborhood will still allow corporate-executive types of either sex to commute to and from their urban domains: it will simply allow, as well, more placid and introspective people to stay away from those domains for longer periods of time.

VI. The Freedom of Families to Make Neighborhoods

So far, I have argued that settled, neighborly communities would be highly likely to reemerge in North America if individual citizens and private businesses were simply relieved of a whopping and manipulative tax and regulative burden. Human beings do not require compulsory legislation to act in a humane fashion: they require, rather, to be liberated from a duress that squeezes them toward an inhumane conformity, a desperate frustration, and sometimes even a violent reaction of some sort. I have not yet written of the reduction in crime certain to occur in more tightly knit communities, but this benefit is surely worth mentioning. Not only are young men less likely to commit crimes when they have jobs, and people of all ages more likely to be law-abiding when they find their work environment personal and rewarding rather than the equivalent of an assembly line or an anthill; children and adolescents, as well, will more likely grow up honest and decent if their years are passed in a single locality where neighbors come to know them well.

The crucible of such uplifting values is indubitably well worth preserving—and, no, such a precious incubator is not generated merely by removing artificial restrictions on behavior. If people can be driven to bad deeds by bad circumstances, they also carry within them the seed of malevolence. A functional neighborhood, then, must assist the individual in keeping buried that which must stay buried as well as in freeing him from the suffocating pressures of faceless, remotely centralized power. I have referred to the necessity of safeguarding public health by limiting what sort of livestock a resident may import into a neighborhood. The principle does not stop with animals. All rational adults would further agree that no resident has the right to set off fire crackers at random hours of the day or night on his property; that no resident may build a glass room atop his house wherein he and his friends dance nude before the surrounding block; that no resident may throw up an earthwork in his back yard and practice a fast-draw "fanning" of his revolver into it; that no resident may give a pet python free range among the trees of his front lawn; and so on, and so on. There are innumerable constraints to how one may act on one's private plot of land in a communal setting. Ownership of land differs from ownership of a coat. You may shred a coat if you wish, or clothe an image of Satan in it, or set it on fire with photos of your worst enemy in its pockets. The purchase of land within a neighborhood, however, carries a tacit consent to employ that land as part of the neighborhood. The recluse may buy a country plot and do any of the antisocial or high-risk acts cited above to his heart's content. In purchasing his quarter-acre within the city limits, however, he submits and subscribes to the idea that he will practice ownership in a neighborly fashion.

Now, big government—remotely centralized authority—is NOT the best arbiter of the standards determining a neighborhood. It may well be the worst, at least among all practical options. One reason, among many, is once again that it may yield to the persuasion of big business. The preeminent example of such sabotage must be the grotesque abuse of imminent domain in recent years. Those who fear how the lawless, rowdy bravos of capitalism would shoot up a town if the state capital or Washington, DC, were not walking the rounds of the local sheriff should ponder some of the cases all over the nation where huge speculative enterprises have, through government and the courts, literally chased people out of their homes. No doubt, the advocates of centralized power (which always means power and force to the maximum) will scream "murder" if we allow local communities to pass and enforce ordinances pleasing to local populations. They will shriek, first of all, that we are inviting a return to the days of racial segregation. Indeed, certain overarching principles must not be violated at the local level. Citizens must not be banned, anywhere in the United States, from living in this part of town or working that job because of their race. The truth is, though, that segregation remains very much alive in American residential areas—self-segregation, where people choose to reside among their "own kind" because they feel more "comfortable" in that setting. If anything, centralized government's attempt to desegregate the nation by *emphasizing* racial identity (in diametrical opposition to Dr. King's vision) has been a major force in creating such comfort zones.

A huge majority of mainstream Americans is immensely more concerned about the appearance of new construction in the neighborhood than about the appearance of new residents. A strip mall requires acres of flat, soulless tarmac for parking in a way that businesses operated out of the home and serving local customers do not—which was precisely the reason, in the beginning, for zoning laws. Yet residential property-owners (especially those with a little clout at Town Hall) can readily have their land re-zoned if it sits near a residential-commercial seam. Such situations initiate a series of falling dominoes whose final state of rest is neighborhood collapse. A new motel is currently rising at the edge of my own neighborhood, next to a busy highway loop. Once operational, this enterprise will multiply traffic congestion tenfold at certain times of day. A steady flow of trash will find its way into adjacent yards. Homes immediately beside the motel will seem less private. If the establishment should degenerate over the years, its clientele could even pose a degree of danger to nearby residents.

Home-owners begin to sell their property in such circumstances, one after another. A few even follow suit in having their land re-zoned to appeal to a broader market, using the spearhead business as a legal rationale. At the very least, and in the immediate future, the neighborhood does not *look* the same. It now possesses a great wide gap, like a smile missing an incisor, and its quiet is fractured at dawn and dusk by departing and arriving cars in vast volumes. The individual home-owner can do little about this. Typically, nearby residents may receive notice of a public hearing where they can voice their disapproval—and if that disapproval reaches some vaguely defined volume, then they win the day. Yet the arrangement is notoriously prone to abuse. (The BBC Radio classic, *The Hitchhiker's Guide to the Galaxy*, satirized such a meeting at its beginning to account for the destruction of Planet Earth.) I have known of at least one case where not a single resident was demonstrably informed of the impending issue before it was decided. Thus the community-minded citizen is stuck with the hard truth that his neighbor enjoys the "right" to begin the process of collapse at any time, or to sustain it without any general consultation. A piece of property, in this regard, is considered to be like a coat: you can sell it to whomever you please.

My one and only "more government, more regulation" proposal, then, would be that neighborhoods possess a *veto power* over such matters as changes in zoning or sale to an entity whose intent for the land's use radically differs from the surrounding community's practice. I mean, to be clear, that residents on the actual city blocks affected should have this power bestowed upon them, and that they should be explicitly, formally, and inclusively polled—not summoned to a meeting announced on the back page of the local rag. A person who "buys into" a community—who chooses to integrate its setting and values to his family's style of living—should not later be permitted to "sell out" that setting and those values for a handsome personal profit. Many new neighborhoods already claim the right (which apparently has legal standing) to require that new construction meet certain specifications: so many minimal square feet of brick facade, so many minimal feet back from the curb, etc. The preservation of the neighborhood from "drive-thru" culture seems to me of incalculably greater importance than such cosmetic concerns. (And I would add that, if neighborhoods were indeed to integrate functions in the manner described earlier, this kind of menace would almost disappear; for instance, the number of "bed and breakfast" arrangements in private homes would satisfy the demand for travelers' accommodations while absorbing or removing the motel's attendant risks.)

Let me conclude by applying this suggestion to a type of problem whose specific cases are growing exponentially: the construction of mosques. The view is much publicized (ironically, most often by people who regret the existence of private property) that the owner of a plot of land enjoys the right to build whatever he wants on that land; or, at any rate, that if the land is zoned for churches, then the owner may build whatever kind of church he wishes. In a predominantly Christian neighborhood, a mosque would likely have an irritating or even subversive effect. Islam's holy book does not cultivate the impression that "the true faith" can coexist peacefully with others, non-Muslims as well as Muslims are keenly aware of this in the twenty-first century, and the mosque itself—if constructed along traditional line—would thrust a physically dissonant image into the heart of most Western communities (an effect much magnified if the muezzin is broadcast several times a day). The question must indeed be asked, Why would devoted Muslims *want* to worship in a setting which produced such friction with their beliefs and customs? The only rational answer is that they hope to see the friction disappear one day—which will only happen when the character of the surrounding neighborhood is completely transformed. The mosque itself, in other words, is a beachhead in a war of cultural conquest. One may consult Brigitte Gabriel's *They Must Be Stopped* or any of a dozen other analyses of the post-Khomeini expansionist game-plan to assess the body of evidence.

The residents of a predominantly Christian community should have a preemptive right to block such construction. Similarly, the residents of a predominantly Muslim community should enjoy the right of nixing a Christian church in their midst. A community whose majority is hostile to religious faith in any shape should be able to stop any church at all from going up. Neighborhoods are extensions of the private home. Just as a tastefully decorated home does not mix early-American designs with contemporary furniture, so a pleasant neighborhood whose residents willingly pass decades of their lives within its confines project their shared values to the casual observer through the character of their public parks, the quality of their private landscaping, the supply of general walking space, the sort of small business thriving on street corners, and so forth. Indeed, American tourists often go to such places (usually in spots far from home, since their own nation now offers so few) though they have no cultural or ideological sympathy with the forces behind the unique structures they see. The joy of the trip is simply to savor the aesthetic pleasure of coherent human habitations.

It would be perverse to read my example above as "religious bigotry". It is cultural imbecility, rather, to maintain that people of a certain faith are bigots if they prefer not to raise their children amid overt and visible challenges to their faith (though big business, to be sure, piously preaches such sermons about "tolerance": the more readily we put up with anything, the easier everything is to market). In rebuttal, I might mention my disapproval of a huge Protestant church that has slowly devoured the neighborhood in which my parents once dwelt. Their former home is now all of one block from the latest parking lot, whose way was cleared by the destruction of at least a dozen homes. No doubt, each owner was richly compensated; but the cost paid by the neighborhood, as a place of settlement and seasoned beauty, is well beyond what any dollar figure can ever equal. The congregation in question would have done far better to amass its cars in the parking lot of some shopping center closed to business on Sunday mornings, then shuttle itself a few blocks to the church in buses. Its present envelope of flat asphalt proclaims to the surviving community not yet sealed under a frozen gray slab, "To Hell with the rest of you!"

Of course, even a church can be big business. Local churches whose congregants tend to walk to services do not rake in enough cash to salary ten ministers, build recreation centers, or lobby the state legislature… so the cycle of dehumanization and top-down edict begins again, this time under the aegis of spirituality. May God in heaven lead us out of this wasteland!

A Return to the Castle: Enhancing City Life by Restricting Population

*First published in **Praesidium** 15.4 (Fall 2015).*

Having delivered my son to the campus where he has lately transferred his college credits, my wife and I were invited to a parents' meeting that turned out to have been ill planned. The number of attendees was nearly twice that of available chairs in the room. As I sweated out the hour (all too literally) and marveled at the heat generated by sedentary bodies, I recalled my own place of employ's state-sponsored paranoia in such matters. The "fire marshal" (a faceless abstraction whom I nonetheless always picture in a red helmet with a long brim bending over the neck) would never let us get away with packing a space like this, bless his oil-skinned heart.

For some reason, that thought clung to me throughout the afternoon and the following day, when we abandoned my boy one more time to seek his adulthood among strangers and fought our way through Denver traffic. I mused upon all the spaces that have mandatory, and perfectly sensible, occupation limits. A dormitory has only so many chambers, and each of these accommodates only so many recumbent bodies. A college campus has only so many teachers and classrooms: when the maximum is reached, further applicants must be shifted to a waiting list or go elsewhere. Restaurants are the same way. You can't seat customers on the floor or in the parking lot. They can line up out the door and await a table, or they can drive off in search of another watering hole.

This is all common sense. No one, even in our insanity-friendly era (when "fairness", for instance, seems to license robbing Peter to finance Paul's deadbeat lifestyle), would think to demand that a school accept enrollees beyond its teaching capacity or a restaurant admit customers beyond its feeding capacity. You go to school in order to learn, and to a restaurant in order to eat; why sabotage the transaction's purpose by clogging its arteries?

You get on a road to travel. Why, then, do we allow cities to grow so large that travel through them becomes impossible at certain times of day? Dallas, Fort Worth, El Paso, Oklahoma City, Tulsa, Kansas City, Phoenix, Denver... I have seen them all within the past half-year, and they are visions of hell by mid-morning or mid-afternoon. Why do we allow the room to grow so full that its occupants suffocate?

The crisis is much more than an inconvenience. Traffic congestion fuels pollution. It leads to costly, sometimes fatal accidents. It causes tempers to flare and induces violent crimes on occasion. It elevates blood pressure and damages long-term health. It promotes a creeping existential despair that can make even a prosperous citizen yearn for retirement.

Why do we not, instead, distribute stickers or "passes" to as many vehicles as the city can effectively handle? The steadily employed and owners of residences or businesses would automatically be accommodated; so would those who had graduated from a local high school or could otherwise demonstrate historical roots in the community. Others would receive their pass on a first-come, first-served basis. Waiting lists would be created. A specified number of visitors could be given one-day passes for a fee—or perhaps rental vehicles with passes could be made available. Mass transit would enjoy enough patronage by this point that it could be operated smoothly and profitably through private enterprise rather than royally funded and incompetently run through the public sector.

The above provisions having been made (and the preceding paragraph is only the crudest of sketches, I realize), cars without passes would be pulled over and rendered inoperable by traffic cops... I'm not sure how; perhaps by a heavy spike locked to the front bumper. As they awaited transport (for a horrible backlog of malefactors would be sure to develop), they would sit harmlessly along the roadside. The wait's extreme protraction and tedium would be one way of discouraging violators—perhaps a more efficient way than the fine payable to recover their vehicle.

Naturally, the question of interstate traffic would present special problems. What to do with cars that are just passing through? What if they need to exit for fuel or a bite to eat? Greedy municipal governments, frankly, have created this layer of the nightmare. Eager to grab federal dollars and also to draw long-distance travelers within the Siren-song of local entrepreneurs, they have often insisted on routing the interstate system directly through their peaceful boroughs. Inevitably, commuters would start to use the same highways on their twice-a-day pilgrimage between work and home. In a tragic irony typical of any chase after short-term gain, the interstate highway's bisection of the city actually enhanced suburban sprawl, making commutes more numerous and lengthy; for as traffic within the city destroyed peaceful settings and surrounded village-like harmony with "fast-food alleys" and shopping malls, the more well-to-do quite understandably wanted to live farther away from it all.

Now, none of this can be directly addressed by a system of distributing passes: the weeds have rooted too deeply for just a little spadework to clear them. Yet my proposal might induce further stages of cleaning out the garden. I think the enforcement of pass-purchases could certainly be suspended on and around interstate highways; and though such a modification would not solve rush-hour headaches, it would begin to mitigate them. Semi-resident "gypsies" looking for a bit of work for a month or two—fortune-seekers with no particular plan in mind—would be removed from the daily mix of commuters and interstate travelers. The reduction would be significant. Since such vagrant hordes are also proportionally well represented in the criminal class, life in the city would become safer and more pleasant with their removal.

It would not be at all antagonistic to observe that the previous paragraph's formula targets illegal immigrants. Indeed, it does: my proposal is a way for municipalities to strain out certain unwholesome elements that higher echelons of government ignore (despite legal and electoral mandates to take action). In most of the large cities I named above, the influx of illegal immigrants, especially from Mexico, has been the major—and almost the exclusive—cause of extreme traffic congestion. If we have a "moral obligation" to receive intruders so massively into our streets, then I suppose we must have the same obligation to let them occupy a spare chair at our table in the restaurant, or the spare bed in our hotel room, or the spare floor-space in our children's classrooms (which can all be shifted outdoors to appease the fire marshal). If one of these "obligations" is real, then all are so; if none of the latter three is real, then why is the first?

I do not claim that illegal immigrants are unwholesome people *per se*. I claim that people who uproot themselves from their native environment to drift without any specific purpose or destination are unsettling, by definition, to stable areas of population. The more restless and footloose of Appalachian pioneers certainly unsettled Cherokee villages. Syrian refugees, though highly sympathetic figures, are destroying once-stable communities in their vicinity. Hoboes were unwelcome during the Depression because clothes seemed to disappear from clothes-lines in the towns where they passed. To this day, the Irish know that things go missing when tinkers wander through. In my footloose youth, I was once an itinerant foreign national seeking work in southern Ireland. The red carpet I had observed earlier as a tourist had mysteriously disappeared from beneath my feet, quite without a trace. I learned an important lesson the hard way.

Mexico should keep her Mexicans. She needs them to stay home, where their ancestors were raised; she needs for their voices to demand the reform of corrupt local and national governments. Frankly, she needs a Second Amendment so that they may defend themselves from the consequences of her rampant corruption. Instead, she sends them north to plunder her rich neighbor and wire their earnings back (to the delight of arch-crook billionaire Carlos Slim, who charges extortionate rates on all such communications networks—a plunder delivered into his lap by well-bribed officials).

But the kind of person also discouraged by my system is the legal American citizen who just wants to "try his luck" in Austin, or Santa Fe, or Memphis… the "big city". (I had originally written "try her luck", recalling a girl who once asked me the way to Austin's Driscoll Hotel—and who was pretty obviously bound there to deliver a service to a customer.) Such homeless waifs often leave behind sad experiences only to hurl themselves into disastrous ones. Urban drug addiction and prostitution are largely sustained by recruits of this order. There are no "sanctuary cities" for them. On the contrary, any city that doesn't filter its incoming population is an abyss of despair. *Is sleamhain iad na leacacha an bhaile mhór*, goes the Irish proverb: "Slick are the stones of the big city." Just because a person is bored to death in Mudville doesn't mean that giving him or her a bus ticket to Chicago is an act of charity. Without far more supervision than that single act implies, the "gift" is indeed very close to criminal fraud.

I hasten to add that very wealthy "refugees" from horribly congested northern cities (which have no room to expand, and which have increasingly waged war on the successful with punitive taxation policies) would have to take a number and stand in line along with everyone else. The responsibility for turning Austin, Denver, Santa Fe, Phoenix, and other major southwestern cities into pullulating termite mounds indeed rests with these transplants from socialist-inclined regions of the country as much as with ruthless developers. When such silver-spooned *émigrés* express their "gated-community generosity" in referenda, they turn their adoptive homes into the forementioned sanctuary cities, lobby for illegal-resident driver's licenses, oppose identity checks at the polls, and so forth. The same sort of self-righteous hypocrite votes to deprive public schools of armed security guards while sending his own child to an elite campus safely removed from high-crime areas. Any program which would slow the unwarranted and unwelcome impact of silk-carpetbag snobs on local politics would justify its existence on that ground alone, to my mind.

It should also go without saying that the program I have outlined is "exclusionist" only with regard to cars. The objective is to thin out traffic, not to target certain segments of the populace for banishment. Anyone who can survive in the city without automotive transportation, or who can borrow a friend's vehicle as needed, is welcome to come on in and settle down. Given our cultural addiction to the private ownership of cars, however, merely restricting this single resource will have the practical effect of shuttling thousands and thousands of human beings to other locations.

Back to the city under a restricted-growth policy... local businesses would of course be forced to draw their employees from the community's resources rather than to import cheaper workers from the outside. If the costs of employing locally proved too expensive, then businesses would raise their prices, and the entire city's cost of living would escalate. In response, employed residents would be brought to realize that their wages had perhaps risen unrealistically high, and a healthy appreciation of economic reality would set in. Daily life in this restricted community, in short, would be an education of the very practical and highly useful sort that Americans appear no longer to receive in school. The need for and operation of unions would be questioned. The absurdity of a minimum wage would become transparent. The opportunities for business start-ups would proliferate. The possibility of a mega-corporation's moving in and driving small competitors under would be vastly reduced (since already employed labor would have to be lured away: no throng of drudging recruits could be smuggled through the gates). Ambitious mavericks would be free to crank up their operations beyond the city limits, and then to restrict their evolving communities or not, as the local population chose; but within the walls of the restricted municipality, the rules that bestowed meaningful freedom upon inhabitants would not tolerate infraction.

The walls I mention are invisible, yet the resulting space is not at all unlike a medieval walled city—a castle. People need walls (conceptual ones much more than solid ones) to live, prosper, and be happy. They should be able to know and trust their neighbors. They should be able to occupy a house more than two or three years. They should be able to get from A to B without severe risk of life and limb. They should be able to breath reasonably clean air and drink reasonably clean water. Politically progressive solutions jeopardize all of these aspects of the civilized life as much as any nineteenth-century robber baron's slave village of factory workers. They do so in the name of "diversity"—a lever that overthrows the mainstream cultural traditions and extended-family structure that leftist social engineers so loathe, but also topples the environmental rhythms and colorful mom-and-pop shops that they claim to adore.

Since the "diversity" crowd has gained a throttle-hold upon national politics and (to a great extent) the federal court system, the duty falls to more regional levels of government to raise walls, close gates, and declare limits. Unless and until we are required to allow vagrants free entry into our kitchens and a free go at our refrigerators, our property rights and basic need of health and safety appear to have enough purchase upon common sense that population restrictions could be enacted. Why wait for states to do the heavy lifting? Why not begin at the nuclear level of government?

Floating Cities: A Better Option Than Going to Mars

Based upon a post to my personal blogsite on Feb. 3, 2019.

Climates change, by definition—at least by extended definition. Solar activity fluctuates, continents drift, volcanism lifts mountains while broadening plains, and evaporation turns inland seas to salt flats. All such contributing factors to climate consume centuries as they shift; most require eons. The severity of this year's winter compared to last year's or even this decade's summers compared to last decade's does not constitute a relevant datum in climate study, in and of itself. Rather, measurements must span hundreds, if not thousands, of years systematically and reliably for conclusions to have value. We have no such measurements. We have computer software that runs various models, attempting to match up short-term observations with long-term projections.

As popularly bandied about, then, the phrase "climate change" designates, not a fact, but an academic industry. In the current *political climate*, an academic researcher in the physical sciences doesn't attract grants by discovering that a given climate's vagaries are staying within the range of normal deviation, any more than his colleague in the social sciences would see future grants after concluding that maleness is not toxic or that gender is biologically based. (I say "a given climate" because, also by definition, climates are regional. What climate-change profiteers mean to argue when using the phrase is that the *planet* is warming—a claim which is demonstrably untrue of every particular region.) The academy is grinding out propaganda in this fashion because professors are busily crafting careers for themselves. There is big money in building a case for a vaster, more intrusive centralized government—the solution (the *only* solution, apparently) to "climate change". Money talks. In academe, perhaps it whispers... but academics have very good ears.

Now, carbon dioxide, the favorite culprit of "climate change", is less than **half of one tenth of one percent** of our atmosphere. Its abundance appears to have ticked up infinitesimally in recent years—actually fueling a growth in global vegetation, which in turn causes more surface absorption of water. Yet absorbed water also evaporates, eventually, and I must not appear to claim a competency in the minutiae of geophysics which my advanced degrees cannot verify (as, for instance, does the ever-vocal Bill Nye). So let it stand, for the sake of argument, that an increase in vegetation also leads to an increase in rain. No one would deny that the thickly vegetated tropics see heavy rains, though I would question in my ignorance whether the former causes the latter or is caused by the latter (and possibly even reduces the net amount of the latter in some complex loop of the cycle).

Heavy rain: so be it. May this ignorant writer further question why such a new abundance of rain would not beneficially replenish our catastrophically dwindling groundwater supply? Twenty years ago, that concern was among the top five which preoccupied earth scientists alarmed over our lifestyle's sustainability. I haven't heard a peep about the levels of continental water tables for years, even though human beings die a lot faster from water deprivation than from having their Myrtle Beach time-share washed under. Odd, that silence… but then, I suppose the problem has been solved, and all thanks to "climate change"!

Speaking of scientists… please allow me to observe that no cardiologist, or phoneticist, or archaeologist, knows any more about climate than a truck-driver—and meteorologists are themselves not necessarily qualified to air out an opinion on climate. I grow very weary of the remark, "We should trust the experts! Ninety-nine percent of scientists say the climate is warming globally!" Even if we permit the phrase "global climate" to pass muster, and even if we ignore the falsehood of the sweeping generalization offered about that inclusive climate, we should pay some small attention to whom we identify as "experts". Then we should also ask ourselves what kind of game the less conscientious of these (for being an "expert" does not inoculate one against moral depravity) might be playing with our future. Neils Bohr, Werner von Braun, and Philipp Bouhler were all expert in their field in the Thirties and Forties. How did common humanity make out under their watchful eye?

"Climate change" has been to the alternative-energy industry what the cry, "Gold!" was to Sutter's Mill… but in all candor, wind and solar power are neither clean, cheap, nor sustainable. The Rare Earth Elements required in the assembly of these "alternatives" are ghastly contaminants of those communities forced to mine them; the exaggeration of their performance-parameters is perhaps the great unreported scandal in the new century's already long history of corporate rip-offs; and their constitutive hardware actually functions, not forever, but for two or three decades before needing replacement. Turbines and solar panels would also claim almost every inch of free space around us to have even the remotest chance of replacing fossil fuels. Paul Driessen is an excellent source on the subject: he's an *expert* (though the Oracle of Apollo at Wikipedia is pleased to call him a "lobbyist" because he opposes the academic/statist complex—and we all know that Wikipedia's contributors are utterly free of bias!).

Nullifying our conventional energy resources as we pay out billions to Third World nations and also allow China and India to continue belching pollutants into the atmosphere will save nobody—but it will surely tighten the noose around the necks of Americans. Is that the objective, then: mass suicide? Are the Paris Accords the third and final great act of Jonestown and

Heaven's Gate—is that how we achieve escape velocity into the next life? Do most of our naïve, idealistic young citizens understand that such is the choice to which they are being urged by their "leaders" and "experts"?

A new idea, if I may: why not spend our time and wealth on a solution which would truly alleviate the problem? What about creating a series of *floating cities*? The level of the world's oceans would be a matter of virtual indifference to their residents. Many distinct existential advantages would also cling to such unattached island-states. Their governments could control intrusions much more easily that landbound metropolises, and their inhabitants would hence be much safer from crime. Floating cities could evade major storms and so escape the cost incurred when devastating hurricanes make landfall. They could supply many of their essential needs directly from the sea (probably even tapping into wave and current somehow to generate electricity). Most significantly for those who honestly care about world peace and prosperity, they could reduce the risk of global conflict almost to zero; for nuclear assault on targets so widely dispersed would mean death to the assailant as well as the target. The highly effective dissuading factors behind Mutually Assured Destruction would be revived. Most of the world does not share the Green Movement's craving for a propitiatory mass suicide.

The blueprints for such cities are already on the drawing board. Why has the political Left no interest in solutions that actually hold promise of working? Why is the response of its adherents always some version of, "No, no, no! I'm not listening! I've stopped my ears! Nah-nah-nah! Not listening, not listening!" Is this any way for votaries of scientific expertise to behave?

Does it not seem altogether probable, in fact, that people who so resist open discussion and consideration of alternatives may either be a) mentally unstable or b) working an angle too sinister to make known publicly? Indeed, is it not credible that a few from Category B are exploiting a great many in Category A?

I don't remember the date of my first encounter with the subject of floating cities. I would guess that the television documentary I viewed on the subject must have aired well over a decade ago (on PBS *Nova*, perhaps, or the Discovery Channel's *Mega-Builders*). At that time, it seemed that the engineering problems were already well along the way to being solved. The proposed substructure consisted of hundreds (or potentially thousands) of discrete units that created just enough flexibility to even out wave-effect virtually to nothing. Shocks were simply absorbed. I can't recall how the whole was to be motorized—but the claim was made confidently that these islands would be capable of avoiding dangerous weather systems. Perhaps independent ships would drag them from harm's way.

That, as I say, was a while back. I must assume that the technology is much farther along today... and yet, one hears nothing whatever about it. Why is that, if not because special interests (or covert operatives) prefer a solution that undermines our economic wellbeing? Consider for a moment all the problems that "sea cities" could effectively resolve if the polar ice caps started to melt. They are in fact *not* melting... but let us imagine that our coasts have begun to creep in on us. All of the plans on the board to reduce carbon dioxide emissions (assuming that these were responsible for "coastal creep"—another whopping and unsubstantiated assumption) would merely plunge us into abject poverty while applying far too little antidote to the crisis far too late. Such "plans" are idiotic, to be blunt. A floating city, on the other hand, is an obvious and complete solution. So where are the drawing boards featuring *that* plan?

To repeat and elaborate an earlier point, floating cities could tightly control access. Crime would diminish to a fraction of current measures. Undesirables and unwanted substances could be kept out with high efficiency. Indeed, one of my concerns about the paradigm is that we could be contemplating crucibles for horrendous despotism, where abject obedience is enforced and flight is about as difficult as we find it, say, from Castro's Cuba. Yet if we really wish to grow more Balkan and more tribal, as appears to be the case... then here's our chance. Island A could be all heterosexual or all gay, if you like; B could be all Mormon; C could speak only Breton, an enclave of Celtic revivalists; D could require all citizens to carry a gun—or to give up even their pocket knives. Landbound communities are always compromised in such endeavor by the ease of "infection" from the outside. Here such frustration would be virtually removed. Numerous blueprints for utopia could receive a trial run with maximal control of variables and minimal menace to unwilling populations.

It occurs to me that islands might also exert an influence *against* despotism in one respect. The greater federation operating on the mainland would face a challenge in enforcing its most Procrustean decrees if dozens of island-cities declared, "Hell, no!" and slipped their moorings. What would Mainland Nanny do? Send patrol boats out to harass the rebels? But the islands would be equipped with their own defense systems (necessary to stave off piracy and invasion), ratcheting up any such act of chastisement to a bloody civil war. From the air, islands would pose slowly moving targets— but targets capable of movement, nonetheless. Given an hour's warning, their security officers could probably draw them out of an ICBM's bull's eye, if not liberate them from the ruin rained down by coastal rocket launchers. Yet I imagine larger islands as having anti-aircraft capabilities as well as their own small defensive fleets, which might well include submarines—useful for hauling them about, but also equipped to take out hostiles along the coast.

This discussion opened as a response to "global warming" hysteria, so it is worth remarking that an island environment could greatly reduce energy consumption and facilitate energy production. Trailing islands supplied with solar panels could be created, and perhaps something less cumbersome and space-consuming than the standard wind-turbine could be designed. Ocean currents could be harvested for energy. Inhabitants would live in a relatively confined area, so they would do much walking rather than gadding about in wasteful, needless conveyances. Life could also be lived in a less horizontal, more vertical manner to address temperature extremes. A substantial underwater community could serve as a retreat when the surface became either very cold or very hot (for water provides excellent insulation against both cold and heat). Surface activities, however, would keep residents in touch with their Circadian rhythms—and often, as we know, the temperature at sea level is very pleasant.

With plenty of sun, the surface would also feature roof-space and slanting walls thickly planted in edible vegetation. Naturally, as with solar panels, food provision could also be addressed through a kind of archipelago whose trailing islets were dedicated to agriculture. And need I say that the sea herself is an abundant provider? If the island produced quantities of "garbage" fully edible and healthy for populations of marine animals, then these latter could be harvested regularly and readily without any risk of depletion incurred.

How to make garbage edible or recyclable? That may be the golden question... but it appears answerable, if one considers that designers of interplanetary transport are already well along to creating biospheres where all waste products are put back into service. Why, may I ask, are we so very far advanced in our plans to leave Earth, yet we seem in no hurry at all to develop a healthy and secure method of existing on her oceans?

Could it be because populating the ocean, as I have shown, would likely liberate our planet's various peoples to a degree of political independence and cultural autonomy that her megalomaniac elite begrudges the human race? Could it be that the only dreams we are allowed to pursue on any drawing board are those that promote centralization? Why is it that "progress", in the warped minds of certain Global Warming Hystericals, necessarily involves the transformation of the human species into an anthill?

PART TWO

The Contemporary Mind's Eroding Grasp of Reality

A Taxonomy of North American Society's Narratives of Catastrophe and Dissolution

*This article first appeared in **Praesidium** 7.4 (Fall 2007).*

To assess clinically civilization's chances of surviving another century, or of surviving in a certain form, would be an Aristotelian endeavor, open to charges of being dry or (the cardinal sin these days) *without passion*. Yet the passion for passion is itself highly toxic, and may be regarded (I certainly regard it so) as a symptom of cultural collapse. When I was little more than a boy, Sir Kenneth Clark was assembling his magnificent BBC series *Civilisation*, an epic documentary which integrated visual art and architecture seamlessly with the music and literature of shifting times and customs. (The series has grown more valuable than ever today since, all unwittingly, Sir Kenneth committed to film several of Europe's most historically rich metropolitan areas just before they would dissolve in the sludge of traffic and contemptuous alien populations.) I distinctly recall the scene—it has been haunting me for years—where the grand old man crunched through the riverbed gravel beneath a Roman aqueduct in southern France and delivered the following lines: "There is a poem by the modern Greek poet, Cavafy, in which he imagines the people of an antique town like Alexandria waiting every day for the barbarians to come and sack the city. Finally the barbarians move off somewhere else and the city is saved; but the people are disappointed—it would have been better than nothing."[1]

How well I know that sentiment from observations of my fellow Westerners during my own lifetime! I recall also, a mere twenty years ago now, an excursion to the ancient Irish site of Emain Macha which I took in the company of several young scholars, all of us enrolled in the Dublin Institute for Advanced Studies' summer program. The talk in the bus at one point became snagged upon the image of our being stopped by an IRA roadblock (for Emain Macha lies a few miles within the Ulster border). There would be bearded men with machine guns (my compatriots fantasized with shivering delight)—and if we made a break for it, the machine guns would shoot out our tires. I drew only dark stares when I laughed that a bus moving at 40 miles per hour would not only shatter any *extempore* obstruction, but would advance so far along our twisting rural road that, by the time the blackguards could extract themselves from "the furzy hedge" (as John Millington Synge has dubbed it), their hiccoughing automatics could never hit any target so small as a tire. I quickly realized that these thin-shouldered, well-washed Ph.D. candidates *wanted* to be detained by road agents. Perhaps the women wanted to be kidnapped and ravished, and the men to be recruited under duress. Such was their boredom. The learning which had been heaped upon them seemed, if anything, to have multiplied their impatience and disgust with the resources of Western culture for bestowing coherence and value upon life. They wanted to be profoundly shaken up: they wanted to become passion's next prey.

Anyone who has ever endured immense emotional strain knows that the calm voice of an analytical Aristotle, far from being tedious and deathly, is a lifeline back to sanity. You cannot *not* cultivate a cool head and still survive in circumstances where people behave like ravening animals. Actually to court the excesses of *taraxia*, the opprobrious turbulence of emotions universally condemned in ancient philosophy, is to grow infatuated with lunacy. Yet it is an inescapable truth that many of our best educated and most influential citizens long to be somewhat "out of their heads". Why is that, and what prognosis does it suggest for our sickly ruin of a culture? I should like to make my own best effort at taxonomizing the possibilities, as surgically as I can. Though my attempt is doomed to be more Theophrastian than Aristotelian as I inventory my experience of people, I solemnly vow to purge irony of bile.

I. Natural Calamity

To begin with, allow me to dispose of roughly half a dozen lurid scenarios much publicized in popular fiction, made-for-TV movies, and even—lately—the political forum, all forecasting the collapse of our civilization due to a natural calamity which mankind will either provoke or fail to neutralize. I have global warming very much in mind, to be sure; but it is only the early twenty-first century's most compelling projection of our species' suicide, for reasons to be discussed shortly. As well as I can recall, it was preceded by 1) a high alert that the Western United States, in particular, would run out of water; 2) an alarm that acid rain would massively destroy crops, voiding several vital links in the food chain; 3) a fear of the impending earthquakes that are sure to devastate major population centers along the West Coast; 4) apprehension over a large meteor's colliding with the Earth and plunging the planet into a "clean" nuclear winter; and, just before the recent heat-up of Global Warming Anxiety, 5) a nerve-racking rumor that a tsunami like that which scourged Southeast Asia on Christmas of 2004 could well wash over the East Coast's population centers with unspeakable slaughter.

Now, all such doomsday scenarios have several elements in common. Each enjoys a certain amount of scientific plausibility. In fact, of major earthquakes out West and perhaps even the asteroidal menace, one might say that the risk is 100%: "not *if*, but *when*". Most of these scenarios also involve at least a small degree of human complicity with the forces of doom. Water is being depleted because we choose to waste it, rain is acidifying because we choose to pollute the air, and even the catastrophe wreaked by earthquakes depends somewhat upon our choice of where and how to build our cities. I should stress the obvious in the matter of human choice, as well: none of the calamities has been projected as the grim consequence of *deficient personal morality* rather than of social and economic policy. That is, when "we choose" to pollute or abuse or ignore, we are not really choosing individually at all: those in charge of our lives, rather, are failing us. Dour prophets warn that large factories are permitted to foul the air, that Las Vegas is permitted to sap the Rocky Mountain water table, that pork-barrel politics has robbed the public of adequate tsunami or asteroid detection outposts. The suggestion is never floated that the typical American citizen has turned his back on frugality to embrace frivolity—disdaining close-to-home jobs for better-paying ones, gambling and partying too often, hitting the beach in a kind of gluttony for sun-bathing. The natural threat is invariably related, sooner or later, to our technology, whose liabilities are in turn related to greedy, wicked people in positions of power.

Finally, and not without connection to the previous point, I observe that most scenarios insist upon truly catastrophic die-offs in spectacular events of flame, tumult, and collapse. Only the water-shortage and acid-rain options lack this aspect. Both of them—surely not by chance—were roiling the public mind before the dissolution of the Soviet Union, when nuclear holocaust still seemed an imminent possibility. In other words, with the disappearance of the nuclear threat as a likely "extermination event" for the human race, natural disasters have proceeded to buy up the available shares of terror (as it were) which flooded the market for mass hysteria.

I do not wish to imply that I view all of these gloomy forecasts as the alarmist exaggerations of a public incapable of enjoying the quiet life. They mostly highlight real dangers, in some cases imminent dangers. I honestly do not know the status of the mid-continental water table or of the predations of acid rain. The threat of earthquake to southern California, however, is immense—a major event during rush hour could easily kill thousands, as quakes have recently done in China and India. In the case of collision-course asteroids and tsunamis, we appear to enjoy a rather more advanced system of detection and early warning. (Since tsunamis are an effect of mid-oceanic earthquakes and volcanic eruptions, they offer us a kind of built-in recovery time even when the earth's crust takes our seismographs by surprise.) In either case, we could probably avert catastrophe. Even a metropolitan center could be largely evacuated in a day. That New Orleans was given almost a week to clear its streets before Hurricane Katrina made landfall and still bungled the job deserves a closer look momentarily. Local evacuation would make little difference in the final tally of casualties inflicted by a meteorite of, say, a mile's diameter, for the vast majority of deaths would ensue months after impact, as crops failed globally thanks to a thick haze of debris high in the atmosphere. Yet we possess the technology at this instant to intercept such an apocalyptic missile with a nuclear weapon whose detonation would fragment it. The most heavenly of the menaces is probably the least of our worries.

I wrote just above that I am ignorant of what inroads have been made against the problems of depleted water resources and acid rain. I am not a scientist or a specialist in any field relevant to such issues. In a way, this is precisely the point I wish to draw from the foregoing discussion—for I was no more a specialist when water and rain were front-page news than I am now. The front page thrust them into my face.[2] These matters, that is, though they deserve to be taken seriously, consistently have not been so over the past half-century, during which span "impending natural calamity" has been a favorite means of soliciting readership and viewership. They have been handled exactly like "stories"—like primetime serial melodramas whose denouement is referenced to a ticking clock. Bored people enjoy them: bored people enjoy being scared. Will the bullet be dodged at the last possible instant, or will Mr. Jones, CPA, be one of his species' hundred surviving members? Which scenario would Mr. Jones *prefer* to see? (Mrs. Jones, he might reflect, is a bit long in the tooth; as forlorn castaways, the last beautiful women could not well afford to be too choosey about which of the last men they allowed into their bed to regenerate the race.) Ms. Smith, teacher's aid, a single parent with few prospects for advancement, generally feels that the world has ganged up on her. The notion of cosmic forces ganging up on the world is not unpleasant—but there is also the child to think of, and Ms. Smith has a quasi-religious faith in the ability of avuncular authorities to defuse ticking time-bombs (which may say much about how she has allowed men to reduce her personal life to a ruin).

All in all, the "catastrophe" theme is good for sales and ratings. It appeals to a great many latent fears and longings in a society with a great many frustrations. If Catastrophe did not exist, Man would have to invent it.

I repeat that I am not dismissing such high-risk behaviors as our high-tech culture routinely adopts in its straining or violating of natural law as the text of a wry joke. It is because these risks are substantial—sometimes very substantial—that our melodramatizing of them is itself risky. We cry wolf. Eventually, those among us who are bored with this antidote to boredom will mock our cries by wearing wolf's ears. There is a kind of person who installs a back-yard swimming pool and buys a gas-guzzling Humvee to putter around town in just because he has tired of what he regards as "alarmist whining". The whiners are far more apt to inhabit the political Left, and the polluters-and-proud-of-it the political Right. One can well imagine that any tug-of-war between two such adversaries is unlikely to reach a truly responsible conclusion, no matter which finally amasses more muscle on its side of the rope. For both are responding to *passion*: the leftist is "passionate" about protecting the environment, while the rightist is "passionate" about protecting consumerist free enterprise.

The one truly relevant datum here to mapping our most likely path of descent, then, is the omnipresence of passion as a tolerable (or tolerated) motive for major decisions. The leftist wears green baseball caps, drinks green tea, sorts glass and plastic from his garbage, rides his bike to work, lets his lawn's grass grow unshorn, eats vegetarian, and buys only recycled paper products. His lifestyle is a role, a mission: it offers lines to utter for every situation and gestures to mime in every crisis. Some of his tactics may actually benefit the environment (e.g., bike-riding), some are mere tokens of tribal loyalty (e.g., clothing and diet), and a few could even prove destructive of the cause to which he claims abject dedication (e.g., the messy lawn: ticks, mosquitoes, and other vermin complicate, aggravate, and sometimes abbreviate the existence of higher life forms). He may also cancel out all the virtuous petrol-abstinence so arduously practiced on a bicycle's seat by jetting to a couple of conferences or "wilderness" vacations per year. Passion rules good sense: acting the part trumps promoting the desired end.

The rightist, meanwhile, manicures his lawn to golf-course perfection, prowls the city needlessly every evening in search of "take-out" food and amusement, plunges for the latest electronic gizmos, spends Sunday afternoons sprawled before a wide-screen projection of the football game, and packs his children off to soccer practice and Tai Kwan Do after school. The traditional virtues of thrift, temperance, industry, modesty, humility, and gravity are little in evidence (though pressuring clients to buy more insurance or computer upgrades or motor vehicles may qualify as a certain kind of industry), or else patently contradicted (grass trimmed beyond a certain point and kids forcibly enrolled in costly extra-curricular tutelage are among our time's pre-eminent forms of bourgeois ostentation). But how could he live otherwise? For he, too, has fallen prey to passion: his inclinations weave a chain around his neck. His acts and utterances have all been choreographed and scripted to flatter basic appetites. The space beyond his part's well-worn limits is needless hardship.

In short, I contend that the least resistible influence upon the West's collapse is not "the big one" due any time now along the San Andreas Fault, but the incapacity of its citizens to live as individual moral agents, rationally accepting or rejecting options on the basis of their relation to objective goodness. For instance, the automobile is a necessary evil: no other portrayal of it makes any sense at all. It is dirty, dangerous, and socially disruptive, and our common moral ambition should be to eliminate it. To the extent that we need it to cover the vast distances between home and workplace and marketplace which we have allowed to open up (largely in accommodation of the car's technical parameters), our problem is one of reconstructing the spaces where we sleep, eat, shop, and work. Yet neither side—neither Left nor Right—has any such plan on the drawing board. The Left periodically proposes higher emission standards which would force hundreds of American businesses to shut down or higher gas taxes which would force millions of our poorest citizens into destitution. The Right racks its collective brain for ways to continue the existing dilemma—thereby offering the single defensible explanation for its curious commandeering of the word "conservative". The privileged bureaucratic class, in other words, cannot understand why commoners are not eating cake when the price of bread goes up, while the private-sector middle class cannot understand what's so wrong about wanting the latest model of car with a TV and DVD-player on board. Neither side understands: there is a crisis of moral understanding. Both sides have laced their emotions through and through a certain "way of life".

The natural calamity, I believe, is much more than another diversion to these people in full flight from responsible self-examination. Now is not the time to psychoanalyze the two political polarities and discuss in detail just what appeal either of them finds in tales of a contemporary Deluge or Vesuvius. Obviously, the crowd on the Right could be expected to take rather more pleasure in the scenario's fireworks and special effects. Not only does the Right appear to enjoy spectacle more (as opposed to the catharsis of mass hysteria, where the Left's affections incline): anything on the order of *The Last Days of Pompeii* offers ample scope for individual action and unhampered freedom during the critical hours when survivors struggle against chaos. On the Left, consumers of so nightmarish a narrative are more likely to perceive it as an allegory of corrupt leadership—or even of an outraged Mother Earth punishing the entire race for condoning the hubris of a few. To the Left-leaning audience, that is, the scenario is less entertaining than sacral—i.e., enabling of proper worship. For I should say nothing new in remarking that environmental causes are the Left's religion: the sequence of garden, custodianship, violated command, and severe punishment is clearly visible just beneath the surface of any left-wing crusade in this direction.

A Right-tending filmmaker, we might summarize, might choose to threaten the Earth with a rogue asteroid, while a Left-leaning one would prefer the rupturing of the government's hush-hush nuclear waste dumps in an earthquake... but, as I say, such is not my theme here. I would stress, instead, the remaining member of the Doomsday Scenario's recurrent characteristics: the refusal to admit any genuine personal culpability. For if the Left postpones guilt until it clings to the highest levels of leadership, the Right tends to evade the issue entirely: again, one hears no homilist on either side exhorting us simply to shut down Las Vegas-style playgrounds, simply to resuscitate farming as a livelihood, or simply to stop dividing our residences from our scenes of business and leisure. Indeed, my perception is that the alleged phenomenon of global warming has considerable traction in both camps, *and that both are comfortable indicting mysterious forces atop the political-economic hierarchy for it.* A rightist is infinitely less apt to reproach certain senators for not supporting the Kyoto Accord's limits on emissions, and infinitely more to mention China's ruthless charge into the future, asphyxiate who may. What we do not hear from him is an entirely different program for living in the tradition of New England Puritanism or Ohio Valley Quakerism or Southern agrarianism. The residue of the "hippy" fringe is perhaps closer to making an "alternative lifestyle" proposal... but then again, maybe not. Just as electric amplifiers were essential to that fringe in its original form, so its present *morphos* relies heavily upon digital amusements. At some relatively superficial level, responsibility for the planetary crisis always shifts to the Establishment. One's personal conveniences and fantasies must not be jeopardized.

Global warming, as a socio-political phenomenon (whatever its climatic truth), is the crystallization of our collective finger-pointing and role-playing. Companies market products by touting their absurdly minuscule reduction of some minor pollutant. Schools announce the planting of a few trees about the campus with much fanfare, though their buses continue to belch soot all about the city twice a day. We all rush to embrace the "do your little bit" approach, since it is the reverse side of heaping a guilty onus upon a select few: a personal conscience cleansed with a dime. Traffic is indeed cited as the primary contributor to greenhouse gases in all the summations of the theory that I have seen, yet citizens of almost every political persuasion cannot seem to stake out a coherent position on any series of issues related to transportation. Municipal governments persist in constructing loops around their city limits to ease rush-hour "slow goes", despite ample evidence that more roads draw more traffic as a magnet draws metal shavings.[3] Car manufacturers boast of cleaner-running engines, yet the miles-per-gallon averaged by their products have diminished or held stationary over the past decade in response to the public's clear preference for heavier, higher-suspended vehicles. The most zealous environmentalists—people who, perhaps, ride bicycles to work—are among the most enthusiastic supporters of open international borders (about which, more anon). Yet a vast infusion of day-laborers, constantly driving to new temporary work sites in vehicles neither properly inspected (if not legally registered) nor state-of-the-art, has immensely exacerbated air pollution in southwestern cities.

We are a shallow people, and the major threat to our civilization's sustained survival is, precisely, our shallowness. The thick lather of indignation over the flawed evacuation of New Orleans before Hurricane Katrina made landfall is surely the most stunning monument to our absurd ineptitude. Hundreds of people perished needlessly, some of them having freely chosen to take their chances, some of them allegedly having lacked the resources to depart. Yet the resources necessary were minimal, since a high alert was publicized five days in advance; and, in any case, one must suppose that local government and volunteer help from private organizations like churches would or could have taken up the slack. Of course, subsequent indignation centered upon the failure of state and (especially) federal agencies to provide timely relief after the catastrophe. The decision fatally embraced by the victims to stay put—and other decisions not to dissuade them vigorously which their neighbors must have reached in many cases—never fall under scrutiny. The personal ensuing tragedies were packaged as nothing less than a plot hatched in the White House.

II. Plague

At first glance, the plague appears to be an entirely natural phenomenon—and so it is, if one considers it strictly *as* phenomenon (i.e., as a fact whose reality begins as soon as it becomes visible). Massive die-offs due to infection are common throughout all tiers of biological existence, in both plants and animals. Indeed, our own time's tendency is again to belittle or ignore the element of choice in human epidemics, as if we were so many microbes in a Petrie dish. Nothing could be more absurd—or more patently illustrative of why human plagues are often *not* natural calamities—than the selling of the AIDS epidemic over the past two decades as a guilt-free thunderclap: essentially, a stroke of bad luck. In North America, where most of the HIV-infected were not born so, this is plainly inaccurate. Homosexual activity is definitively unnatural if one simply builds statistics upon mammalian behavior, the specific high-risk behavior here has always been the *opting for promiscuous activity*, and intravenous drug use is also a deliberately chosen series of acts. Yet AIDS has been aggressively represented to the public as a fatal version of the common cold. Apparently, it was not unheard-of in the early days of this scourge for certain men infected with the HIV virus to spread their contagion to unsuspecting women with careful premeditation so as to "upgrade" the disease's moral status to a pure misfortune. As we have already seen, the American masses were well primed to adopt the desired view, for Americans tend to see any sort of catastrophe—public or private, medical or natural or financial—as engineered by wicked authorities rather than admitted by personal decision. Furthermore, a few homosexuals in recent years have publicized their active attempts to become infected, a suicidal behavior which once more reminds us that catastrophe is an antidote to boredom.

But what about the common cold—or a common case of winter influenza? Our society has lately been harrowed with rumors that a major outbreak—a pandemic—of "bird flu" (borne by migratory wildfowl from Southeast Asia all around the world, then spread among domesticated fowl and thence to other animals and to humans) is poised to cut our numbers in half, perhaps. Might some particle of "lifestyle choice" affect the dreadful progress of such a scourge? At a certain level, yes: certainly more so than in the case of an Earth-asteroid collision or a volcanic eruption. One of the major factors in the spread of any plague is frequent long travel. European merchants didn't understand this in the days of Marco Polo, nor European explorers in the days of Columbus. We understand it very well now, however—yet never have so many people traveled so far so frequently. We travel for amusement as well as for profit: we travel simply to "get away". The best-educated travel expensively to conferences several times a year, even though staying at home and reading dozens or hundreds of position-papers has never been easier. The wealthy travel in order to spend their wealth; the retired travel in order to convince themselves that the shackles of routine have truly been struck off.

Besides compounding problems involving traffic and pollution, and besides wearing the traveler's physical resistance down due to decreased exercise and irregular diet, these habits jeopardize everybody back home who is likely to come in contact with the returned globe-trotter, now a breeding ground for opportunistic infections. Yet I must repeat (at the risk of belaboring the point) that nobody during the bird-flu scare's opening volley of advice and reproaches ever hinted that our North American lifestyle is really rather frivolous, and that we would have to worry far less about this sort of misery if we would make our local communities more habitable, learn how to read for pleasure, and take up gardening. To this day, such a strand of argument has not worked its way into the public debate. Because of our continued resistance to changes in our basic habits, and now because the first bird-flu alarm has proved a false one (the "cry wolf" syndrome again), we are probably more vulnerable to decimation by plague than we have been since the discovery of penicillin.

For the fact remains that wandering people, not migrating geese, are responsible for all of the few reported cases of Avian Influenza in this hemisphere; yet the unsanitary conditions which nurtured the flu in Southeast Asia are being replicated—with an official determination to court disaster and an official indifference to the risks—even as I write these words. Diseases such as tuberculosis and leprosy have grown exotic in our part of the world, the scourges of distant times and places (like the Black Plague itself). Now, however, with the throwing open of its southern border to millions of destitute immigrants unschooled in basic hygiene, the U. S. is transforming its cities into incubators for such all-but-extinct contagions. In Dallas public schools, diagnosed cases of tuberculosis have skyrocketed. Most disturbing is that new strains of the bacillus are proving untreatable with existing antibiotics: as we saturate our national pharmacopia in thousands and thousands of cases bred not only in dense populations, but also newly and constantly mixed populations, we are writing the perfect recipe for the invincible infection. The phrase "melting pot" is acquiring a new, morbid meaning.

Of course, penurious refugees from the wastes of Chihuahua can be supposed to understand the mechanism of bacteriological infection no better than (if even as well as) Boccaccio's Florentines. The typical American citizen, however, is fully aware that sneezing in somebody's face, drinking from somebody else's glass, or eating a morsel that has occupied an unclean place can cause illness. Yet many very well-educated Americans, apparently—occupying positions of private ownership and public leadership— are not alarmed at the probable consequences of unleashing Third World health habits upon the high-tech metropolis, where people of all walks of life can cover vastly more miles and mingle with vastly more sub-populations during the average day than they would in Mexico. When a treatment- resistant strain of TB finally sweeps across the nation (and, as with the 8.5 earthquake in southern California, it's only a matter of time), the response will be the same as it was to the first tiny outbreaks of bird flu—and, for that matter, to Hurricane Katrina and to the "Christmas tsunami": "Where were the reinforcements? Why were our rulers not fully prepared to intercept this threat, or at least neutralize its aftermath? What plot is being hatched against us good, ordinary people at the very highest levels?"

III. Technological Short-Circuit

Most of us have known the frustration of being stuck in a power outage after a violent electrical storm or, perhaps, a wintry blizzard. Practically every amenity in our environment, all of our tools at work, all of our amusements at play—our garage doors, our lights, our heating and air conditioning, our ovens and microwaves, our clocks, our hair-dryers, our computers, our televisions, our stereos—*our whole world* is electronic. Suddenly deprived of this magical current, we are apt to reflect (if we are at all thoughtful) upon what utter havoc a protracted breakdown would wreak. Water would not be treated at municipal plants; essential transactions would not be made at bank windows; traffic lights would not work. In the Robert Wise sci-fi classic, *The Day the Earth Stood Still*, the benign but stern Martian visitor impresses upon the world's recalcitrant population the gravity of his mission by shutting down everything electrical for one hour. His point is soon taken.

Computers have probably heightened our awareness of vulnerability. In the early days of the word-processor, many of us were introduced to the exquisite misery of losing every trace of an important document because we had not saved it properly. Such lapses were almost routine. In the case of yesteryear's typed or printed document assembled from handwritten notes, an entire building would have to burn down to wipe out one's hard labor so completely. Important e-mails continue regularly to go astray in ways that the layman cannot begin to understand, and cell phone reception is notoriously unreliable.

The notion of our slave Technology's rising up like Spartacus and throwing our empire into chaos, therefore, is not at all far-fetched to us. It is an experience which we have known on a small scale, and which hence need only be magnified to produce a disaster narrative. In contrast, most people cannot begin to formulate an image of what assault by tsunami or asteroid would be like. This particular pest, because we have already been dosed with its toxin in tiny amounts, seems less exotic all the time. The 2001 in which Stanley Kubrick projected his *Space Odyssey* has now come and gone; the Mutiny of the Computer, having become part of our cultural drill in a small way, has lost its teeth. The boy has cried "wolf" too often.

The truth is that we are probably less prepared for this kind of calamity, more exposed to its real occurrence in some devastating form, and more inept at reading its early rumbles than in the case of any disaster so far discussed. Earlier in this essay, I have accused North Americans of not understanding, of being shallow, and of not recognizing the significance of personal choice in their affairs. These charges are fundamentally the same charge, and it has repeatedly surfaced when technology was under consideration. Technology is what we do not understand adequately; technology is rendering us shallow; technology obscures to our eyes the importance of our own choices—and even the existence of those choices. We are uniquely exposed to technological abuses or miscues, in my opinion, because we seldom have any notion of just what's at stake in a high-tech crisis of the simplest kind.

I admitted that I myself have only the weakest intellectual grasp of what issues currently surround our water supply or the acidification of rain. I am clearly not alone in being puzzled about the degree to which global warming is fact rather than theory (I am indeed joined, it seems, by a great many climatologists); and this, like the various concerns about ground- and rain-water, is at last a matter of how the modern production of energy and material affects the environment (for no one would be very exercised about rising temperatures or falling water tables if the trend turned out to represent a natural cycle). We are outraged when "science" doesn't warn us of a coming earthquake or tsunami, or when it fails to predict a hurricane's path reliably enough that some prankster at the National Weather Service can be suspected of crying wolf. We tend to view the persistence of heart disease and cancer as a national disgrace, just as a fairly common opinion holds that AIDS could be cured next year if the medical community would really apply itself.

These views, I would emphasize, come from people who are shocked at the damage done by a motor vehicle "barely moving" at 30 miles per hour, who will chatter away on a cell phone while watching an electrical storm, who believe that an old keyboard tossed in the trash will disintegrate at the landfill like apple cores and leftover spaghetti, and who expect to cheat sleep year after year with caffeine while suffering no long-term ill effects. North Americans are ignoramuses about every kind of science, from physics to meteorology to anatomy. So is virtually everyone else in the world, for that matter. The scientist's calling is that of a specialist—and few people can specialize, by definition. (Even the nuclear physicist usually knows nothing about engineering, and the cardiologist nothing about nutrition.) But the great danger is that we are immersed in applied science as no other culture on earth, although many are overtaking us rapidly. They, too, will soon share our dilemma. Their lives will be awash in gadgetry which makes no more sense to them than a wristwatch to a caveman. They will grow very familiar only with what these marvels are supposed to do when the right buttons are pressed in the right succession (and making such sequences simple is known as being "user-friendly"—a euphemism for burying every last trace of the mystery and enhancing the false sense of security). Were a vast network of such things to malfunction in unison, whether by accident or design, not one in ten thousand of us could take effective action.

The most homespun and "scaled down" example of this risk is the minor catastrophe of a fatal car wreck. Drivers have grown quite anesthetized to the risks they incur when traveling at 60 or 70 miles per hour—to the point, indeed, that they suppose themselves freed up to handle phones or food or radio dials. We feel ourselves to be entirely in command. What we do not feel is the extremely fine edge of that command: one instant of inattention or one over-correction, and we could end several lives on the highway around us as well as our own. Imagine now that a mechanical failure were to occur at high speed. Even the most conscientious driver, ignorant of the warning signs and of the malfunction's immediate effects, would be diving off Niagara Falls in a barrel, just as if he were one more drunk behind the wheel. The tally of traffic fatalities per annum is already approaching that of the entire Vietnam War. It is symptomatic of our dense insulation from such realities that we do not even style the figure—more than double that of China's Tangshan earthquake in 1976—as a calamity.

Yet the most relevant class of cases involving misidentified or ignored technological menace may be found in the file devoted to terrorist attacks. From the evening of September 11, 2001, until this very instant, the techniques of Al Qaeda have been praised or damned as "sophisticated". They are nothing of the sort. They are astute, but not sophisticated. They involve the mere exploitation of loosely stitched seams in our high-tech lifestyle's fabric. We happen to have many such seams. One of these is the number of conveyances moving at anywhere from three to 15 times a racehorse's fastest gallop with a high volume and density of travelers on board—at least dozens, often hundreds. One stumble, and the contemporary iron horse spills all his riders like grape shot fired out of a cannon... so the trick is to figure out how to catch a hoof. In the case of a bullet-train or a jetliner, this turns out to be remarkably easy. No one remembers now, but shortly before 9/11, a favorite scenario for disaster was widespread "metal fatigue" in commercial jets (a theme at least as old as the classic James Stewart film, *No Highway in the Sky*). To our terrorist-obsessed mentality, every new plane crash or train derailment is immediately assumed to conceal another dastardly plot; yet the plain truth is that such disasters were already occurring frequently of their own accord before twisted young men armed themselves with box-cutters.[4] Our techniques of mass transportation are quite terrifying in and of themselves.

Another seam ever ready to split in contemporary habits of living is the skyscraper. Terrorist masterminds were at first somewhat overmatched by the task of destroying a high-rise's inhabitants in North America, where building codes are more stringent than in other parts of the world. Yet the edifice need not be toppled: if simply set on fire, its occupants will be trapped like rats on the proverbial sinking ship. Civilian targets in tall structures could also be struck by a massive curb-side explosion—the equivalent of an IRA "supermarket bomb" ignited in a locality where the supermarket is a multi-tiered complex. Timothy McVeigh did not induce the Murrah Building in Oklahoma City to collapse—he simply took off one of its faces at a time when most of the chambers were occupied, and this with no more than a rented truck and some fertilizer. Timing, of course, is of the essence. A commercial tower leveled in the dead of night would not only possess little photogeneity: it would claim relatively few victims.

We remarked that time would be a major factor, too, in determining the devastation inflicted by a Los Angeles earthquake. Our masses move to the clock's tempo: many of our machines require some sort of chronological coordination—perhaps internal, perhaps with other machines—in order to reach their peak performance. Yet many also do not. Indeed, I can think of no apparent reason why office space would not be maximally utilized if workers came and went around the clock. Traffic would certainly be diminished, fuel consumption would be reduced, opportunities for ancillary businesses (e.g., all-night coffee shops or gyms next to office buildings) would be multiplied, and general stress would be relieved (assuming that the round-the-clock regimen translated into greater flexibility of schedules). In this case, I believe we may divine one of the machine's greatest menaces: that its habits are infectious to neighboring humans. Instead of acquiring greater freedom thanks to the machine's having liberated us from the sun and the seasons, we spring to life far more rigidly at the alarm's claxon than any farmer ever did at cockcrow. We steadily create new technology that allows us to "cheat" a little—drugged drinks to wake us up faster or new conveyances or routes to get us to the job on time. We do not, however, seem to spend much thought on creating jobs that begin or resume when we're ready—at dawn, at sundown, at 2 a.m. The truth is that there were many more such jobs in the past than there are now: the carpenter's, the seamstress's, the baker's, the writer's.

So technical catastrophe is not invited only by the physical structuring of contemporary North American life, with its emphasis on breakneck speed and precariously juggled population densities; the short-circuit may also occur in our own nervous systems, one individual at a time yet with plague-like abundance. It is difficult to compare the nature and extent of nervous disorders from one generation to another, and certainly from one century to another: many ailments were not even identified as such in the past, many today are obscured or mitigated by advanced treatments, circumstantial factors such as diet and exercise have changed radically, and so forth. Nevertheless, the deterioration of manners in recent generations has achieved an acceptance so near to the universal that it has grown to be a cliché. People certainly seem to be more tense. Anecdotal evidence abounds—some of us can even remark an increased aggression in our own deportment as the electron has sped up everything we do. To argue that North Americans already suffer from a plague of machine-inspired neuralgia, then, does not seem at all far-fetched.

Of course, the most popular scenarios for cultural dissolution involve something more explicit and dramatic: a take-over by robots, for instance (the projection, one might say, of *2001: A Space Odyssey* into the terrestrial and the bourgeois). Several reputed scientists and technicians have lately created a stir by suggesting that robots will, in fact, supplant the human species eventually.[5] This narrative seems to have enjoyed a considerable magnetism upon our audiences for generations already, if one may view the highly mechanized aliens in H. G. Wells's *War of the Worlds* as robotic (or, to adjoin the ridiculous to the sublime, take those devils-on-coasters, the Daleks, from the campy *Dr. Who* series). What most interests me about the scenario here—

which has probably captured the popular imagination more than any other I've named—is that it once again minimizes the citizen's willful collaboration in the process of decline. Yes, we drive cars, we hop aboard elevators, we log on to computers... but we have no apparent hand in "artificial intelligence". Some Frankenstein-like figure in a white coat invented it, perhaps an evil genius, perhaps simply a naïve introvert who failed to foresee his plaything's ruinous consequences. In any case, the fault is not ours. We may admit it as a collective guilt, for such guilt costs us nothing personally (and may, indeed, ennoble us personally for "admitting" to a sin on behalf of others). Nothing we do in our quotidian routine, however, seems to bear the remotest relation to this reified menace of circuitry. By agreeing to fear our technology in this form, we have yet again succeeded in missing the point.

IV. Weapons of Mass Destruction

No discussion of doomsday scenarios would be complete without The Bomb. The Baby-Boomer generation was raised in the shadow of a mushroom cloud: some North Americans can recall actually drilling for nuclear attack in school the way youngsters do today for tornados. (The tornado sirens used in early warning systems around the US were actually developed back in the Fifties as alarms for incoming Russian missiles.) Nuclear weapons have the "advantage" over other forms of catastrophe, from the standpoint of "doomsday credibility", that they have indeed been used and that their ruinous aftermath was indeed immensely more widespread in time and space than anyone had predicted (another example, by the way—the preeminent one—of technology's tendency to exceed even the understanding of its specialist creators). The track record of A-Bombs and H-Bombs well supports the thesis that a general exchange of them would end life on Earth. They constitute a unique class of technology which we need not—probably should not—attempt to squeeze under the rubric of "technological short-circuit"; for, while as distant from most of our daily lives as robots, they have none of the robot's potential for farming ocean bottoms and mining planetary surfaces. They are invincibly *extraordinary*: their purpose is to obliterate the ordinary and plunge reality back into primal chaos.

This malodorous reputation clings to nuclear power even when attempts are made to harness it as domestic energy. In the popular mind, it will remain a "bomb", first and foremost. The identification may not be ill-advised, especially with the proliferation of terrorism around the world and the painful revelation that none of our security systems is fully secure. For all that, I suspect that the most popular narrative is once again among the least likely: not the least serious, but among the easiest to avert. A missile or a bomb must be delivered, and airborne weapons can be detected and destroyed in flight. Something like the defensive net of satellites proposed by President Reagan, and which was at once derided with the tag "Star Wars", will probably soon be in place over North America. An infinitely more disturbing WMD, given the relative ease of introducing it into the target society, is the bacteriological weapon. A vial poured into a major city's water supply or a highly infectious bacterium like anthrax dusted over a few large crowds could leave millions dead, and its lingering effects could be just as difficult to purge from the environment as radioactive fallout. The evidence that Saddam Hussein was developing such weapons included the blunt fact that he had already gassed dozens of Kurdish villages (leaving tens of thousands of non-combatants dead in their tracks) and that his own scientists confessed to having developed such a hellish arsenal.[6] Yet both the popular mind and the Bush Administration fixed upon the image of a mushroom cloud. The question of where, exactly, Saddam's vials and dishes of "Satan Bug" ended up has been left not only unanswered, but unasked.

If the nuclear bomb overlaps with the renegade robot as a portrait in high-tech evil, then the bacteriological weapon overlaps with the naturally occurring plague. To infuse a population with smallpox would be to "jump-start" Mother Nature down one of her most destructive paths. The factors which make of the pandemic a harrowing possibility today—enormous concentrations of people moving over unprecedented distances with unprecedented speed and frequency—also elevate the planted contagion to the status of a "dirty bomb". The suitcase-bomb with fissionable material would at least give a quick death to immediate bystanders, and its long-term effects could be circumscribed and anticipated within a fairly specific area. The infused bug would have neither redeeming quality. Let us not suppose, either, that only governments, or government-sponsored paramilitary groups, would have access to it. A deranged lab technician could conceivably slip a vial into his pocket and head for the mall. The scare created one week after 9/11 over certain items of mail dusted with anthrax points to just such an individual or minute group.[7] The coverage of that story exposed that such living time-bombs as anthrax and smallpox can be rather easily obtained from their "secure storage" for purposes of "research".

V. The Most Likely Scenario

I am a great consumer these days neither of science-fiction novels nor of "disaster genre" movies. I have tried to create an inventory of what appear to me the most widely circulated narratives into which our national anxiety about the decline of the West has been compressed in recent years; and I have tried to leaven this mass of material, furthermore, with what I perceive to be less publicized and less naïve versions of the story. That is, I have sought to knead the whole from inventory to taxonomy—to impose certain priorities, at least by implication. The metaphor of raw dough is not entirely inapt, for the substance with which I have worked does not lend itself to clear separation. We have seen that commonly styled natural calamities tend to overlap with the effects of our technology on the environment, that plagues are also part natural and part consequence of "lifestyle" choices, that technology itself is widely perceived by the masses as a "given" of nature and its malfunction hence as "bad luck" or "an act of God",[8] and that weapons of mass destruction substantially intersect both the region of high-tech and that of nature (in the form of plagues). The ultimate end of such an exercise as this, of course, cannot be simply to produce a curious arrangement of diverse objects. A responsible investigator must look over the whole and attempt to reach a reasonable conclusion about which scenarios are the more likely ones—for we are not, all metaphor aside, merely surveying beads on a string or a recipe for making bread: we are contemplating the possible collapse of North American society, as precipitated by a catastrophic event that will prove too much for its waning or overstretched energies. Anyone who can raise a warning should do so.

I will immediately observe in response to this challenge that a major catastrophe may surely occur without jeopardizing society's survival. Earthquakes, volcanic eruptions, and tidal waves *will* happen, and some of them will claim thousands of lives despite our best efforts at prevention and preparation. I find that one of this topic's most fascinating lessons, therefore, lies in the popular mind's tendency to associate such events with societal collapse. The earthquake, the tsunami, and especially global warming have all been presented in fiction and on film lately as *likely to disrupt the North American way of life irreparably*. A foregone conclusion of personal vulnerability and general ineptitude seems to rest at the bedrock level beneath every narrative. These scenarios, at least as much as anticipations of natural cycle, are symptoms of an advanced moral anemia. Americans do not feel in control of their lives, and they readily flinch when the shadow of some major event requiring radical readjustment falls over their shoulder.

I remarked time and again throughout my survey—I could not restrain myself from a commentary so patently justified—that all varieties of disaster show a tendency to thrust whatever measure of human responsibility may exist onto the "higher-ups". The proliferation of a dreadful disease has no more to do with one's personal decisions than whether rain will fall tomorrow; the failure of traffic to move smoothly indicts poor planning on the part of corrupt or stupid politicians, and the pollution dumped by so many cars into the atmosphere clearly proves that manufacturers have bribed Congress to settle for low emission standards. The jet which struck the first World Trade Tower was (though nobody now recalls this) immediately assumed to have veered off course through pilot error, and we were told that such accidents had in fact been fearfully anticipated when the towers were constructed; yet the emphasis at once and permanently shifted when the terrorist plot surfaced (except for some talk of suing the construction company because the interior sprinkler systems malfunctioned). The presumptuous height of the Towers ceased being an issue: *they* had done it—the others, the bad guys!

Several pieces of the puzzle's most likely picture, then, must be drawn from a condition which precedes all specific disasters: the persistent and characteristic evasion of personal responsibility notable in Americans' responses to calamity. Why have we surrendered to this sad ebb of morale?

The chief culprit in my view would be our technology: we are so accustomed to having vast amounts of labor done for us by systems which we don't begin to understand that shut-downs, break-downs, and melt-downs may always credibly be laid at the door of "them". How can we be responsible for something which we personally didn't build, can't repair, and can't explain? A house was constructed, and we bought it: what did we know about mud-slides? A desirable apartment in a high-rise came available, and we rented it: were we not entitled to assume that *someone* was protecting us from stray aircraft?

I believe that the average American's profound ignorance of how his technology works is a major national problem, and growing day by day. We are asked to approve a bond for a new loop around town in order to reduce traffic, having no knowledge whatever of the rigid connection between such projects and *increased traffic*. We are asked to oppose the construction of a nuclear power plant on a ballot initiative, abysmally ignorant of what environmental costs a conventional coal plant will exact or of whether the nuclear option can in fact function safely. The personal computer has been part of my life for about twenty years: has there been a single study of entering college freshmen, from the cradle to the present, who grew up before the PC? Parents were once warned not to let their children sit within five feet of a television: what unwholesome effects may be observable in a generation whose members have spent their entire life within two feet of these new screens—or nestled them upon ear or in lap? Is such a study being designed even now? Do we know the long-term effects of wearing an earpiece all day long which pipes in loud music? The public bristled a few years ago over rumors that cell phones produce brain tumors, and a few years before that over rumors that power lines over one's residence produce all kinds of cancers. Both rumors were eventually shot down derisively... but how many more plausible worries will never reach the status of a rumor because the boy has already cried "wolf" twice?[9]

At a subliminal level, if not consciously, most of us must surely be somewhat nervous. And there are more practical, even political reasons to fidget. When all of your financial transactions are at last done online, how vulnerable will you be to the kind of savvy depredation which plunders life-savings from a terminal? How will you guard your identity and private information? What if the whole system "crashes" in a massive and protracted power outage, caused either by accident or malicious design? What if the public is allowed to vote by computer—how difficult will election fraud be then, when online surveys are already notoriously hard to police for "stuffing the box"? How much personal information will intelligence agencies extract about us, with or without legal permission? How much truth are we likely to be told by our leaders when rhetorical "spin" can be vetted before a focus group in an hour, then finessed and fed to the general public according to cues from electronic polling? How easy will we be to lead about by the nose—how hard will we find it to dig in our heels and *not* be led?

The kinds of situation I have just sketched out are already first-tier disasters for our society. Natural disasters will occur on their own time and without our provocation—but our moral disaster will compound them. People unwilling to leave their homes as a hurricane descends, or all too willing to build homes on a fault line, because "it's out of their hands" and, in any case, "they will be taken care of"... people unwilling to change their travel plans just because the flu season has turned virulent, or all too willing to engage in exotic sexual activity, because "you can die slipping in the bath tub" and, in any case, "modern medicine can handle it".... what more obliging cattle could any slaughterhouse ask for? Such crises will certainly be exacerbated by the misplaced fatalism and obtuse trust in higher powers typical of contemporary North America.

Technological malfunction will abound, for the same reason. Seismometers will *not* prove quite accurate enough, antibiotics *not* quite potent enough, because this population will have allowed itself to pressure existing resources to the breaking point. Traffic will grind to a halt, and computer systems will black out—but the public outcry will demand only more highways and more fiber-optic cable. Malevolent souls will exploit the universal stress of every network for their wicked ends, tossing in a wrench, loosening a rail, crossing a couple of wires. Public outrage will demand more police, better-welded joints, and "hack-proof" software. Though an excessive reliance on technology has created the problem, the only solution recognized by our citizens' passive mentality is yet another technological appendage; for, since they did not understand the original miracle before it malfunctioned, they cannot understand why a supplemental miracle should not correct the malfunction.

In such a scenario, an elite coterie high in the central government could conceivably transform the political landscape. Elections might well be engineered, or voters otherwise manipulated. A deceased hero might even be resurrected digitally and appear on screens everywhere to solicit votes or support. The potential for propaganda would free itself from all practical limitation—entire nations could be invented and then obliterated, invasions by interplanetary pirates mounted and repelled, without the viewing public's being any the wiser. Contagions could be selectively released and "steered" like a raging forest fire so as to eliminate certain undesirable demographic elements. All sorts of comic-book caliber narratives could suddenly find accommodation in the twenty-first century's now highly plastic reality.

I return to the affirmation, though, that these exotic nightmares are no more than the endgame of a society whose primary catastrophe was to lose its will power. If I put it thus Delphicly in closing, I hope I will now make sense: our best defense against an asteroid on a collision-course with us may be to stop buying every new gadget. We should begin striving to understand as well as we can whatever technology we allow into our lives; what we do not well understand, we should allow to affect as small a part of our lives as possible.

Being surrounded by incomprehensible switches, levers, and buttons is diminishing—not enhancing—our technical skill. What good would an asteroid-shooting laser-gun do us—a device understood by all of half a dozen people on earth—if not even these happy few could calculate how the original rock's fragments would behave? How will we know whether the elite six would misuse the gun? How would *they* know whether its side-effects might poison the atmosphere? How will we know that the asteroid or the gun exists, either one, and that we are not being manipulated by a propagandistic fabrication?

Free people cannot live like this. If we are to inhabit so complex a world, then our society can only preserve its freedom by placing an immensely greater value on seeing things clearly and weighing things soberly.

1 This scene comes early in the initial episode, entitled, "The Skin of Our Teeth." I have copied the text from the volume in which Clark eventually published series transcripts and photos, *Civilisation: A Personal View* (New York and Evanston: Harper & Row, 1969), 4.

2 Within hours of writing these words, I discovered on the cover of *U. S. News & World Report* for June 4, 2007, a dried-up lake's basin spanned by the alarming title, "Why you should worry about water." Yet the cover story (pp. 37-46) in fact addresses a crisis in water purification as facilities age and funds diminish. A trail of brief related features ignores actual depletion of subterranean sources, both in the US and abroad. As for the sensational cover photo, it turns out to be attributed to no locality, and frankly looks more like the Dead Sea region or a shriveled Lake Baikal than any North American site. The editors appear to have decided that a *new* high alert about our water's cleanliness did not lend itself to apocalyptic images (microbes swimming under the microscope indeed lack sublimity), and so retreated to vistas which stirred anxiety three decades ago.

3 Cf. Andres Duany, Elizabeth Plater-Zyberk, and Jeff Speck, *Suburban Nation: The Rise of Sprawl and the Decline of the American Dream* (New York : North Point Press, 2000), 88-94.

4 When American Airlines Flight 587 crashed into Belle Harbor just after take-off on November 12, 2001, just two months after the terrorist hijackings, the assumption was instantly made by the general public that Al Qaeda had struck again. Yet the culprit turned out to be faulty tail structure.

5 Cf., "Will Spiritual Robots Replace Humanity by 2100?" a symposium held at Stanford University on April 1, 2000. Conference notes appear at http://www.ceptualinstitute.com /nuc/robo-souls-more.htm.

6 Reporter Jane Corbin narrated a documentary for PBS *Frontline* titled "Chasing Saddam's Weapons" which first aired on January 22, 2004. The following are Corbin's own words in summary of her findings: "So far, the strongest indication that Iraq may have continued a clandestine program is the ISG's discovery of 97 samples [of bacteriological matter]—reference strains. A scientist had kept them hidden in his refrigerator at home for the past 10 years. One of the test tubes, or vials, contained an organism called botulinum..." and later this: "Dr. Rihab Taha, the woman U.N. inspectors called 'Dr. Germ', had used her skills in Iraq's past bio-weapons program. She admitted that in the 1980s, she'd played a key role in developing anthrax and botulinum—for Iraq 's self-defense, she claimed." Corbin retained a coolly skeptical tone throughout the presentation, yet the claim of a captured technician working on methods of mass murder surely deserves at least as much skepticism as that of intelligence officers concerning the probable end of such "experiments". As for the dismissively tendered presence of deadly

bacteria in homespun storage, it can only raise suspicions about what vials were deemed important enough *not* to sit languishing in an old refrigerator. Ultimately, however, the Bush Administration preferred to shrug off the paucity of pieces for nuclear missiles lying about rather than pursue the many biochemical leads, and neither the Fourth Estate nor the public has demanded answers.

7 The first contaminated mail was discovered on September 18, 2001, exactly one week after 9/11; the offices of two U.S. senators were eventually among the known targets. Though the case has never been solved, the very absence of useful leads flowing from organized terrorist cells suggests that a single disgruntled functionary may have been "freelancing".

8 Of course, José Ortega y Gasset noted decades ago in *The Revolt of the Masses* that citizens of modern Western societies view their technological amenities as a natural and self-sustaining endowment, like the air they breathe. See especially Ch. 6, "The Dissection of Mass-Man Begins."

9 I may volunteer anecdotally that I have struggled for years to combat certain side-effects—headache, insomnia, indigestion—induced by long sessions before my computer. I now sit before it in relatively comfortable truce halfway across the room, with an improvised Faraday Screen shielding me (I hope) from the main unit's electricity. Medical people scoff when I recount my troubles; but from others, I gather an increasing supply of similar evidence.

When the Wheels Come Off the Wagon: Contemporary America's Inevitable Descent into "Progress"

*First published in **Praesidium** 12.2 (Spring 2012); the endnotes that originally accompanied the piece have unfortunately been lost, and not all could be reconstructed.*

It is the destiny of every seed to rot, but some turn into trees. I was shocked and delighted to discover that the old coffee grounds and tea leaves of our household, if sealed in sandwich wrap and placed under sunlight, provide the perfect medium for nurturing apple seeds to germination. Yet the unpromising period before the first tinge of green appears, be warned, is a frightful outbreak of rioting mold; and if you should remove the wrap after the incubator sits a couple of weeks on the window sill, the chemical released into the air is unmistakably the same as patrols the most densely populated regions of a barnyard.

The human animal, though endowed by his Creator with free will, has nevertheless a proclivity to certain such metamorphic sequences—and many of them, alas, seem to produce only foul odor and mold in their terminal stage, with no green sprout in sight. Medical minds tell us that our bodies, even in their healthiest state, harbor harmful bacteria and a smattering of cancer cells. These we repel under normal conditions; under a bit of stress, however, our defenses may flag and a major war for health or survival may ensue. So with the spirit: our hearts—even the purest of them—are mottled with the taint of our corrupt nature. If not placed under inordinate pressure, we usually abide by the rules of common decency and humanity. Let one or two existential variables change ever so slightly, however, and we begin a descent into the abyss.

The most alarming thing about this universal penchant, indeed, is that the changing variables themselves often seem to result from fully natural tendencies: they don't require the stimulus of some thunderclap or wholly arbitrary Darwinian mutation. Take Moore's Law: though never having heard of it until last fall, I have been aware for years and years (who of my age hasn't?) that technological innovation always accelerates.[1] What Mr. Moore didn't understand that Ortega y Gasset and I know well is that the median creativity, emotional maturity, and moral responsibility of a given society decelerate in direct proportion to this ascending curve. The machine does our work quicker, it does our heavy lifting easier, and it never makes efficiency suffer by yawning or blinking; hence we rely more upon it after a little use and proceed to get lazier, flabbier, and less competent than ever; hence we need a new machine to pick up the slack in our rising levels of ineptitude; hence, thanks to better machines, that level continues to rise. As Ortega y Gasset noted (and this was almost a century ago), we end up—the rank and file of us—with scarcely enough sense to invent the wheel, yet we believe ourselves to be the brightest hominids ever to walk the planet because our pigmy achievements sit atop such giant shoulders.

High-tech guru Bill Joy opined in the early years of the new millennium that our doom is now sealed. We shall become so much stupider and less able than our computers that robots must eventually judge us redundant, and phase us out. The more optimistic Ray Kurzweil insists, rather, that our biological system will fuse with nanobot technology. Either way, the essential species terminates.[2] Oh, happy day!

Recoil now to a fundamental level, and consider what happens to human beings as they pursue happiness. What does that mean, in the context of human beings? More than anything, they (we) appear to desire security. At first, fixed settlements congeal; then thriving markets emerge; finally, states with civil laws and police forces arise. Now we have advanced culture, if not civilization—and beyond this point, security can only be enhanced in two ways: possessing enough money to create buffer zones around oneself, or reducing one's needs sufficiently that one needs very little of the material environment. Bourgeois society inevitably prefers the former option (hence the strange admixture of admiration, dread, and loathing with which it greeted Diogenes, Socrates, and Jesus). People compete fiercely to make the greatest financial profit: those who advance the farthest often embrace the most cutthroat tactics. As these elite few look down from their lofty, self-engineered fortress of wealth and power in later life, they are often overcome by boredom. Like Alexander on the coast of India, they have no more lands to conquer, and they weep.

In contemporary political terms, they change from free-market capitalists to left-leaning progressive social crusaders. Some of them, I am willing to admit, may be stricken with sincere compunction for past misdeeds or with a sincere desire to help their fellow man amid the astounding affluence that has overtaken them. Yet even among most of these, I would wager that at least a tincture of the "game-player" circulates. Having moved in half a lifespan from pawn to knight to bishop to king, they now transcend the chessboard entirely and view all of us as curious little pieces at the beck of their fingertips. Bill Gates tinkers with the notion of overhauling the entire educational system so that drones will not consume resources needlessly preparing to be guard-bees or pollinating honey-collectors. Warren Buffett whimsically speaks of reversing the magnetic polarities that drew fabulous wealth into his pockets (which gamesmanship, however, seems to position him well for acquiring yet more wealth). George Soros undertakes the destruction of national economies and the fashioning of quaint new societies as a kind of hobby.[3]

Meanwhile, what happens to Diogenes and Socrates… and to the would-be Christ-followers among us? They have lived commendably ascetic lives: they have become models of moderation, and even abstinence. They mortify us with their degree of spiritual elevation, while we excite their sublime pity with our various addictions to folly and frivolity. They are true saints, perhaps… unless and until they begin to take their sainthood seriously. Unfortunately, this happens more often than not—for they, too, turn out to be merely human. They chide us publicly for our servitude to material things, perhaps from a high pulpit or a diocesan cathedra. They virtually command us to follow their own example, their own conscience: to renounce our long hours at the job and our quest of promotion and pay raise, to desist from hoarding our harvests for a rainy day or a legacy, to rise above our physical terror of unsafe streets overrun with nomadic Visigoths. Their vision, too, is intoxicatingly progressive (as Mark Levin's bestseller has observed of the airy republic designed by Socrates).[4] Though they began with both feet set squarely in a traditional belief system emphasizing self-discipline and mistrust of flashy gadgetry, they end up preaching Utopia with no less fervor than Bill Gates or Ray Kurzweil. These Pastors and Popes may know nothing of nanobots, but the surrender of our free will which they require for the construction of their City of God nevertheless transforms us into robots.

A naïf might suppose that some eloquent, public-spirited person would warn us if this toxic brew were fermenting under our noses. The truth is that the men and women of the Fourth Estate—the vigilant watchdogs of the Republic—themselves drink heavily of the same progressive distillation. Why does any young undergraduate study journalism, to begin with? Because he or she is convinced of the importance of "news". Who would reach such a conviction? Obviously, not a person who inclined to believe that human events are more or less locked in eternal cycles—that there is nothing new under the sun. This person, rather, would assume that the community desperately needs to know "the truth", "the facts", or else its members may make disastrously wrong decisions.

The young journalist, in other words, likely believes that a nation's political future is significantly shaped by what information is broadcast to its citizens.[5] People who hold such beliefs tend to see human society and its individual components as very malleable. Given this malleability, they further tend to believe (naturally) that "better change" is preferable to "worse change". Hence, finally, they are predisposed to reveal facts that adduce to "better change". After all, some kind of triage of all available facts must take place in the newsroom: a reporter cannot communicate everything. Important facts therefore become those whose possession will most probably finesse a malleable citizenry into supporting—or even advocating—change in the direction of tomorrow's improved, more humane and enlightened society.

The reporter's descent into "progress" is thus almost as inevitable as a final domino's fall when the first domino in a close file is pushed over.

In our time, all of these vectors have converged. Whatever ebb and flow pulses in each of them has fallen into a synchronicity of the whole. Technology has never so clearly and thoroughly reduced the masses to Ortega y Gasset's state of the spoiled child. Billionaires have never enjoyed so many resources (thanks to technology) for playing God. Ascetics have never been so cleverly tempted into worldly crusades by such wanton frivolity on so wide a scale. Journalists have never commanded so many media with such narrow windows of broadcast time requiring such a severe triage of so very, very many recorded events. The wheels are all about to roll right off the wagon at once: all four hubcaps are already rattling and chattering.

Nor should a quaint metaphor confine us to supposing that only four such trends are motivating our degeneracy. I might have added some expanded notation about the professoriate's inevitable decline into progressive fantasies, for instance: maladjusted children turn to their books, children who turn to their books do well in school, children who do well in school go on to grad school, young introverts in grad school carry the scars of their childhood maladjustment, axe-grinding scholars gravitate to wild theories vengefully promoting social upheaval, etc., etc. Scholars were selected from a certain scribal background throughout the Western world until recently: now anyone with "book smarts" can go to graduate school in English or History—and virtually every kid in the nation has been deemed fit for undergraduate work. Never before: only now. The incubator of malaise has never been so fertile.

Once our nation descends precipitously into the progressive vision under the baleful influence of these converging trends, life will no doubt continue, at least in some quarters. Detroit has become a killing zone as of this writing; but even in Detroit, some residents have rediscovered the self-sufficient art of gardening. Perhaps, as well, the rotting ruins of the United States of America will feed a new political plant. The scent of manure sits so tenaciously in my nostrils that I can scarcely imagine a flower... but perhaps that is only natural. Are the days of "a more perfect union" at hand? Are we finally ready, or almost ready, to form a looser federation whose components are based on regional needs (inasmuch as the central government has voided our contract by refusing its constitutional duty to defend our borders)?

One can only hope.

1 According to Wikipedia, Gordon Moore's formula runs thus: "The number of transistors in a dense integrated circuit doubles about every two years." In other words, technological growth is exponential.

2 Bill Joy's gloomy prophecy, "Why the Future Doesn't Need Us," appeared in *Wired Magazine* on January 4, 2000. As for Ray Kurzweil, a sampling of his curious optimism may be found in "Promise and Peril," *Living With the Genie: Essays on Technology and the Quest for Human Mastery*, eds. A. Lightman, D. Sarewitz, and C. Desser (Island: Washington, DC: 2003), 35-62.

3 The Gates Foundation has mingled (or meddled) in education for years and to the tune of several hundred million dollars. Among other endeavors, it has promoted a quasi-European "track" system which would designate youngsters at quite an early age for white-collar or blue-collar training. Buffett famously remarked (in promoting the candidacy of Barack Obama) that he pays less tax than his secretary, obscuring the fact that the minions tending his affairs do not have access to his tax shelters. George Soros has insinuated himself well enough into the infosphere that attempts to uncover the depth of his presence through major search engines inevitably draw warnings of chasing after mere "conspiracy theory". Yet the egregiously misnamed Southern Poverty Law Center, for instance, has been a Soros ancilla since the millennium turned over. Its revised mission: to tar all organizations as "hate-mongers" that impede his intrusions into the corridors of power.

4 See Mark R. Levin, *Ameritopia: The Unmaking of America* (New York: Simon and Schuster, 2012).

5 The impact of the Marxist-revolutionary Frankfurt School (Theodore Adorno, Herbert Marcuse, *et al.*) upon the curriculum of Mass Communication programs at universities has mushroomed since the Sixties. The gist of the consequent pedagogy is that all news has an "angle" and no story a closer connection to the truth—which does not exist, in practical terms—than any other. Therefore, the reporter is freed, and indeed obligated (if possessed of a "professional conscience"), to represent that side of issues which promotes rejection of bourgeois capitalism.

Progressivism on Trial

*First published in **Praesidium** 13.2 (Spring 2013).*

If I were called to speak on behalf of a twenty-first century progressive—if I were being paid, for instance, to present a summation of his case before a dull jury composed of citizens of the universe—I could harangue more eloquently than my addle-brained client. I would expect to be paid very handsomely, however.

"Ladies and gentlemen of the jury," I would say, "my client is really the victim in this case—as are you, and as are all good people. The plaintiff grandly styles himself pro-life, whereas he is truly anti-life, anti-freedom, anti-progress, anti-choice, anti-philanthropy, and anti-humanity. He calls himself conservative—and so he is. He wishes to conserve the hierarchy of the past, the special privileges of the past, the archaic gods of the past, the superstitious taboos of the past, the hatreds of the past, the bigotry of the past, and the servitude of the past. He desires you to have more children that he may have more slaves, but he has no intention of empowering your children with the skills and education necessary to work their way free of chains. He desires you to have more hunger and misery so that you may be driven to find work and to fend for yourselves, but he has no intention of making your work safe or easy to procure or tolerably pleasant to do. He desires you to love God—his God—so that you may be conditioned to expect less of this life, but he has no intention of obeying the universal law of brotherhood that would require him to share the profits he makes on your backs.

"The entire human race is this man's victim—and yet he charges my client with sedition!

"And what were my client's crimes? Let us review. He is said to have stolen from the wealthy. How many times, though—for how many generations—have the wealthy and their forebears stolen from you and me? How many long days have you labored to come home with no more in your pockets than what barely suffices to put food in your children's mouths? How many high-priced marvels have you bought, after a long period of frugality, only to discover that they don't work or aren't safe because the wealthy ordered corners cut in their production? How many doors have been shut, locked, and bricked over against you and yours that might have provided entry into better-paying work and higher privilege? The wrong man is standing in the docks!

"My client is said to have lied repeatedly about matters of critical public importance. How do we count the number of lies—and over how many generations—that have been ground out by the wealthy and their propaganda machine? How many of your fathers worked at miserable jobs throughout their lives, retiring just about in time to drop dead of exhaustion and despair, because they had always been told that hard work pays off? How many of our fathers' fathers were raised as children in schools that told them over and over and over that this system is the best in the world—not perfect, perhaps, but scarcely to be improved upon? How many of our mothers and their mothers were told to stay home and keep having children—to stay out of politics and the work place, to keep their minds blank, and to keep their men chained down with so many little dependents that they, too, would have no time to stop and think? The whole system is a house of lies... and my client is on trial for trying to fight a firestorm with a matchstick? The wrong man is in the docks, I say again!

"My client is said to have murdered unborn children and to have subverted public morality. Yet how do we count the number of children born into this system who would have been better off dead—who were born dead, in effect, since they were born without a future? The wealthy have seen to that! Should we say a child has life, then, just because he breathes? Is it life to be dreaded, avoided, and hated by your very parents because they can no longer feed you? Is it life to be sent for years to a prison called school where you're constantly given work that you can't understand and then punished because you can't finish it? Is it life to be spat upon and called stupid until you can't take it any more—but when you rebel and stick up for yourself, you're introduced to the first in a long, long series of real prisons? And how many such children die—how many are killed—before they reach the age and estate of a man who might have sired and reared his own children, a stage that was thought a normal stop along life's journey in every human culture before ours? How do we count the number of those unborn children, those millions and millions of unborn victims whom the wealthy cannot even imagine? Yet my client stands accused of killing the unborn. He shall have to make so much room in the docks for those in this one building who deserve to be standing there more than he that we'll find him back on the streets in one minute.

"And what is it, after all, that my client really wants? What is the source of those actions which have stirred conservative ire against him? Why, just that he wants to see things progress. He sees so much misery around him that he can no longer stand by idly and watch—for make no mistake, ladies and gentlemen: if you free my client today, he will be up to his old tricks tomorrow, or this afternoon. He will be trying again to see that the hungry have food to eat, that the ailing have medicine, that the homeless have shelter, that the young have a future, that the oppressed have liberty, and that the imprisoned have hope. His worst deeds are only those that aim at creation—at bringing to light what has hitherto, in this corrupt and gloomy swamp of a society, been stifled and submerged. It is a lie, perhaps, to say that a seed should not be planted under a house's eaves because room for growth is lacking: next year and the year after, yes, there will be room enough. But the year will come when the aspiring branches will rake the house, and the two will war from then on. It is a lie, in the dead of winter, to say that a well should be dug because the stream hasn't enough water. The fall rains have fed the stream, the melting ice will feed it further, and throughout the spring it will run powerfully between its margins. Yet the summer will come, the stream will dry up in July, and for three months there will be no water.

"Lies are all in how you see them from time. The present's truth-tellers are often the biggest liars in the future. My client is an artist, a visionary—a prophet. He sees things that do not yet exist. He sees a happiness that is not yet possible. People who live only in the present—and, even worse, people who can live only in the past—will never share his views. You cannot climb that mountain, they say, because it has never been climbed. People will never share their wealth and care for their fellow beings, it is said, because they never have. Humans—these conservatives say—are incurably selfish. But my client has the cure. The medicine may be bitter to some because the disease is virulent: but the cure is to cut away all that is diseased. The way to climb the mountain is to put beneath us all that is above us. My client has the will to do this: his persecutors have none. They would have us roll back down to the mountain's foot, curl up, and die of slow rot.

"The wrong man is in the docks; but his accusers, even if they escape trial, are already sentenced. They will die of their own decay if they do not embrace his cure. Even for them, he is the only hope."

Upon consideration, I would not, in fact, deliver that speech—not for any amount of money—because it is too dangerous. Too much in it is true—and the falsehoods riding on the coattails of those truths might themselves usher in murder and mayhem. To speak in such terms to masses of people without rhetorical sophistication or fine discernment would be grossly irresponsible. Of course, progressive politicians understand this implicitly: hence their desire to "water down" the electorate with hordes of unskilled laborers from Third World cultures who have no rhetorical sophistication at all—who, in many cases, not only don't speak the language of their host nation, but cannot read or write the language of their homeland. Hence the progressive tendency, as well, to draw often and shamelessly from a treasure chest of demagogic imagery: the weeping widow, the starving child, and the scapegoated migrant.

The rhetoric itself, if effective, is rudimentary. You take the plaintiff's charges and, without addressing a single item or detail in any of them, you reverse each one and send it back where it came from. Magnify the payload ten times. If they charge that you lied about your campaign donors, counter-charge that they and their ancestors have always lied about their plan for the nation's poor. If they charge that you have never attended the church where you claim to be an alderman, counter-charge that they violate every day all the core principles of the faith they profess to follow. This might be called the "see your raise and double it" technique.

Notice, too, that the raise must always be made in the very vaguest terms. Details about campaign donations are a matter of public record, and can be verified: accusations about the attitudes and prejudices of an entire class or ethnic group, perhaps spanning several generations, are patently indemonstrable with any degree of precision or fairness. Likewise, a behavior such as church attendance could be investigated either by interviewing other church members or examining church documents: a behavior such as degree of practical adherence to a faith's moral teachings is scarcely discernible even in an individual case—and is certainly not so for a vast group.

If I charge you with chopping down a reverend old tree, then, you should charge me with eradicating traditions left and right that once made life meaningful to people. If I charge you with beating your wife, you should charge my entire congregation, community, or race with having tortured helpless innocents for centuries. See the bet, and then raise with every coin you can find whose national currency is unknown and indeterminable.

As I have acknowledged, however, some of the counter-charges in my imaginary summation are true. Winners and losers are often predetermined in our society, as in all societies—and they are so on both sides of the political aisle, and in all religious faiths and denominations, and among all species of pagan or atheist, and within all fraternities and sodalities. People inevitably form cliques, gangs, coteries, cabals, and musketeer threesomes within musketeer companies. I have noticed dozens of times, for instance, and always painfully, that my editorials never receive a hearing when I send them to sites that enjoy a national renown, even though I believe my writing to be quite the equal of many syndicated columnists. All ventures and industries have their "old boy" networks, and some of us will be forever on the outside looking in. No amount of "hard work" will make any door open for us, although a well-timed, well-placed marriage or the discovery of a felicitous second-cousin connection might bring out the red carpet.

This sort of thing is highly annoying, and to hear the system's defenders insist that it doesn't exist—to hear them warble sanctimoniously about the direct proportion connecting jobs well done with material success—can send up the blood pressure and make fists clench. The System is just another system; if it lacks the vices of some, it also has the foibles common to all. Tall men with deep voices get along better than diminutive, shy men: beautiful women fare better than their plain sisters. Life can be rather horrid that way.

It is also true that some of the young men, perhaps many, who languish in our prisons are not at all bad people, and may indeed have extraordinarily good qualities. There's no denying that a certain percentage of them were "set up" by social malaises whose cancer tends to be passed along almost genetically. The ambition to redeem these men for a life of honor and decency is admirable; and if the path to redemption were capable of being made somewhat programmatic, then we might even dare speak of "progress" in our public policy. Not everything old is good. Sometimes the potato crop has to fail before one can understand that eating only potatoes was never very healthy, to begin with.

This brings us, though, to the matter of poetry (for lack of a better word): for you may have noticed that my "summation" closes with a couple of little allegories. Tropological language can very powerfully condense complex ideas into simple, dynamic images. The compression can be excessive, however; and, on a progressive's tongue, it usually is. Life is neither a mountain-climb nor a disease to be cured. The truths I have just conceded above are indeed half-truths as used in the summation, in that they more properly indict the human condition than any particular political or economic system. To insinuate that a capitalist republic produces abnormally high levels of crony-ism and criminalization of racial-ethnic minorities is grossly abusive. In the same way, to suggest that removing such ills from our midst equates to curing our body of a disease is, as a logical claim, idiotic. A more accurate allegory would be to say that we could rid our body politic of all inequity by shutting down its voluntary systems entirely and putting it on life support under the supervision of an external healer—an infallible prophet, a god. Then we could review the credentials of the real-world applicants for that exalted position. Such images would do much less violence to the truth... but, of course, they would also attract far fewer adherents in a naïve electorate.

The allegory of the visionary creator who brings forth something from nothing (if I may digress slightly) is especially inept when applied to entire human communities, and often even when applied to certain kinds of individual endeavor. Who, exactly, ushers a wonder into existence where there was no such wonder before? An artist. But human beings are not an artistic medium, and to imply that their lives may be treated as canvas and paint or wet clay is disturbingly hubristic. Of the several words that we might use to describe the person who would thus play God with his fellow creatures, none is untainted by some implication of moral depravity or insanity.

In matters of strictly, narrowly physical achievement, we are often able far to exceed our self-expectations. A pitiable light-weight can become a marvel of muscle with disciplined body-building. An athlete can train himself to perform complex maneuvers with either the left or the right hand after hundreds or thousands repetitions. Olympic gymnasts are not born, but molded out of years of agonizing practice. Mastering a musical instrument, as well, while considered an artistic achievement, partakes liberally of the athlete's conditioning program. In such cases, stunning progress is indeed possible. There seems to be little room for carrying over this optimism, however, into more cerebral matters. One can become reasonably quick at mathematics or fluid in Pashtu with years of intense study—yet some people are simply born with a gift in these cognitive areas, and no amount of labor can make up the ground separating the gifted from the more pedestrian. A master pianist may never be a very good composer. We human beings are not infinitely malleable in every direction.

Perhaps this is nowhere more true than in our moral character. To the extent that societies have ever existed whose members sacrifice their time and effort for the benefit of their fellow beings without any hope of remuneration, it is because the remuneration is invisible. The pay-off may be either positive (e.g., high praise for services rendered) or negative (e.g., public disparagement in return for a lackluster performance). Though we may consider such duty-driven people to be paragons of virtue and a sure sign that progress in character is collectively possible, we are deceiving ourselves: our little utopian knights of public service are mere automatons, deprived of personal will power rather than liberated into moral choice. Properly seen, this sort of situation (which has never even existed in convincing detail outside the fictions of Plato's Socrates and Thomas More) is indeed more regression than progress. Only a mind that envies the anthill its unanimity and efficiency could embrace such a vision for human society.

I do not say—Heaven forbid—that saintly people have never existed, nor even that the rest of us should not try to emulate their example in our piddling way. I say only that we must not suppose any tinkering with the political or economic systems around us capable of producing a society of saints. Spectacular moral triumphs are all individual, and always individual. This is the most critical blunder made by progressive thinking. If "good" is to be defined for human beings in moral terms, then it must refer to the choices they make. A behavior cannot be designated as good if it has not been freely selected by the moral agent—for instance, if it is forced upon the citizen by systematic brainwashing or by laws that punish contrary behaviors. The progressive proposes that we require generosity and self-sacrifice of all citizens by confiscating "excess" earnings, dissolving family ties, severely limiting private property, suppressing individualism in favor of group-think, programming young children to ignore the "background interference" of parental and cultural influence, etc., etc. By definition, this agenda cannot produce good people, since it concentrates on removing choice from the lives of the rank and file. To the extent that the Brave New Hive does not permit either good or bad choices, but only grinds out worker-bees, it is in fact an evil place. It robs human beings of a free will whose exercise is their inalienable right and which, above all else, distinguishes them from mere animals.

It is sometimes difficult, I realize, to imagine a more hive-like existence than that into which free-market capitalism has lured or coerced millions of people. Wake up at the scream of an alarm, fight through the crawl of rush-hour traffic, sit at a desk or stand behind a counter for eight hours a day, navigate another rush hour, crawl into bed exhausted and quite without any sense of having benefited oneself or humanity... wake up to another alarm....

This misery is rightly ascribed to our way of life, it does not belong to the inevitable human condition, and we should certainly struggle to be rid of its dreariest elements some day. Yet greater centralization is not the way out. Being assigned daily a certain time to leave the house, for example, and a certain route to reach work so as to dispel traffic jams will only magnify the degree of regimentation in the individual's life. Being paid to stay home might seem more attractive... but where, then, will one's pay come from if one has withdrawn from the productive work force; and for how long, in any case, can any human being remain content while doing nothing?

The best antidote to the daily grind would be more freedom. When a brutal employer shortchanges his poor wage-slaves, their only alternative is not (or should not be) unionization: a far better one is competition. Let the abused laborer market his skills under his own shingle. Let him quit his job and open up a small shop in his garage or den. His income would greatly diminish, no doubt—at least in the beginning—but he would also save money in gasoline, car maintenance and insurance, child care for little tikes who cannot be left home alone, and doctor's bills that would otherwise have loomed if his high-stress lifestyle had continued. The security of his neighborhood would improve, the locals up and down the block would know each other better and forge stronger ties, and life in general would have more sunny days.

Naturally, our oppressed worker cannot do any such thing. Building permits, zoning laws, local taxes, OSHA regulations, wheel-chair access, fire codes... the morass of "nuisance" rules is impenetrable to any ordinary person. What I would emphasize in this context is that all such rules originated in the desire to protect the little guy. Nobody has ever stood before a local, state, or federal legislating body (as I pictured myself doing when this essay began) and proclaimed, "We need more rules to make it thoroughly impossible for small entrepreneurs to compete with huge corporations." The arguments advanced always claim to defend the poor, the underprivileged, the powerless, the disenfranchised, the overlooked... yet they simply wrap more chains around the common man's neck.

My jury, consisting of average citizens of the universe, would perhaps understand few of the arguments I have made in rebuttal of my own summation. There is too much "dependency of thing upon thing", as the Bard says: the chain of cause and effect has too many links. The victor in the debate will simply trot out weeping widows, starving children, and scapegoated migrants. All pageantry, no discussion. And my jury will vote to hang itself, without ever recognizing that it, far more than either the defendant or the plaintiff, is on trial.

But the good news is that there are too many citizens of the universe to hang. Eventually we will run out of rope, out of hangmen, out of gravediggers. Our elite rulers will have walled themselves away in such a high palace or such a deep bunker that they will have no interest in the waifs moving about the rubble of Cincinnati or Tallahassee or Spokane or Reno; and their elite police force, though authorized and equipped to shoot any waif on sight, will be more interested in staying warm and sharing confiscated narcotics. That will leave the rest of us to begin again—and we will do so precisely as I have just described.

The first step, then, is to survive the Great Slaughter of Freedoms, with the help of much patience and... well, vision. For when unhinged progressives lead us into a steep regression, all of us who would cling to our freedom must formulate a plan for real progress.

Postscript

Inasmuch as the essay above addresses the possibility (or, I should say, the improbability) of fortifying ordinary American citizens against the rhetoric of manipulative "change agents", an experiment with our youngest voters suggested itself to me just after I finished the piece. I assigned the text of this essay (being very careful to dissociate myself from it) to a class of college freshman in January of this year, at the very beginning of the Spring semester. Students read (or were supposed to have read) the essay as homework before their third class meeting, whereupon they were asked to write a brief response to it. I might observe immediately, by way of warning, that all responses were handwritten. The absence of an automated word-processing program trailing the student's fingers and mopping up his or her sloppy orthography is painfully evident. Is this an incidental comment, I wonder—or does it not rather drive right to the heart of the matter: the inability of many young people even among the educated to see any kind of thoughtful endeavor through without the aid of time-and-labor saving devices?

For besides almost universal complaining about the vocabulary's difficulty, the most common criticism of the piece appeared to be that it didn't quickly fit itself into some well-worn template—or that it seemed to do so at first, but then "deceptively" doubled back on itself. These young readers, for the most part, did not much appreciate the descent into one genre by way of exemplification, and then the clinical autopsy of that genre. The 180-degree turn disoriented them, and the disorientation irritated them. They wanted the game finished according to the same rules that presided over its start. The level of abstraction that was instead demanded of them by the rhetorical masquerade struck them as cynical—or, in the word of one, "sarcastic".

On the other hand, how many students (I found myself asking from time to time) in fact understood that the courtroom defense was a mere figure and not the author's expression of his own views? The following assessment of one good-natured young man certainly doesn't seem to see a distinction:

The author's criticisms are exagerated [sic] a little but he agrees with them. I think he is over doing [sic] his point to infasize [sic] it better. He had the point where school is a prison, but I think he meant at a certain age students should be allowed to decide if they will attend or if they will join the work force.

The "school is prison" equation, of course, belonged to the courtroom, not the autopsist's lab, and thus cannot be ranged among the "author's criticisms" except by mistake. The student cited below obviously made the same error (or else simply never read the second half of the essay: that possibility must not be discounted).

> The author had the ability to turn every accusation around into something positive. In a way his statements were true but at the same time highly exaggerated. I think he is exaggerating to show the so-called "jury" that his client should not be convicted but applauded for correcting society.

The next comment I offer is not so gullible. This young woman "gets it"… but not fully. Indeed, she names as her "favorite part" the advancing of a strategy that the author not only didn't promote, but roundly condemned:

> At first, I actually thought that the first part was real. I had no idea he was pretending to give that speech. Then, all of a sudden he starts analysing [sic] it and breaking it apart. I think he did a good job of representing the other side. My favorite part of this piece was when he shows how to respond to accusations from his opponent. He says that if they accuse you of doing something blame them for doing something with out [sic] giving detail, that way you dont [sic] have to prove it because its [sic] vague.

As you can imagine, this sort of response depressed me more deeply, in a way, than the kind that detected no seam in the value systems identified by the essay; for this girl, having located the seam, proceeded to admire the fabric on the wrong side! (Then again, maybe I missed her point: maybe she was merely admiring the astuteness of the rhetorical trick, not applauding its moral propriety.)

Then we have varieties of misreading that show more initiative—that distort the essay into the sort of adversary, apparently, at which the student-writer most likes to tilt. This sample accuses my argument of gross misanthropy:

> In my opinion the author stretches the truth to prove his point. He make [sic] it seem that all people were bad people. When in truth, they are not. Their writting [sic] mainly talks about how everyone has poor morals and only care about themselves [sic]. He not once gave an example in which a person performs a good deed to help others."

I assume that the rebuke here is at least leveled at the essay's second half rather than at the courtroom burlesque: for the "defense summation" oozes with pie-in-the-sky optimism. It is the second half alone which warns of how rigorously self-interest tends to limit human action. Still, what could the specific passage have been that drew such indignant fire? Was it my claim that hard work won't always get you to the top (a concession to the imaginary progressive advocate, by the way)? Was it my mention of all the rules and regulations that throttle small businesses? Or should I simply never have claimed that the American electorate is a jury that will generally vote itself to ruin these days if manipulated with the right rhetoric? What relevance does the occasional person's doing a selfless deed have to the fairly fixed quality of communal behavior? Are we bound to believe that our system will promote universal goodness just because good individuals exist among us?

This manner of indignation became a recurrent theme. The following respondent, for instance, virtually accuses the paper of enslaving him as a dictator would a helpless populace and leading him to places where he would rather not go:

> The writer... establishes a dictatorship with the people, leading the reader throughout the paper to think, see, and feel the same way he does. The extra energy displayed by the intensity of the writer could easily be seen as over the top and unorthodox. It shows how much passion he has for the subject, but leads the reader to believe that he is fanatical. The mock trial is a clever way of introducing everything in detail to the reader in order for him or her to come to a conclusion, but the writer's exagerration [sic] of the magnitude of injustice imposed by those he is actually accusing is not supporting the argument like it should.

It may be that we have here another response focused exclusively on the courtroom tirade: I really don't know. If so, then the student has again failed utterly to notice that the essay's true intent is to reject the "fanaticism" of the defense's summation. Yet this particular student must have detected that the essay breaks into two distinct pieces, for he refers to the "mock trial".

I think the next sample, however (the last I shall adduce), has the piece as a whole in its angry crosshairs:

> Throughout the whole passage, I had a feeling that the author did not feel strongly about the topic. There was a sarcastic tone throughout the entire piece. It felt as if he was literally writing just to write. I can honestly say that I was annoyed with the author. It was as if he was just some guy off the street; not a credible source. Albeit, some of the things he said were true. He mentioned that the wealthy steal from the poor, and that happens all the time. The way he went about explaining it, however, was not very feasible [sic]. He was so sarcastic that it almost made me believe he was part of the wealthy that steals [sic] from the poor.

This young woman was practically unique in not ascribing the author's "passion" to a wholesome motive, I might remark. Many responses not cited here were partially won over by the energy of the essay—though I must presume that the courtroom defense generated most or all of this energy in the students' minds. Hence, once again, they would be evaluating the author on the basis of an example that he creates merely to castigate. Evidence of "passion" in a point of view appears to earn it special points among the young, even when its logical connection to that view is almost haphazard. Passion trumps reason these days as rocks break scissors.

The response I have just quoted, for that matter, is probably denouncing my essay's failure to sustain its passion—my "betrayal", as one might say, of the courtroom's fervor in casting the summation upon the dissection table. This student is very clear about directing her scorn at the "entire piece". I'm guessing that the element of sarcasm noted repeatedly, then, is the essay's very withdrawal from the courtroom tirade to a more analytical level. I believe this young woman finds my piece repugnantly aloof precisely because it does not immerse itself in the opening scene's passion, but rather warns against and even derides the exploitative strategies of that passionate outburst. I am "writing just to write" like a "guy off the street". I am apparently coming across to her tender young mind as a bloodless, condescending kinglet—the "dictator" of another student, or the wealthy thief she mentions who shares the plunder taken by those he condemns—because I shift rhetorical gears: because I seize upon that fire-breathing lawyer and expose his passion as tawdry calculation. Do I not believe, then, that anybody ever does a good deed (in yet another student's formulation)? Do I not realize that passion is the true and ultimate measure of moral value? Do I not understand that my icy analysis chills to the bone and ends my own trial before it has begun?

All I can add, then, by way of postscript to my essay in the light of about forty college-freshman reactions is this: Q.E.D. We're in big trouble as a nation for at least another generation. The sooner a salutary degree of hardship reintroduces our children to common sense and immunizes them to theatrical displays that amuse rather than analyze, the better.

Progressive Economics: The Starship *Enterprise*, the Good Ship *Lollipop*, and the *Titanic* in One Blueprint

*First published in **Praesidium** 16.2 (Spring 2016).*

For some odd reason, I devoted an evening a couple of months ago to watching a documentary on Netflix about the creation of *Star Trek: The Next Generation* (titled *Chaos on the Bridge*). Though never a fan of the series in any of its multiple incarnations, I have friends and relatives who swear by this stuff, as a somewhat younger set of cultists swears by the *Star Wars* saga (none of whose branches, likewise, I have ever been able to sit through for five minutes). I'm glad that I invested the evening as I did, primarily because of a single "find". I learned that Gene Roddenberry, the original serial's creator, made life impossible for most of the new show's writers with his insistence that there should be no more friction among crew members. It seems that Roddenberry, an outspoken atheist, had long envisioned the generation of star travelers after Captain Kirk (William Shatner narrates the documentary and interviews its contributors, by the way) as having shed the human propensity to quarrel. In practical terms, every episode had to bring the Starship *Enterprise* in contact with yet another less evolved civilization so as to manufacture something resembling a plot. I suppose the odd mechanical malfunction might have served as well… but you can do only so many of those before the Superior Race's engineering competence is called into question. Writers being writers, furthermore, there was an invincible tendency around the drawing board to give the major characters assertive personalities. Roddenberry's formula, in contrast, demanded robotic little Maoists flitting about in harmony as the Klingons threatened to neutralize the defense shield.

I realized that I was looking at the progressivist psyche's snapshot in full frontal nudity. On Planet Roddenberry, nothing that goes wrong in life is ever OUR fault: it's always THEIRS—the others', the ones who won't accept our vision and play by our rules. Our vision cannot be flawed, and our rules cannot be skewed. That never happens. The guarantee against it may be taken on faith. Things go awry because the backward infidels who surround us haven't yet heard the gospel. That the United States national debt stands at around twenty trillion dollars as of this writing, for instance, would pose no problem if the troglodytes who weigh our society down would not view a debt as something in need of being paid off. Money itself isn't a necessity. It is a convention that lubricates our trade of goods and services until such time as we finally understand, collectively, the meaning of trade itself. When we trade, we "gift" (a new verb that blends five grams of mysticism and one of LSD with "give"). In the Next Generation of Captain Picard, we will have ascended to a more cosmic level of consciousness. Our paper currency will turn worthless, yes: glory be to Roddenberry! Then we shall realize that we need only have been giving (or gifting) each other what we individually needed, all along.

I have just offered a thumbnail version of Marina Gorbis's 2013 mass-marketed opus for Free Press, *The Nature of the Future: Dispatches from the Socialstructed World*. Gorbis holds a Master's degree from U Cal Berkeley (where else?) and is currently executive director of a Silicon Valley non-profit, the Institute for the Future. Berkeley, of course, is just a Planetary Disembarcation Module's ride from Hollywood. Roddenberry's retreaded galactic band-bus eventually went on tour after he himself grew too decrepit to meddle under its hood (though the writers, one and all, expressed admiration for his worldview). If the real thing ever launches, I enthusiastically nominate Ms. Gorbis to be its Chief Officer of Morale and Propaganda. Is there a chance, I wonder, that the entire population of California might be beamed up to staff the fleet?

It's not that Gorbis's interpretation of our future is dead wrong. On the contrary, what I find most perplexing about her little book (and about progressivist thinking generally) is its blindness to highly significant distinctions in sorting through genuine evidence. My original bone of contention with her thesis concerns centralization in the high-tech world: a topic on which I had two classes of freshmen writing last fall. Indeed, thanks to my recent immersion in the subject, I wanted very much to read Gorbis's work upon seeing a brief description of it. I soon grasped that her and my perceptions of the centralizing (or centripetal) phenomenon in contemporary life are diametrically opposed. Gorbis views the Internet as the great liberator from centripety. No longer is there any point of triage through which everyone must pass in order to participate (as, say, in the early days of the telephone). Now you may contact your desired party directly. Your initial solicitation and subsequent flow of data move through a loose, flexible web rather than traveling to the congested hub of a wheel and then back out along a different spoke. You can put together groups of tailored interests whose members physically inhabit every landed area of the globe. You are free to create or shape these groups with very personal touches, as opposed to yesteryear's compulsion of taking whatever Town Hall or the local church or marketplace had to offer.

This, to me, turns everything on its ear. I am not particularly concerned with the network's technical dynamic—with whether it has one nexus or a thousand nodes. In either case, and in all possible cases (as regards the Internet), the experience remains one of an infinitesimal participant's having utter dependency upon several factors and forces wholly beyond his control—and, usually, his understanding. If the power source switches off locally or nationally, no Net. If software is "upgraded" into something whose download is a bit cryptic... no more group. If hardware "advances" to a form whose cost is at first beyond one's means... goodbye, distant friends. If the government (a government—somebody's government) should decide to impede certain kinds of traffic... hello, isolation. For that matter, if a ruthless hacker should decide to "capture" one's devices on a lark... back to smoke signals. Nothing in all of this has any of the autonomy implicit in taking a walk and greeting a new neighbor.

Gorbis makes our brave new world sound like a utopia of enriching social contacts. Leaving aside the absence of direct human contact in e-communication, I would stress from the outset the gross dependency of it upon a multitude of complex circumstances. If our transmitted photons are not streaking to one receptor before being redirected, they are nevertheless the minions of faceless entities (perhaps not even fully human) that determine how the message moves, and if it moves. We have not grown decentralized just because we can no longer put our finger on a geographical center. Centralization, as I understand the word, is the experience of having *en masse* to submit to a fixed protocol and conform to certain behaviors in order to appear on the human grid. I would have thought that someone whose mother had lived most of her life under Soviet despotism would comprehend as much. Does Gorbis, then, believe that her mother—a physician—inhabited a decentralized environment just because her patients would sneak food and shoes to her *sub rosa* when the shelves of shops were empty? It was centralization that forced such exchanges to go underground; and it is centralization that leaves me, at this moment, not even knowing if the words I type are being monitored by some new NSA monstrosity in Utah.

(In fact, all of our exchanges—including cell phone conversations—can be recorded now. Our major defense is precisely that so many *are* being recorded. As Dana Priest and William Arkin report in *Top Secret America*, the collection of private exchanges has become so sweeping that those assigned to review the data are hopelessly inundated.)

That Gorbis's "success stories" consist almost entirely of unencumbered people (as in "no mouths to feed") who volunteer their expertise online is not an economic drawback utterly invisible to her. Of that, more later. Yet even before I come to her handling of the little snafoo involved in paying one's bills, I'm bound to cry foul at her styling of the Internet as a collection of deeply enriching personal experiences. I will hasten to say that my own work through The Center for Literate Values has introduced me to persons whom I consider true friends, perhaps the truest I shall ever know; but I say that also with a certain sadness, since I understand that I have little chance of ever meeting any of them face to face. Why are the academic colleagues whose bows I cross (often at some risk) every working day so unfriendly, by comparison: why have I needed to surf the Net in order to find people more open to honest exchanges and less prickly about any hint of tarnish to their reputation? The Age of the Internet must be held at least partially responsible for creating people who are so disappointing in the flesh. The very proliferation of alternative "virtual" societies" has suborned us (some of us—

far too many of us) to neglect the society before our eyes. There is something of the phenomenon here of the "perfect partner" found through a dating site who turns out to be a predatory sociopath. Not that I suspect any of my *Praesidium* friends of being such frauds (I have encountered so many types of personality so intimately through my writing over the years that I'm an expert profiler: I have indeed evaded further contact with a couple of would-be contributors after noticing how often their emails were "on the prod").... Yet it remains a distressing fact that these neighbors are not and cannot be my literal neighbors. The arrangement is not ideal, and clearly not an improvement over yesteryear's calm, mannerly village.

To see Gorbis warble on and on about our "technology-enabled sociality", under the circumstances, leaves me rather dazed. Cheerfully acknowledging that digitalization and robotics are rapidly squeezing warm bodies out of the conventional workplace, she seems determined to transform lemons into lemonade, if not water into wine. Sure, people are losing their jobs, as jobs were once understood. "But the new work is all about the social and personal," she announces breathlessly. "It draws on the power of personal connections and the diversity of personal tastes, talents, and quirks" (28). The Internet and related technology, in other words, only *appear* to have exiled us to the unemployment line. What they have really done is to liberate us from regimented, mind-numbing drudgery so that we may reach out to our fellow beings with generous offers emanating from our unique qualities. Like so many technophiles, Gorbis uses the economic gun at our heads as a reason to alter our perspective and leap with joy. "This shift is likely irreversible, which is why we are increasingly going to be called on to capitalize on our unique human skills to engage in new types of production that socialstructing is facilitating" (37).

Happy, happy day! Now we can not only go AWOL from our jobs (because we no longer have any) but enjoy a perpetual vacation doing just what we always wanted to do, like children in a dream! Researchers can invite field workers or test subjects to participate in projects that trace the spotted owl's movements or explore the effects of a cinnamon-rich diet. Writers can ask readers whether the butler should prove to have done it in an unfinished manuscript. Cooks can enlist chocoholics to try out a new recipe. School's out—it's summertime!

If I present Gorbis's sunny economic forecast with an acerbity that renders it extraordinarily insipid, I may nevertheless plead on my behalf that I have stayed well within her parameters. And let's face a few facts. We live in a time when joggers can raise hundreds (or thousands) of dollars by recruiting "sponsors", and when video-gamers can make tens of thousands (or more) by gunning down virtual helicopters or picking the weekly line-ups for sports teams. Perhaps the joke is on me. Self-promotion on outrageous YouTube videos has carried the possibility of lucrative reward for years now.

Such, however, is not the kind of economic viability that Gorbis foresees as sustaining an entire society of quondam machinists and secretaries permanently dismissed from their employment. Before I come the details of to her stunning alternative, I must emphasize one last time how immensely unconvincing I find all these collaborations as the face of resurgent of social skill. Endless strings (or threads) of chatter and counter-chatter are not necessarily a triumph of cooperative labor. One can find on the stalls in men's restrooms (cover your eyes, girls) tasteless serial commentary that successive occupants have filled out, sometimes with illustrations or diagrams. Is that, then, an enhancement of "sociality"? Back in the days when the office or the factory still hired bipedal primates, didn't women exchange recipes during breaks, and didn't men make friendly bets about the next weekend's playoff game? Why is our species being ushered into a higher phase of its evolution just because people with time on their hands are commenting on each other's Facebook posts? Is this really a warm, profound kind of interaction such as the human world has never before witnessed?

One gathers, though, that the Great Step Forward awaiting us may, in some sense, be a return to our primal state. This sort of conceptual vacillation, verging on unconscious contradiction, appears so often in what we might call "romantic" thinking that it well deserves to be classed as a distinguishing characteristic of progressivism (which is a mainstream variety of romanticism). Progress is primitivism: to move forward is to find the way back to an all-natural simplicity. Gorbis cites Bronislaw Malinowski's work on the Trobriand Islanders of Melanesia (42-43) in explaining how the electronically "linked in" life will allow us to dispense with money. The Trobrianders apparently observed a ritual passage of seashells among themselves—called Kulu—that initiated exchanges of vital supplies along the way. For good measure, our futurist guide then tosses in the annual Burning Man gatherings in the Black Rock Desert of northern Nevada (44), whose attendees take a break from farming medical marijuana and tracing tattoos to barter old guitars, bowls of chili, Tai Chi instruction, spare tires for VW Beetles, beadworked moccasins, tallow candles, origami butterflies, and haircuts (well... probably not) for a few hours or days, until they wake up. No coin or bill of tender ever besmirches a finger. This, of course, is a mirror-image of what the Trobrianders did with their seashells... kind of.

Again, I am dumbfounded. One might protest that the Melanesian island clan was essentially using seashells as currency. (Certainly our currency at this moment is nothing but stamped paper; no serious adult can believe that gold and silver underpin it any longer.) Yet even if a preliterate tribe of fisherfolk is merely giving (or gifting) in an open generosity elicited by the seashell ritual, embracing this sequence of events as an analogy for how a high-tech society of three hundred and fifty million might operate is alarmingly naïve. A fish may be caught by anyone, though some fishermen are surely more adept than others; and in a climate where leafy huts sufficient to ward off rain pretty much fulfill the list of habitation requirements, just about anyone may also become a master-builder. How, though, do I convince New Balance to send me a pair of shoes for a pair of poems? Or if we keep our discussion on that richly personal level of "enhanced sociality" (where it's practically impossible to locate Hans the handy shoemaker), how will I convince a programmer to make The Center's website more spiffy? By overhauling his résumé for him? That might work… but what if I don't like what he does to our site? Should I demand a re-do? How? Do I deliberately mess up his résumé, so that he becomes unemployable (always assuming that he can still be employed somewhere), and then agree to straighten it out if he does the same for my site?

I will offer a real-life example of "charity" exchanges from my own recent experience (so recent that I am pained to write of it). I volunteered my publicizing assistance to an Iranian Christian living in Germany whose conversion from Islam, she claimed, had placed her and her congregants (for she is a minister) at grave risk from the new influx of Middle Eastern refugees. Since I supposed lives to be in danger, I proceeded with all dispatch to circulate her letters on every blogging site to which I have access, keeping her apprised of my efforts at every step. This cost me no little bit of time, but I was eager to help. For my troubles, I received a curt email advising me to desist and accusing me of betraying the trust implicit in confidential correspondence. Since neither of the minister's letters (and I had received only two) contained anything substantially different from what she had trumpeted over a loudspeaker in Nuremberg and posted on YouTube, I was stunned… and I remain so. I had offered "free gifts" and was prepared to sustain the shower indefinitely. My end of the swap was a slap in the face.

Ms. Gorbis, can you tell me what happens when someone throws the plate of food in your face that you exchanged for a book—or that you gave *gratis*? Or do you suppose that such things happen only once in a blue moon (as opposed, say, to almost half the time)? May I come to live on your planet? Or, that failing, would you please consider not making mine more miserable than it already is?

Of course, canny readers will recognize in such pabulum the daily fare served up by an academic establishment that loathes capitalism and loves to reduce complex economic issues to "either/or" propositions. Though the "c" (as in "Red") word is never invoked in Gorbis's book, utterances are abundant that equate competition and acquisitiveness with a learned perversion highly destructive to human happiness. And I, for one, will not vigorously disagree with that thesis: we are fallen creatures, and the *libido dominandi* corrupts even our most altruistic efforts. Capitalism has certainly run amuck in our time. The most successful capitalists have steadily yielded to visions of dazzling power; yet in doing so, they have increasingly commandeered the tentacles of progressive government. They have stifled the ability of smaller entities to compete with them and limited the ability of ordinary people to acquire, all so that they might rule the roost uncontested. The degree to which starry-eyed products of the Left's educational assembly-line like Gorbis play into the hand of corporatist monopolies while decrying the inhumanity of competition is enough to make one long to live on the Moon. Who, one wonders, does she think provides the "technology for enabling socialstructing"? Does she suppose that Internet search engines are a year-round atmospheric condition, like the magnetosphere?

Granted, then, that capitalism can grow into a monster that strangles free enterprise, and perhaps even does so inevitably without certain checks that we as yet poorly understand: the pitfalls of "charity" are scarcely less numerous or less deep. If I might tip my hand a little, I intend to conclude this discussion by observing that so many West Coast professionals and intellectuals are so passionately committed to destroying our few surviving cultural traditions because they have amassed thick layers of material comfort yet have no family, no "other", for whom they might sacrifice. They therefore require a cause—and the more improbable and hare-brained, the better (since a bottomless pit will receive sacrifices *in perpetuum*). Gorbis preaches the "money can't buy happiness" sermon at some length. She even draws a very disturbing (to me—not, alas, to her) citation from Jonathan Haidt's *Happiness Hypothesis*:

> We are, in a way, like bees: our lives only make full sense as members of a larger hive, or as cells in a larger body. Yet in our modern way of living we've busted out of the hive and flown out on our own, each one of us free to live as we please. More of us need to be part of a hive in some way, ideally a hive that has a clearly noble purpose. (62)

What a staggering passage to have drawn the admiration of someone who claims to celebrate the decentralizing effects of modern technology! The "insectification" of humanity, even as a metaphor, is no less revealing, in my opinion, than Machiavelli's comparing the mastery of flighty fortune to the rape of a coquettish woman. Yet perhaps the "clearly noble purpose" at the end is most troublesome of all. What, pray, is the definition of nobility? And what makes nobility clear? Clear to whom? Is this not just another version of Chairman Roddenberry's maxim that WE never quarrel because only THEY misunderstand the good?

To state the obvious: the manufactured "charitable" ends of social-revolutionary progressivism partake of just such self-serving circularity. Imagine an elite of pampered, privileged darlings of the system, vaguely guilt-ridden about their comfort yet also thoroughly invested in their personal pleasure, who eventually feel a calling to dedicate themselves. That calling is natural enough: most sane, responsible adults have known it. A cause or "noble purpose" must be found, therefore... and it is. The "team" experience—as in the annual Burning Man Socialist Cookout—proves quite satisfying, as a communal effort; and, since the participants are wholly absorbed in the orgiastic "team" thrill, they fail to notice that their act is really one of rank self-indulgence. Competition and acquisitiveness, after all, have their redemptive side, too: the competitive person pushes his potential to the limit, and the acquisitive person generates energy and becomes a resource for the more dependent types around him. These and other characteristics turn squalid only when they fester in personal egotism. Charity decays through the same process. The *sacrificant*, the self-styled Christ-figure, the romantic idealist, the eternal "gifter", can be just as egotistical in his bid to lead the team in giving.

What we need in our worrisomely mutating economy is a means of catching our own fish, building our own hut, and then guarding the fruits of our labor both from freeloading marauders and from "gift-crazy" mandarins. I speak of "we" as those who have families dependent upon them, who do not rest regally upon a government sinecure or an inherited fortune, who are susceptible to being replaced by software, and who have too much pride to live off public subsidies (and too much sense to believe that such subsidies can be funded indefinitely). To such as we are, quoting the "eminent economist" Duran Bell offers little reassurance; yet Gorbis volunteers, "To increase the benefits of trade, the decision makers in the gift economy attempt to make improvements in the technology of social relations, given the technology of production" (45). In my dull, plainspoken way, I interpret this as meaning that we need to keep convincing each other—or, I should say, get better at convincing each other—to browse in the marketplace of "stuff". We need, apparently, to retain our acquisitive breeding, and even to whet our appetite for acquisitions, especially of the frivolous sort; for only then will we be content to trade a seashell necklace for a pound of garden-grown potatoes. Socrates' exclamation upon wandering through the well-stocked agora—"How many things there are of which I have no need!"—will not do at all in this impending utopia.

The idea, rather, is to get out there and get chattering. Be social (i.e., be active on social media). "I'm Suzanne. Eat my *torts de chocolate*." "I'm Ricardo. Let me design your website." But if my children are starving, they don't need cake; and if I must find work right now, it isn't because I need a website to advertise my dry-walling skills. There is an urgency to real-life financial crises that Gorbis, Bell, and the Burning Man Gang just don't seem to understand. I will confess that no single passage in *The Nature of the Future* annoyed me more than the vignette about one Robin Sloan, "a strategist at Current TV [who] left his job and decided to pursue something he's been passionate about for a long time: writing" (57). Mr. Sloan ended up raising fourteen grand online for his new novel by playing at huckster the way boys once played cops and robbers, cutely promising various upgrades of the book for higher contributions. As someone who has labored unsuccessfully to market books on the Internet for two decades, I found Gorbis's "see, it's that easy" assessment of Sloan's experience altogether stupefying. I will not question that the young man made out handsomely in hawking his tome, nor even that "peer-to-peer websites like Prosper, Lending Club, and Kickstarter" have raised millions of dollars and are showing a healthy profit-margin (57-59). I do very much question, however, whether all this activity is strictly apolitical: I strongly suspect from Gorbis's evidence, rather, that many "donors" are major promotional engines for political propaganda. Even our more stodgy lending institutions are being pressured into becoming money-launderers for social-revolutionary causes. A conventional bank today, for instance, dare not ignore the applicant's race when reviewing a request for a housing loan. On the other hand, if Mahin Mousapour wished to publish a little book about the persecution of resettled Iranian Christians by Syrian "refugees" in Germany, would the people who ponied up for our burned-out communications "strategist" do the same for her?

In short, if these New Age, cash-exempt marketers are addressing others of their class with their heightened "sociality", they may be quite successful. We may see Burning Man in Malibu. And that, frankly, may be precisely the objective. The rest of us, the ones who don't fit the Roddenberry vision of perfect harmony, will simply be written out of the script. We will go somewhere and do whatever people like us do when they disappear... and the world will be a better place. As one progressive has put it, to make an omelet, you need to break some eggs.

Finally, I must say a few words about alternative currencies. When Gorbis discusses these (46-53), the plastic chips in betting games, the Bit Coin, and the Greek Volo are indistinguishable. All simply show us that "creating alternative currencies is only one way we are beginning to bring the social bank into our economic relationships" (53). Well... yes and no. As with most of her assertions, this one contains a grain or two of truth—although, as I have already suggested, one can hardly argue that the paper dollar of 2016 stands upon anything but blind trust. And therein lies the unhelpful line-scuffing of treating alternative currencies as tokens in some sort of board game. An elite, well-educated, tech-savvy group of Gen-Xers can afford to go wrong with the Bit Coin: for them, the whole venture is a cool experiment in how to move commodities and exchange services in the twenty-first century. I can assure Ms. Gorbis that the Greeks are not so toying with the Volo. Their currency has collapsed, and some of them are trying to put bread on the table. We Americans may soon be following suit. When and if I offer to educate my neighbors' children in return for cow's milk or fresh eggs, I will not view myself as journeying into the future so much as sinking into the past. Makeshift currencies probably await us tomorrow, I agree—but not as a lubricant for some Internet-based socialism. They will rather designate the last step before we redescend into a medieval bartering system. Our seashells will circulate among those whom we trust (i.e., not among economists who believe that two minus two equals four), the better to remember that Jim has taught Joe's child for one month and Jill's three daughters for two. They will resemble beads on an abacus.

And is a higher quality of socializing involved herein? Certainly: if I don't know Jasmine at all, I will not risk agreeing to teach her children for a year—not on airy promises, and not when I need exchanges to keep my own children alive. Such trust, however, will have to be built through face-to-face contact. The Internet will not only prove insufficient to the task: as a favorite refuge of rogues adept at projecting false personalities, it will throw up one prohibitive red flag after another during the screening process. To be sure, if we are trying to imagine the Weimar scenario where sand dollars become silver dollars as realistically as possible, we should assume that neither Jim nor Joe nor Jill nor Jasmine will even enjoy Internet access. Things, by this point, will be pretty basic.

This essentially ends my discussion of *The Nature of the Future*, though I have scarcely covered a third of the book. (Had I any interest in mockery, I would have devoted a few paragraphs to the long chapter, "Governance Beyond Government"—whose title, perhaps, says about all you need to know regarding the author's brand of decentralization and independence.) I have not intended to write a book review, but rather to fathom some of the almost unfathomable absurdities of progressive economic thinking. I do not perceive Marina Gorbis as a sophistical ideologue and devious propagandist out to snare as many naifs as her net will hold, despite the terms that I have used occasionally. She seems sincere in her claims—which only alarms me all the more, because she is plainly perceptive and intelligent. I will go farther: I believe she evinces genuine concern about humanity. Her later comments about her son's frustrating experience of our education system after enjoying a non-traditional school for his eight initial grades remind me of my own son's bittersweet schooling adventures. I hate our system. I hate the regimented curriculum, the game of chasing after the A, the standardization of testing, the ice-cold "instruments of measurement", the "goals and objectives" behaviorism… but I have seen these and other ruinous tendencies grow exponentially worse in my lifetime as government bureaucracies at all levels have intruded themselves into the classroom. The systemic failures belong to the new and evolving system, not the "little red schoolhouse"; and that new system is defined by nothing so much as by gadgetry and "information" lifted from vital context. Computers and the Internet are not liberating us from this cage; they are padlocking its door. I have heard *ad nauseam* the refrain about students now being able to look up the capitol of Uzbekistan in an instant. And so what, exactly, have they learned thereby? How to use a smartphone? If Gorbis's more science-based model of the educational process can gather input from brilliant minds all over the world in mere hours, how is this superior to a child's being challenged to build a miniature windmill that withstands a box fan at full blast and doesn't collapse when wet? How do "data" and "solutions" substitute for forming useful questions and making— with one's own hands—instructive mistakes?

At best, I think what Gorbis is inadvertently describing is the home-school movement. Here is the ultimate hands-on, barter-friendly, face-to-face, flexibly scheduled, debureaucratized answer. Naturally, she wouldn't dare mention it in her book. She is bound to have sensed that the people who trade cupcakes for downloaded songs are also passionate enemies of charter schools and the Religious Right.

I've written many an essay (for not so much as a cupcake) about the indispensable value of truth to our spiritual growth. Nothing so isolates us from our fellow beings as falsehood, and nothing so hampers our escape from a childish egotism into the objectivity of the responsible adult as pampered fantasy. One would think that arguing for a currency supported only by thin air (i.e., not even by the stable production of necessary items) would partake of patent falsehood to most sane minds. If we all agree to admire the emperor's new clothes and employ his tailors to make similar suits for us, then perhaps we will be better off in some sense as a nudist colony; but the fact remains that the tailors have gotten very rich by doing nothing. Or if they accept my classic novel filled only with empty pages as payment, then they and I both should probably be fitted for a straitjacket: real variety.

The people most responsible for filling our daily lives with lies, however, are not overtly mendacious. They deal in half-truths—and they cling for all they're worth (since their self-worth is the vapid currency of these exchanges) to the truthful half of their story. Most of us, I suppose, want or need to believe that the dragon of advanced technology is smiling and not leering at us. We cannot accept Bill Joy's prognosis that the human race is doomed to be rendered obsolete by its robotic creations; we prefer the mantic Ray Kurzweil's vision of human-robotic hybrids that live for millennia in perfect health and without anguish. In the same way, if we can regard the accelerating digitalization of life as paradoxically increasing our opportunities for warm human contact, we're apt to embrace the story-line. Why should we make ourselves gloomy? A mushroom cloud is a beautiful thing.

But at some point, by easing the passage of misconceptions into the popular mind and even the cultural psyche, we become the worst (if not the greatest) kind of liar in our *complaisance*. We make those around us more vulnerable to lies. That we ourselves may believe the fabrications underlying a given fantasy may somewhat redeem us... but it is the redemption of diminished capacity—of the lunatic or the fool. And if the evidence shows that we are, after all, fully sane, then... then, yes, folly unnourished by lunacy eventually becomes mendacity.

Say that I wanted to cast a rosy glow over the *Titanic*'s story. I could write that her catastrophe taught many lessons that saved countless lives in subsequent sea travel; there would be some truth to that. I could write that we don't really know of very many deaths resulting from the sinking; except for the bodies that floated to the surface, no casualties were confirmed. That would be strictly correct, but also ridiculous. I could write that the ship carried a high volume of the exploitative wealthy class, and that the demise of such people improved society and even stood as a lesson to those who would flaunt their plunder-based success in luxury. That would be an opinion clearly justified neither by the statistics of the victims' income level nor by good taste. I could write, finally, that all of the supposed casualties remained alive and well in some parallel universe, like the survivors on the television serial *Lost*. That would be a fantasy whose truth or falsehood was wholly indemonstrable—but whose evasion of the raw material facts might license a cavalier attitude toward safety issues in the future.

I have seen one "academic" study after another in recent years that modeled my approach to the *Titanic* above. To paraphrase what the Claude Raines character in David Lean's *Lawrence of Arabia* says of half-truthers, we have not merely hidden the truth: we have forgotten where we put it. And pretending that the immovable veil shrouding the future licenses us to utter nonsense about tomorrow is unworthy of a trained mind. I should like to ask Ms. Gorbis and the Burning Man Brigade what they foresee happening to the millions of unskilled immigrants pouring across our borders (often illegally). What is their likely role in the Internet revolution? To be sure, many are already bartering staple items; their families haven't stopped doing so since the Anasazi settled Chaco Canyon. But how will Ms. Gorbis's friends pay them for mopping out toilets and changing bedsheets? For they will continue to do dull manual labor for the "foreseeable future"—which means, in this case, until the sun explodes. Certain jobs will never be performed by robots, which are expensive to develop and require maintenance, as long as a helot class exists to do them. Will our helots, then, be literal slaves, paid with room and board? They certainly won't have any use for Bit Coins.

A likely scenario is that they will be bred to manageable numbers, in Huxleyan fashion. They may, indeed, end up being the last surviving full humans, as Kurzweil's hybrids pay them in booze and porn to feed cats and kill roaches.

I offer a concluding speculation, however, whose focus is very much "now" rather than "tomorrow". Reading Gorbis's book and considering many related issues has brought an anomalous condition sharply into focus for me. How, I kept asking myself, can so many elite intellectuals sign on to such blockheaded ideas? Haidt's "beehive of happiness" may have precipitated my moment of epiphany (and Haidt is himself a professor—of psychology). Western society is littered today, as at no other time in history, with unattached people. Gays who cannot have a family, feminists who do not want a family, couples who choose not to marry, married couples who choose not to have children... all of these people have nothing to live for but themselves and their own satisfaction. And most of them are or will become moderately wealthy, with respect to the statistical mean. Why wouldn't they? Their education is exceptional, their jobs are white-collar, their freedom from distraction at home has allowed them to win promotion: they are the economy's equivalent to Navy Seals when it comes to wealth production. And what, then, do they do with all this wealth? Money can't buy happiness... and they have no one in their lives, or maybe a faithful lover who as grown as familiar as old bedroom slippers. What else... who else? As they (along with any lover-appendages) embark upon the downward slope of their fourscore years, what meaning does their time on earth acquire to their highly educated eye?

A "clearly noble" cause must be supported. They must find some such mission upon which to lavish their savings, even as the dutiful footsoldier willingly lies down to die in the breach that his brethren may climb over him and capture the city. And the cause, also, must encounter stiff resistance: it must have enemies far and wide around the land. Otherwise, it might be won while twenty or so years of life yet remain to beguile away. Preferred, therefore, is the cause that never ends: progress! Anything that promises to make us other than we are now will do. "Better" rather than "other" might seem indicated, as well; yet "other" is always "better"—the important thing is always to change. Who are we, in our present state, to judge the right and wrong of evolution?

N'importe où, hors du monde, wrote Baudelaire with exquisite irony of the self-deceptive romantic: "Anywhere out of this world."

Anomalous, marginal, alternative, minority, diverse, non-traditional... whatever we choose to call this socio-economic sector of our high-tech, postmodern community (or whatever its members choose to call themselves), it is immensely influential, due both to its financial resources and to its emotional detachment from everything except "the cause". It is a Petrie dish of prosperous fanatics; and, if I may don my own "futurist" cap for a moment, it is destined only to expand, both in volume and in resources. If contemporary Western societies do not learn how to oppose this phalanx of careerist- and nerd-kamikazes effectively, it is certain to destroy everything our ancestors so painfully constructed.

That is my own dire prognosis. I personally rate its fear factor as superior to Bill Joy's robotic takeover, if only because I'm really not prophesying at all. Just look around.

Some Grim But Necessary Observations on E-Culture

This article was initially a series of personal blogposts uploaded in January, 2017.

One reason I'm very much in favor of simplifying our lifestyle, even though I perceive "climate change" as a boondoggle veiling a power grab, is the ever-lurking, apocalyptic EMP. We depend far too much on electricity. It's probably not good for our bodies. (I might detail my own physical discomforts after extended exposure to computers at some later date.) At this point, electric utilities pump our water and operate our refrigeration. In most homes, they supply heating and cooling to structures designed without a second thought's having been given to efficiency. Automobiles have depended on computerized systems since about the mid-Eighties: if everything electrical were suddenly fried… no more transportation. Even if you could walk to the grocery store, the trucks that deliver its merchandise would cease to run. And if you were retrograde enough to own a vintage car with minimal electrical dependency, it would still need to be gassed up after a few days… and the pumps at the filling station wouldn't work.

Defense experts have estimated that 90 percent of the US population would die within a year if our power grid were destroyed. In other words, the loss of that grid would equate to a surprise trans-continental nuclear attack, minus the lingering contamination—and with the addition of lethality at peak levels even in rural areas.

Books like Peter Pry's *Blackout Wars: State Initiatives to Achieve Preparedness Against an Electromagnetic Pulse (EMP) Catastrophe* consequently make for grim reading. The title of this volume actually hints at a source of optimism not visible in Pry's earlier books: preemptive action by state governments to secure their section of the power grid. This can apparently be done legally; and the federal government, while confronting the crisis with all the energy of a deer staring at headlights, has at least not intervened (in the manner of its contribution to border security) to ensure that our pants stay down and our hands remain tied. Nevertheless, only four or five states have taken effective action at this point.

The kind of pulse at issue need not be administered by a nuclear weapon exploding thirty kilometers above ground, by the way, or by the domino effect begun when certain key power stations are overloaded. The pulse may be entirely natural. Solar flares occasionally create major surges. We haven't seen a big one since the so-called Carrington Event in 1859, which turned all the telegraphs of New England into smoking ruins. We're overdue another such burst—and we have far more than the telegraph at stake now.

Besides equipping all power stations with surge-arrestors (WHY was that not done in the construction phase, as a matter of course???), our leadership should send a very clear message to Kim Jong Un, whose nuclear trials and dry-run nautical missions have left little doubt that he has an EMP attack in mind. This little lunatic must be reminded that our nuclear submarines will survive even after the continent is plunged into darkness; and he must be warned, publicly and with icy clarity, that a devastating nuclear response directed at all of his hideaways will follow, instantly and irrevocably. I know what a gruesome remark I have just written. The prospect of 300 million American casualties, however, requires a strong deterrent. Mutually Assured Destruction worked in the Cold War, but we were dealing with comparatively sane despots. Maybe, in this case, the little lunatic's entourage would pull his cord if it became apparent that he was about to pull theirs.

***

The Affordable Care Act was supposed to make medical records readily transferable from one treatment venue to another. Push a button... and the ER uploads the files from your GP's office. In practice, learning the software is a nightmare for medical personnel, amending and updating it is a hemorrhage within hospital budgets that cannot be stanched, protocol turns out frequently to require the same old paperwork reproduced now from computer files, and the origin of critical errors is often almost impossible to trace. Time and money saved? Efficiency enhanced? What world are you living in?

One is now vigorously urged to liberate one's investment accounts from paper. Quarterly reports are posted online: don't forget your password! And just in case the power grid should go down for any reason, you'd better print out a copy of crucial data, or there might be no record at all of your life savings! I've been very happy with my TD Ameritrade account... for the most part. But when the lion's share of my portfolio was shifted to a companion-operation called Amerivest, I continually had trouble finding my money online. I couldn't remember that I was supposed to log in with the Amerivest username at the Ameritrade log-in box: there was no separate box for the separate entity. Such a simple conflation of procedures apparently needed no explanation to the site's designers; but to me, whose typical day does not allow time for checking in, the "skipped step" is a perpetual stumbling block. Now that I've actually written a few words about it, I'm sure to remember the way in... but how many other such crucial protocols are easily misplaced or obscured because technicians don't think like ordinary people? The minutes or hours of panic that result may add up to months or years subtracted from one's time on earth, since our hearts are still flesh and blood.

142

Your job requires you to employ a certain software program—but the program's designers have so overloaded it with firewalls and safeguards over the years that it runs like cold molasses when it runs at all. So your organization decides to shift to a different software provider and orders you to learn completely new protocols. Yet the shift will not occur for several months; so the valuable time you spend listening to software gurus explain vital details (as well as dozens and dozens of functions of utterly no interest to you or relevance to your personal tasks) will prove wholly wasted, since you will have forgotten everything when—six months from now—you need to recall it. In the meantime, you do your job a little less well thanks to all the distraction, and the raises that might have helped you keep pace with inflation are poured, instead, into the handsome salaries needed to attract more high-tech gurus to maintain an ever more complicated network.

Where in all this chaos do we find a poster-child for efficiency and competence?

A government mandate requires that you now integrate a, b, and c into your normal professional routine. A government functionary chides you for not fully overhauling your routine in a timely fashion so as to front-and-center a, b, and c. You ask that a, b, and c be settled into a certain available free space... but no, "studies have shown" that a, b, and c are most effective when everything else is organized around them. So, essentially, your thirty years of experience doing what you do must be jettisoned, and you must follow in the footsteps of every other tyro who serves a remote, faceless bureaucracy of power-brokers blissfully unfamiliar with what you do. The "studies" show that the new program of indoctrination indoctrinates better if the surrounding program in which it's delivered does little but echo its messages. Well, duh.

Yes: *duh*—the three-letter commentary on our new "culture" which is perhaps the only example of real efficiency to be found in it.

***

What happens when messages can be conveyed easily from one party to another? Messages proliferate. What happens when messages proliferate? Everyone becomes saturated in "information" of widely varying quality. What happens when the good stuff and the bad is all stirred together in the same dumptruck-load of malodorous "communication"? The good stuff gets neglected with the bad. What happens when negligence becomes epidemic? People start feeling isolated and depressed, or even getting chippy and rude. What happens when depression and rudeness suddenly spike? People grow plangent—they want more attention, and they want everyone to apologize to them. What happens to a society of hurt, whining children and sullen, smarting victims? It fragments. You have the children who continue to whine and form groups of whiners; you have withdrawn clams who tune everything out, including the desperate sufferers who are in anguishing need; and you

143

have the whackos who decide to blow themselves and everyone around them to hell since they can't find an audience.

Welcome to our world.

In a professional context, you also see the multiplication of petty tasks to virtual infinity. Since it's now so easy to demand that minions and underlings do thus and so, demands grow more numerous. The manufacture of demands, indeed, becomes itself an arduous chore: the tinpot dictators snuggled behind their keyboards actually manage to overwork themselves. They need more supporting staff, so more funds must be allocated to more hiring. At the other end, the minions grow more stressed-out because the day's hours have not been multiplied to keep up with the rising volume of minute tasks to perform. They cut corners on the work they were intended to do in order to complete absurd surveys, questionnaires, and tutorials. The threat of harsh consequences if they do not accede to every latest demand wears upon their health, as well; for the demands are entirely impersonal and often, therefore, imperious. When you can order someone about remotely, never seeing the person's face or hearing the person's voice, you tend to order a little more often and a little more peremptorily. One thinks of the subjects of the Milgram Experiment, turning up the "pain" button on their tortured victims (who, unknown to them, were just acting), because they nestled behind the anonymity of a command chain and a one-way mirror.

Give a man a hammer, it is said, and everything looks like a nail. Give people the capacity to send messages simply and quickly… and you have a society of people who do nothing but "message", to the extent that they haven't enough time to accomplish anything worthy of report. Applied to an entire society, the model is pretty crappy, really. I could almost wish for an EMP to wipe it all away; but then, most of us would die in the process.

Then again, are we alive right now?

Cell Phones and Celery: How to Create a Polis of Mass Dependency From Two Directions

*Condensed from two posts published by the online magazine, **The Intellectual Conservative**, and later in **Praesidium** 13.3 (Summer 2013). Be reminded as you read that the technology mentioned herein, though it may seem laughably outdated now, was all the rage merely five years ago. The trends associated in the discussion have greatly accelerated, in my opinion.*

I have known for several years that communications technology has altered the way people think—and even, from a certain perspective, their ability to think. Every classroom teacher over forty knows as much. You can tell a group of students five times to do a simple task, having first ascertained that they're not texting and have logged off of Facebook... and ten percent of them will still go to their graves swearing that the instructions were never given. Another ten percent will have needed all five announcements, and another ten at least four announcements. Probably not more than a quarter of the class, or a third at most, would register the original directive after one clear broadcast.

Are these young people stupid? Their behavior replicates that of sad specimens whom, without hesitation, we would have identified as mentally challenged twenty years ago. Rush Limbaugh tactfully refers to them (along with occupants of the cerebral bell curve's rising slope) as "low-information". But why is so little information being received?

There are several theories. Varieties of information are in constant competition today because of the convenience and portability of media; hence more "boring" varieties (i.e., those less focused on the receiver's immediate selfish interests) are neglected. I think there's also clearly a state of mind associated with being wired and online: that is, with having the bud of an iPod in one's ear while texting and keeping an eye on a computer monitor. Inattention becomes a learned behavior in some sense rather than the default condition of untrained minds. It's almost necessary for survival. Human figures beyond the receiver's "noospace", as well, turn into mere playthings. Real persons must compete for a share of the present with realistic representations—and the former have no more right to common courtesy, let alone rapt attention, than the latter.

A sad irony here is that commentators like Limbaugh constantly promote the latest i-tech in the sincere conviction that they are serving free enterprise and Yankee ingenuity. They do not see that this revolution is a collective lobotomy for the electorate, even though it may also be styled a triumph for the Space Race, emergency warning systems, and so forth. The carry-over of these communications miracles into the marketplace has never unleashed the sort of individualism upon the world whose triumph George Gilder prophesied back in the Nineties. Yes, ordinary people have been given instant access to a global forum by the Internet... but who pays any attention to them unless they cipher in the sexy shorthand of instant gratification? Will the number of people who visit a "discussion" website in a decade amount to one tenth of those who "follow" Dennis Rodman or Beyoncé on Twitter in a day? The proportion of the former to the latter, we all know, more closely approaches statistical zero.

The medium is the message, wrote another prophet with far greater truth than he realized. Marshall McLuhan belonged to my father's generation. Neither one of those worthy men would have thought that television would midwife that regressive species, the Couch Potato, when the Box first arrived in ordinary households during the Fifties. It was terrific diversion— stimulating, vilifying, fertilizing. Only decades later did we figure out, as pictures got better and "for TV" writing got worse, that brain activity was flatlining in front of this miraculous "alternative reality".

Communications gizmos are but one high-tech tentacle of the many that have throttled our intellectual and cultural life. Yet I scarcely think that anything can be more important than the manner in which thoughts—words that convey thoughts and, increasingly, full-formed sequences of images—are piped into our brains. Voters follow candidates in the same way that they follow their pop-cultural heroes on Twitter; they "like" a mouthy challenger in the same way that they "like" a snarky post in a chatroom; and they salivate like Pavlov's dog at Hollywood-inculcated cues such as "industrialist", "big oil", "rogue reporter", and "female detective". These New Age electors are people who think associatively: don't give them linear logic—give them icons and keyword phrases. They are low-information because they're instant-processing.

I enjoyed the rare pleasure recently of editing an article about the classic 1968 television series, *The Prisoner*. I believe the serial's supposition is quite right that surveillance technology is merely a sub-species of communications technology. We've already reached the point where we can be watched by our laptop camera as we view the Internet, where cookies monitor our preferences and selections in shopping, and where we volunteer immense amounts of sensitive personal information on Facebook just to fit in—to conform in a counter-conformist way, to be one of the Village's progressive sheep. Changing the content of college History and Civics classes will not save our children from the twenty-first century *assommoir*. The medium is the message. If we continue to let our media rule us rather than learning how to hold them in check, then we will not recognize our grandchildren. We will have about the same level of exchange with them as Jefferson might have had with Washo the Chimp.

The foregoing pedigree offered for our current political and cultural crisis will probably not strike readers of this journal as original. We have sounded the same alarm many times over the years. I stress, however, that electronic media represents only one branching network of a complex family tree, though perhaps no limb points more directly into the trunk. I should like to identify just one more influence by way of giving complexity its due. The causal connections here, I am confident, will not have occurred to very many and are well worth contemplating.

Agriculture, and its decline in the ordinary citizen's life: this is not a minor contributant to our miseries. I hasten to stress that my observation is not made from the pessimistic Doomsday perspective of a fidgety survivalist—though, of course, consumers are indeed buying dehydrated beef stew in record volume for storage in their cellars and bunkers. In a time of utter turmoil, naturally, you'll need to feed your family. "Preppers" who have only stocked Del Monte green beans and corn will eventually empty the last can, even though they may be able to shoot a figure-eight into the torso of any competitor for that can. Over the long haul, food is a resource that will clearly have to be replenished the old-fashioned way: i.e., by farming.

None of which concerns me here in the least: I propose, rather, that agriculture is very beneficial to the psyche—so much so that our republic only began to deteriorate when the link between man and soil was ruptured. The notion that frail individuals need Big Brother in order to survive would never have crossed a true farmer's mind—and, if it had, would surely have turned his strong stomach. (I speak not of agri-business, by the way—not here or anywhere else; most of what passes for occupational farming today is just another species of assembly line *cum* statist boondoggle.) The Industrial Revolution, unfortunately, proceeded in a way that tore farmers from their land and held them hostage to meager wages in unwholesome cities. Things got pretty ugly. The industrialized North enslaved immigrants from Ireland and Eastern Europe in ways practically as binding as those employed by Southern planters upon imported Africans (a population, this last, made available for slavery by northern shipping concerns). Indeed, our Civil War was essentially the result of ever more centralized and monopolistic industrial interests drawing an ever more dependent—but also more resistant—agrarian culture into their Charybdis of ambition. (It certainly was NOT primarily about freeing all Africans on humanitarian grounds, a population whose members Mr. Lincoln himself believed inferior beings unworthy of the vote, of being jurors, or of receiving public education.)

We should have stayed on the farm, perhaps; or, since they say progress is irresistible, then we ought now devise a way to technologize the small family farm, even (or especially) in suburban circumstances. Farming, to repeat, is good for the soul as well as the body. Farmers understand cycle. They therefore grasp viscerally that existential freedom has limits—that terrestrial freedom is really nothing other than the precious gift of choosing how to adapt oneself to the inevitable. All that lives in this world must someday die to this world. A farmer who should fail to understand as much would soon perish. Farmers survive within the rhythms of life and death. They need to know when to plant, when to harvest, and how to read the sky's dozens of moods. Freedom without cost or boundary makes no sense to them. A free man is free to work, free to look after himself and his own—not free to sleep late and then have a government-issue card punched for his breakfast pizza.

A close friend of mine (who always votes for the utopian candidate) is indignant that I allow my son to shoot squirrels with an air rifle. But squirrels aren't as cuddly as they appear. They are metabolically racing omnivores. They destroy fruit trees, they devour eggs and small songbirds, and they sometimes get into attics and chew up roofing and wiring. Their natural enemies—foxes, coyotes, tree snakes, etc.—have been driven far from man's habitat, and so they have wildly overpopulated in back yards and public parks. Holding them in check isn't wicked, but it may seem so to people who think that everything can and should live virtually forever unmolested beside everything else. Those who seem to think this way and are past the age of six are usually college-educated city-dwellers. They don't accept the hard facts of life.

The farm also teaches you (as I've hinted already) what might be called the work cycle. You turn the earth, pull the weeds, plant your sprouting spuds, collect rainwater, give the garden a daily splash, pull more weeds, and finally dig your potatoes. Now you have something to eat. If you don't work, you starve; but if you work exceptionally hard, you may build up a surplus—which you can then barter or sell if (like potatoes) it doesn't store especially well. A person who refuses to work has no "right" to your produce. Common decency demands that you help a poor bloke who's down on his luck, yet not at your children's expense, and not if said ne'er-do-well keeps coming back for more.

We understood this when our sweat and toil translated directly into food on the table. When, however, we increasingly started to draw a wage for selling shoes or cars or stocks, our intellectuals and our clergy could no longer keep the former relationships in focus. Some people had so very much more than they needed, yet only broke a sweat when working out at the gym. Where did all that affluence come from? Why wasn't it shared more evenly?

It wouldn't be such a very bad thing, it seems to me, if our "economic recovery" and our nanny state's time-out disciplining (also known as "austerity") turned every ordinary citizen back into a gardener or farmer. Nature doesn't lurch along with crisis-ridden news alerts, the popular romances of Climate Change and Bush-Engendered Tornadoes notwithstanding. Instead, she plays one cycle into another with patience, rhythm, and relative quiet. The spiral of existence has not been, and cannot be, "straightened out" into a linear progression on a graph just because we are mapping genomes and sending remote-control trolleys around the Martian surface.

True, a Chernobyl may disrupt the smooth regenerative powers of nature for centuries. The irony about that particular case is that the most progressive regime on the planet at the time engineered the reactor's meltdown. Perhaps we may hope that the young zealots of the Green movement may one day recognize natural cycle and totalitarian progressivism to be enemies to the death. The very essence of the progressive program is to manhandle natural order so that we may call our own existential tune instead of dancing to the seasons we have inherited for time immemorial.

There is an axis hiding here that cuts right through party divisions. Big-government Republicans who never saw a seascape that wouldn't look better with motels and casinos are of course no better than big-government Democrats who want to siphon millions of tax dollars into wind farms rather than design a less energy-hungry city. Whether we at last choose to live again within the terrestrial cycle of being or are forced to do so by the mismanagement of greedy autocrats, we will likely recover this most humane and enlightening generator of culture in some measure.

"Corrupted Mind/World Interface": The Black Plague of Our Time

*First published online by **The Intellectual Conservative** (Nov. 2, 2019).*

When Diana West finally mentions Herbert Hoover's *Freedom Betrayed* in her recent expose of FDR's Soviet-infused administration, *American Betrayal* (St. Martin's: 2013), she seems much less impressed by the book than I was. "Hoover doesn't explain the shift in thinking" (she writes) that left the Western world—from the Washington press corps to Winston Churchill—scrambling to obfuscate Soviet atrocities like the Katyn Forest massacre of 22,000 Polish officers (194). Hitler was the only evil on earth: Stalin's satanic regime was forever being rehabilitated for public—and personal—consumption. The number of Ukrainians systematically starved under Stalin (and a lieutenant named Khrushchev) during the Twenties would roughly equal the tally of Jews later gassed by the Reich, and ample news of ongoing slaughter throughout Russia had leaked out in the decade before the Second World War. Nevertheless, Soviet communism was being patiently window-dressed long before Stalin's assistance against Hitler was deemed necessary.

It is in this part of her deeply unsettling tome (about two-thirds through) that West raises the subject of "convergence" in detail: i.e., the theory that Western democracy and Eastern collectivism would harmoniously merge if our side bent to meet their side. In an arrogant naïveté of stupefying magnitude, Roosevelt seems to have answered William Bullitt's warnings about the USSR as follows: "Bill, I don't dispute your facts, they are accurate. I don't dispute the logic of your reasoning. I just have a hunch that Stalin is not that kind of a man" (199). Bullitt summarizes FDR's attitude as "the vice of wishful thinking" (*ibid.*), a phrase embraced by West. And it's a good phrase, but...

But I nonetheless have the feeling that Diana West herself comes short of providing a full motive for what James Burnham, many decades ago, called the "suicide of the West". Infiltration of academe by communist operatives, check; penetration of the news media and the state department by Soviet moles, check; infection of the intelligentsia by the utopian theory of convergence, check; but... but what else? Nothing deeper? Manipulation by malevolent external forces, seduction by a beautiful design that looks good on paper... but why is the design seductive? Were those who so admired it smoking something that had been smuggled to them, once again, by malevolent panders from Hammer-and-Sickle territory? How much of our folly can we blame on master-spies?

It's still going on, after all. It's happening every day. I don't think the "vice of wishful thinking" was distilled into my erstwhile minister's misty brain by a covert operative when she was blaring that the desire for borders is mere "xenophobia". (Yes, I've changed churches.) There has to be some other reason why so many of us are so susceptible these days to childish delusions of such dangerous proportions. Doesn't there?

My own theory is that something potentially fatal happens when a culture begins to lose touch with basic physical reality (emphasis on *physical*). Marxism views the Industrial Revolution as a watershed stage... and maybe the Marxists, like a broken clock, are right sometimes by accident. I, too, think the abrupt deracination of long-settled peoples from the land and their all-but-forcible (fully forcible, in Red China) transplantation to urban centers lies somewhere near the cause's root. The sun no longer shines upon you throughout the day. You never again drink rainwater delivered by a clean brook. You don't know the calls of various birds, or which call signals danger and which a change in the weather. You can't identify a single constellation at night—hell, you can't *see* a single constellation from most of these smoking urban crypts! The exiled millions no longer possess the kind of wisdom embodied in their parents' proverbs. They don't understand that "work is a great teacher" or that "a man's praises are in the product of his labor" (to cite a couple of Irish samples), as simple and earthy as such knowledge is. Instead, they learn that they must conserve their energy when performing servile chores for a paltry wage, and that only strength in massed numbers can resist the power of wealth and privilege.

The Industrial Revolution made human beings less human. It shifted our species from the apex of Nature's pyramid and fixed it firmly within a termite mound, where a few queens were served by thousands of nameless minions. It crushed individuality while promoting conformity; it suppressed the free enterprise of the village's clever artisans while spawning a ruthless kind of capitalism that largely predetermined the big winners.

That's right, I said it (and, for some reason, it remains a highly provocative thing to say in conservative circles): capitalism, far from being a synonym for free enterprise, turns out to be its mortal enemy in the evolved, high-tech economy. Most of us haven't come to grips with this; as a society, we certainly have not. We exhort our children to hurl themselves into mind-numbing, soul-killing careers after college ("Just be glad you found a job!") and expect their generation to discern generous latitude for freedom and creativity in this arrangement. We ignore, most likely, the wreck in which our own careers left our higher ambitions. We seem to think that writing code to keep Amazon from being hacked is something like cutting and stitching good leather saddles or laying chimneys that will last a century.

And it's not just a change in the spiritual quality of labor (the "despiritualization" of labor) that has fueled our corrupt taste for escapist fantasies—our "vice of wishful thinking"; the very feel of stone in the hand is alien to us, and the very scent of a horse in harness. We'll laugh and exclaim, "Well, I'm glad I don't have to smell that horse's calling card out in the streets!" No, we don't have to smell much of anything that's unwelcome. If the woman in the cubicle next to ours wears too strident a perfume, we're apt to complain to the boss. As for those flies that followed horses as mold follows deadwood... Pascal once mocked the philosopher whose airy speculations are ruinously disrupted by a little buzz at his head. Do we even comprehend his reference any more? Our air-conditioned spaces have banished noxious insects. We ourselves have grown as artificial as the indoor climate we have created.

Of course, here I write about the twenty-first century's white-collar bureaucrat, not about a Joe in overalls carrying a lunch pail. But we have ever fewer of those Joes: their grandsons... they are *us*. The Industrial Revolution has produced so many machines to perform so many purely manual tasks that those who still have jobs tend to be punching keys rather than rivets. Our grandads were merely denied a view of the stars: we (and especially our children, if you're my age) don't understand the intricacies of the rotary "land line" phone. The stars? They're those destinations where faintly green humans with pointed ears speak elegant English to Captain Kirk's boarding party--or, I should say, to the next-next-next generation of Kirklings.

We've become practical idiots. Why learn to change a tire when you use Uber most of the time, anyway? What's a washer? All the turning on and off of faucets... Siri or Alexa handles that. A torn shirt, a worn-out shoe? Search Amazon under "apparel". (Or is it under "clothing"? The other word might be confused with "app".) Hungry and don't want to go out? Order pizza. Health-conscious? Google Home Chef or Magic Kitchen (or, better yet, download the app for future ease if you're industrious—and "app", I believe, is now generally spelled with one "p" for convenience).

I don't say that we are idiots. Obviously, we're technological whiz kids. But we are perfect imbeciles where the rubber meets the road (in a cliché I last heard during a Firestone commercial thirty years ago). We have no significant connection with hard labor—with sweat, bruises, dirty fingernails, gardens smoked by a heat wave, poured concrete ruined by a sudden shower... we inhabit a bubble the reinforcement of whose artifice is usually the source of whatever good jobs remain. Ortega y Gasset wrote almost a century ago that modern man (and he says *hombre masa*, our ordinary Joe) lives in greater luxury than kings did a few hundred years ago. The emperor of all that he surveyed was still using a chamber pot less than two centuries back: a kid raised in the Projects today scarcely catches a whiff of his effluent before he flushes it.

What has this to do with embracing Stalinism? Why, everything. It explains why we can embrace the "relief" of communism (no more unemployment, job interviews, performance evals, or constant competition) without sniffing its ordure (no more creativity, novelty, individuality, or free expression). We don't understand how reality works—how it *really* works, off the drawing board and down in the shop (where assembly is now robotic). Our parents once learned something of human nature early on by reading great novels and plays in high school; now a phalanx of utopian evangelists from Education programs force-feeds us on the "narratives" (i.e., the monochrome, cartoonishly stereotyped struggles) of women fighting the patriarchy or Sioux orphans caught in the White Man's world. (Already when I was a mid-adolescent, we were force-marched into reading Arthur Miller's anti-McCarthy screed disguised as a play, *The Crucible*: Diana West had the same insistent douse of teenage mind-control [173] that might have yielded space for studying Marlowe's or Goethe's version of Dr. Faustus.)

Once again, however, when I say "we", I'm thinking especially of our children. We learned little enough about the great wide world, and now they have learned less than nothing (enough, for instance, to think that every tornado signifies climate change). There are pathological consequences to such exile from hard reality—and I truly commiserate. Our so-called "millennials" didn't ask to be dealt this hand of deuces.

Yet before I turn exclusively to the children, I should stress that we and our fathers, as well—and, indeed, our grandfathers—were already suffering from the progressive disorder of "corrupted mind/world interface". (Of course, the pun in "progressive" is intended.) Is it entirely accidental that Woodrow Wilson was an Ivory Tower eremite? It may indeed be accidental that he ended his kingly administration almost as a vegetable, with his wife running the bluff of competency for him; but then, just a couple of stops down the road, we have the wheelchair-ridden FDR, prince of all practical idiots. His anemic puppeteer, Harry Hopkins, was so debilitated by mysterious and chronic ill health that he arranged the rise of the Soviet Union mostly from his bed in the White House. I'll leave the state of Barack Obama's mind/body interface to your imagination. He apparently could lift a golf club and a basketball; but his "hands off our token half-African treasure" upbringing was certainly no initiation in the school of hard knocks, and his very fuzzy orientation to family and sexuality... no, I won't go there.

Remember, in any case, that the real target of this speculative study is the electorate that advanced such people. It's us, and our children. It's my (until recently) minister, older than I; and it's the offense-detecting dynamos who dissolved into ungovernable indignation five years ago when I lightly quipped to a class of college seniors with very slovenly attendance, "Still missing a third of the group—maybe the homework drove them to suicide."

No, we don't behave—collectively—like normal, functional human beings of ages past. And there has to be some other reason than that Boris and Natasha have laced our drinking water with hemp.

Let me cut to the chase. The following observations appear to me to indicate the presence of "Corrupted Mind/Body Interface" in our midst, and especially among our young people. I submit that some of us Americans have lately approached critical moral issues around the globe with a suicidal irresponsibility, and that we have done so thanks to having lost our sense of how physical reality connects with the "noosphere" (the world of mind and ideas). You could say that all societies have always possessed a few members, at least, who struggled with bridging the subject/object gap. All of us as individuals face that struggle daily, in fact... but no more dramatically than we face—and meet—the challenge to get out of bed. Sane, mature people understand that they can't fly from a ten-story window just because, minutes earlier, they were Superman in a dream. The number and extremity of cases in our ailing culture where people actually seem to be sleepwalking through some such fantasy suggests to me that a very distinctive epidemic has broken out.

Here are further symptoms, far more specific to our time and to our immediate neighbors than those I have discussed earlier. Pardon me if I employ the dubious noun "disconnect" throughout. It's perfect in this context: it describes something mechanistic that has been "miswired". We are indeed, I believe, probing at the level of essential circuitry.

Physical Disconnect

<u>Mood-Altering Drugs</u>: We have them in disturbing abundance. Yes, the New World natives were smoking nicotine of hallucinatory potency and drinking mescal that made them think they were walking upside-down... but the consumption was reserved for ritual occasions, and then mostly for shamans. Yes, we've known the God of the Vine for time immemorial; but there, too, drunkenness was usually considered a social *faux pas* when it surpassed certain limits on festive occasions. People seldom got pasted in a lonely room. Today we witness alarming spikes in the use of numerous substances whose effects drive the world far back from the individual's awareness, and such use often knows no ritual kind of boundary. Indeed, it's probably more characteristic of completely isolated settings today than social or celebratory ones. As a society, we're escapist. I am tempted even to cite the proliferation of "dragon-master", "time-traveler", "shape-shifter", and "witch" or "vampire" romances that are advertised on my Kindle every time I power it up—but I don't wish to appear facetious. As a public health crisis, drug and alcohol abuse scarcely belongs in the same category as our adult comic books. Nevertheless, the difference is one of intensity. Both habits can be addictive, both develop a tendency to retreat from the world when it offers challenges, and both eventually allow unaddressed realities to metastasize into major problems.

<u>Eating Disorders</u>: In my youth, anorexia and bulimia were constantly in the news (e.g., when Karen Carpenter essentially starved herself to death). Now we seldom hear about them: our new crisis carries us in the other direction—yet in the same direction, ultimately. We eat *too much*, and we eat foods that immerse us in endorphins, presumably because we're not very

happy most of the time. Happiness is generally (if superficially) connected to social life. Girls of forty years ago were starving themselves to be sexually attractive (though I know that their self-torment rooted much more deeply than that); girls and boys of today are stuffing themselves because they have virtually no significant connections with the outside world at all, and they seek relief from the pain of "non-existence".

Self-Neutering Sexual Habits: If a blank is inserted into the phrase, "drugs and ___", the word "sex" is probably more likely to be supplied than "alcohol". Certainly when casting back in our memory to the Seventies, those of us able to recall that shallowest of decades will dredge up the rapid decline of sexual morals at least as readily as the growing dependency on recreational drugs. I confess that at no time did I foresee the vector taken by the era's libertinage; I figured that new couplings of increasingly bizarre kinds would degenerate into complex varieties of promiscuity ending in something like Huxley's *Brave New World*. Instead... instead, the destination seems to be a kind of abstinence that would shock a monk. Wildly permissive and abusive opposite-sex arrangements apparently inspired a retreat into same-sex alternatives, which themselves are now morphing into sexual self-mutilation as confused young people seesaw between genders (or among them: we're no longer allowed even to speak of a mere two). Sex with robots is offered as an option in some parts of the world. The most credible endpoint, though, seems to me to be that we ourselves will emulate the robot in having no sexual appetite whatever; and the sexual drive, however numerous and frightful the varieties of antisocial behavior it can fuel, has nevertheless always been a motive to learn socialization skills. Now our society is well along the way toward discarding it, utterly and for good.

Ineptitude With Oral Communication: Surely few indicators of "disconnect" with the external world could be more observable than the inability simply to speak at an audible pitch and with basic eloquence. Believe me when I say that classroom teachers of a certain age all have a stock of favorite student gaffes (e.g., "for granite" instead of "for granted" and, of course, the dreaded "cereal killer"). These have grown more abundant and laughable in recent years... but the underlying truth isn't really very funny. Our children are forgetting, not just how to spell, but how to talk. (I used to attribute the decay of orthography to that of regular reading: I now think that the decline of actual speech, especially of the clearly enunciated kind, plays a role.) The lapse in skills includes even (I am convinced) merely producing an oral volume sufficient to reach beyond one's elbow. Toward the end of my own career, I occasionally wondered if my hearing were going bad, given that I had to ask students to repeat themselves so often. Yet I noticed no signs of deterioration outside the classroom. I concluded that, over a span of three decades, young adults had largely lost the register needed to make their voices audible across an occupied space of twenty-by-thirty feet. Such encounters were as alien to their regular existence as parachuting or scuba-diving.

Emotional Disconnet

Neurotic Sensitivity to Insult: As the Word becomes a stranger to us, the few words remaining in our vocabulary must take on meanings they were never intended to bear. A monosyllable as neutral as "rope" can suddenly start an associative chain of dominoes falling... and at the end of that chain is "hanging", as in "lynching", as in "racism" and "KKK". (We could get to about the same stopping point, by the way, with the word "chain".) Now, to suppose that everyone who ever says "rope" is guilty of "hate speech" in "code" is to be suspicious to the verge of paranoid insanity... and yet, hundreds of college campuses and workplaces appear to have bestowed a kind of fearful veneration upon this folly. We are not even allowed the defense of insisting that we had in mind the word "rope's" conventional meaning. The paranoids among us insist, in return, that we don't know what we intended, because we have been subliminally programmed by our racist environment. We are held captive, in short, by the nightmarish fantasies in those who hear us but refuse to listen to us. We end up playing a part scripted in their impenetrably insulated heads which we can't read, but which is nonetheless a particular crime of ours. The disruption of interface here, interestingly, doesn't just put the "offended" party completely at odds with the world: it justifies his or her extreme discomfort with the situation—it objectifies being at odds. "What do you mean, we're not communicating? I heard what you said! Now I'm removing your right to say anything more! Don't you dare say another word!"

Projection of Social Failures: I believe the more accepted word among psychologists is "transfer"—we have an increasing tendency now to thrust our social ineptitude upon others as the cause of our misery rather than to recognize its origin in ourselves. (I ended the previous item by noting that the "I know what you meant!" insistence on registering insults does precisely this.) If people of other races make us nervous, then the cause of our neurosis is the presence of racists all around us (viz., "I know you see a mugger when you look at that black kid in a hoodie!"). If we have unusual or ungovernable sexual appetites, then the cause of our extreme restlessness is the presence of predators or "gay-bashers" all around us (viz., "I know people like you judge me because I have a girlfriend and a boyfriend!"). If an inclination to open hostility poisons many of our encounters with other people, then the cause of our elevated blood pressure is the presence of gun-toting rednecks all around us (viz., "I'm sure you'd like to gun me down just for disagreeing with you!"). Women demand that men not so much as "touch" them with a lingering gaze... and also that access to instant abortion under any circumstances be legally provided (presumably because they have "spontaneous" sex with men regularly). Protesters scream that they want peace and safety... and welcome the support of masked thugs armed with bats and bottles ("They're only doing what your fathers did in the Klan!"). We seem to acquire our awareness of the horrors haunting the outside world by looking in the mirror—without, of course, having the least idea that it's not a window.

Preference for Non-Human Friends: The growth in attachment to dogs and cats in Western society is really quite remarkable. I loved my Welsh terrier when I was a boy (though I never felt much attraction to felines, perhaps because of my allergies). Pets are fine. Who doesn't like Lassie? But the prospect of young people, especially, devoting massive amounts of time and money to a pet or pets in progressive cities like Denver leaves me stunned. For the most part, these are persons of an age when they would have been married and tending to children in previous generations. Now they deeply mistrust "long-term relationships" and are so adverse to child-rearing that terminating an unwanted baby's life *after* birth often doesn't strike them as murder (or so they claim). Yet their hearts melt at the thought of the fur ball that will greet them with a tail wag or a purr whenever they walk through the door. No degree of emotional negotiation or interpretation is needed to cuddle Mr. Mittens.

Phobia of Life Stages: No child can grow up on a farm, or even in a rural setting, without becoming aware of the natural life-to-death cycle. A clock ticks for all of us. The trees lose their leaves, winter sets in, then the world once more turns green, then summer reveals that fallen flowers have yielded to swelling fruit. Small animals are found dead about the property after the first freeze. Birds unleash wild calls heard at no other time of year as cocks contend for mates. Later on, the cat may appear with feathers all over his face (another reason I dislike felines, natural though the cycle is). Our city-dwelling, video-game-and-iPhone-addicted children, however, see none of this. They are vaguely (or perhaps poignantly—even agonizingly) aware that certain events are supposed to happen at certain stages of the "life narrative". After all, acquiring a lover or having a child is all part of whatever Netflix serial or boxed set of romances ("e-boxed") they consume. But they themselves are forever mere consumers, forever mere spectators—or maybe, at most, impersonators participating in meaningful time through an electronic avatar. The years succeed each other, unseen trees shed their leaves and sprout new ones... and the disconnected mind of our new citizen, straitjacketed in progress, remains the same, unfulfilled in an early adolescence that will carry through midlife. Women often marry among us, if they marry at all, in their late thirties, when they must settle for whatever male expresses an interest rather than win the wavy-haired rebel on a motorcycle or the time-traveling stardust-bandit of their escapist Kindle epics. By then, childbearing is almost a physical impossibility. Treating infertility has become a major industry in the medical field—with its outcomes, alas, generally unencouraging. Then aging and death begin to loom even before the exit from youth has been fully accepted... and the race into further fantasies of more extravagant kinds is on. (Herein, perhaps, hides the origin of the phenomenon studied in Diana West's earlier book, *The Death of the Grown-Up*.)

Cognitive Disconnect

<u>Dangerous Naïveté About Human Nature</u>: It shouldn't come as a surprise, when everything above is weighed, that we (or many among us) have only a pre-adolescent's grasp of likely human motivations. Young men especially seem surprised that (for instance) a girl used for sex during a semester should think herself in a purposive, soulful relationship; and young women seem surprised, in the same scenario, that men have no manners and no nobility. College grads of both genders (let's pretend there are only two) assume that police are Gestapo thugs, that soldiers are butchering mercenaries, and that business management always wants to push employees to the brink of starvation for sake of a wider profit margin; yet the same downy-cheeked cynics encounter no obstacle to picturing a safe, smoothly running society where only uniformed figures carry guns, which are only ever used to protect the helpless innocent—and where government bureaucrats daily spring to the defense of the oppressed without the least thought of power, promotion, or pay raise. The degree of emotional incoherence and retardation involved in trusting socialism—the practice of confiscating property by force and redistributing it as willed by an elite few (known in earlier ages as piracy)—to bring happiness to the world is mind-numbing.

<u>Ignorance of How Things Are Produced</u>: This category is probably best appreciated by viewing the next two... but it's important to realize, as an entirely distinct category, that our alienated, unsocialized citizenry doesn't simply lack connection to other human beings. Its ignorance of the material universe is an integral part of the paranoid isolation we have been describing. How many of us fully understand (i.e., *act* as though they understand) that putting a plastic outlet cover on sheetrock does not draw clean, inexhaustible energy from the Spirit World? How many have any inkling that solar panels are produced with Rare Earth Elements mined in miserable locales of the Third World commonly called "cancer villages"? Apparently some do not quite grasp where babies come from, despite having been saturated in "sex education" since Kindergarten.

<u>Qualitative Imbecility</u>: Of course, babies are not "made" in the fashion of solar panels. My final example above leaks from a vast ignorance about how economies function into how natural cause-and-effect works. I'm sure that high school students today are much better equipped with hardware in chemistry or biology class than my generation was; and, we must hasten to add, they have the Internet. There is scarcely any plausible way to explain their degree of ignorance about the basics rhythms and connections of the natural world, then, if we do not posit that their daily, practical experience of that world is alarmingly deprived. How many understand that a year of unusual weather patterns offers up virtually no relevant data to the study of climate? How many comprehend that deadwood left untrimmed in a grassland or forest becomes tinder for major fires? Why do so many not see that human

158

cultures (which are natural phenomena in many ways) annihilate each other unless permitted some degree of isolation? This stuff isn't "rocket science".

Quantitative Imbecility: Plenty of young people are more proficient at math already than I ever was on my best day... but plenty more can't seem to reach an elementary proficiency. Related to our nation's special instance of cultural collision... why is it hard to grasp that resources of all kinds are limited for handling Mexico's itinerant laborers? Does the fact that so many of our citizens cannot correctly write out "twenty-three trillion" in numeral form mean that our debt problem is solved? Is there something about the volume of illegal immigrants pouring into our sanctuary cities that college students cannot connect with congested traffic, deteriorating infrastructure, increases in infectious disease, rises in pollution of all kinds, and escalating crime rates? Or why do these students and their parents believe—why did they ever believe—that the Big Brotherly FAFSA applications they were required to fill out upon completion of high school would lead to "free money"? Why, as a society, can't we count? We're no more obtuse, one must assume, than our forefathers. Could it be that we have lost touch with the world's "thingness"—that we no longer have direct experience of plants receiving too much water, of fireplaces lacking sufficient chopped wood, of gutters too high for a certain ladder?

***

I have perhaps already been prolix, so I will end my list here rather arbitrarily. I've written enough, surely, to promote the point that our awareness of the world is being challenged today in ways unknown to other times. We lack common sense to a degree that, as far as I know, has no parallel in any society's general population—in any society's of any time.

Last week I happened to read two explanations of why more than fifty percent of millennials appear to view socialism favorably. David Limbaugh (somewhat echoing Diana West) blames academic propagandists; Tucker Carlson blames the student debt crisis. I myself have to believe that much, much more is going wrong. The "millennial mind" (if I may be pardoned the phrase) is being won over to suicidal folly neither by professorial harangues nor by economic self-interest. Its collective attitudes and outlook are far more deeply embedded than such causality can explain. The disease eating away at us has gnawed all the way to the bone.

PART THREE

The Dark Elite and Imminent Dystopia

Erchomenology: The Study of Things to Come

*First published in **Praesidium** 14.3 (Summer 2014).*

a) the uniqueness of Now, and of Time to Come

The following four facts about tendencies in contemporary society are beyond argument.

1) Citizens of the "postmodern" world exist in a much higher density than any generation of human beings before them. This is the only of my four propositions that might be initially questioned; for ancient Rome or Alexandria (not to mention the largest settlements of India, China, or the Aztec and Mayan empires) must have seen warm bodies jammed together in hive-like proportions that our automobile-based lifestyle has effectively thinned out. At the same time, however, a sizable percentage of these earlier civilizations clung to life on the farm. Mechanization was insufficient to have things otherwise. Only since the Industrial Revolution have masses of farm folk become city folk; and this trend has accelerated exponentially rather than arithmetically, until today the green spaces between urban centers in our own nation's southeast are almost as deserted as the desert spaces between Las Vegas and Reno and Phoenix.

Furthermore, one supposes that people on the streets of the ancient metropolis would not have chafed upon and against each other as we do. Fast-moving machinery did not menace; turbines of raucous noise, sometimes deliberately amplified, did not surround them; rigidly separated functions within the city did not require that they rush ever and anon to reach job or market or temple or home in time to escape censure; clocks did not warn them ubiquitously, either, of the impending instant when they would be counted absent or branded tardy.

Both in terms of the actual percentage of the populace wrested from the hinterland and in terms of the somewhat subjective feeling of "crush", ancient people were no match for us.

2) *Homo postmodernis* (henceforth HP) possesses artificial means of communication far in excess, not just of what his ancestors knew, but of what they could have imagined. Direct speech was already being rivaled by exchanges over the telephone half a century ago. Now the descendant gadgets of that wired and immobile convenience scarcely even transmit a spoken word, but rather are largely devoted to brief, formulaic messages encoded in an evolving shorthand. The very act of reading has gone high-tech. The words I write at this instant will be processed for a screen

that constantly dangles links to alternative pages before the reader and will also flash or ping notification of new email or awaiting updates.

3) Distinct from the previous proposition is the immensely multiplied intrusive power of "data collection agencies and services". Perhaps HP should have seen this one coming; but he didn't, as a man or woman on the proverbial street (truly proverbial—for what ordinary, innocent citizen walks our streets any longer?). The "smartphone" (one word), for instance, continues to be peddled as a means of instant access to far-flung friends and relatives. No marketing campaign would ever pitch it as a more efficient means, besides, of supplying the central government and the private-sector elite with detailed personal information. Intimate privacy, rather, is emphasized. The sharing of such intimacy with unknown eavesdroppers, insofar as it is even suggested, becomes the source of "negative" marketing strategy: i.e., this or that service provider of email vaunts ironclad security from the invasions of snoopers.

Nevertheless, the eyes over our shoulder are here to stay, and they can only get keener and more numerous. (Indeed, service providers are themselves motivated to facilitate snooping, since enhanced paranoia must feed the public's demand for greater security; in the same way, the manufacturers of shields from computer viruses have always had a hidden motive to keep those viruses evolving.) HP will be watched closely from now on. Whether his spectators will make sinister use of their disembodied powers or, instead, simply drown in a tsunami of information is another matter. Eventually, more and more of the information-processing—and perhaps even the associated soliciting or censuring of individuals—will have to be taken over by machines.

4) The classical Chinese poet Wang Wei writes of crossing the broad Yangtze: at one indefinable point, he grows so intent on the newly emerging shore that he fails to notice the slipping from sight of his home behind him. Even so, the many transformations of HP's brave new world may blind us to the most obvious effect of the change: deracination from the past. We see our flashing, exotic future rising before us; we do not see the beloved haunts and habits of our past disappearing behind us. People move to cities, and they proceed to move often within cities. Their contacts are instantly reached by a handy device (perhaps, in the near future, something like a wristwatch or a collar pin); but the "contact list" itself is in constant flux as jobs and neighborhoods succeed each other dizzyingly and ambitions reach toward far horizons. It probably does not even occur to HP to revisit the streets and playgrounds of his youth until he has consumed about half of his biological span. Then, if he should go seeking them, he will almost surely be frustrated. Should they not be physically plowed under or degraded to slums too dangerous for him to prowl alone, he will still find the human landscape unrecognizable. People in his society no longer bequeath residences to

their children. The residences themselves turn as insipid as a thirty-year-old hair-do after one generation has been reared in them, and are thereby doomed to the auction block and the bids of less affluent wanderers.

If it is important for the human being to preserve some kind of connection with his or her past, then HP loses something vital in this transaction. Perhaps he supplements the loss in other ways; yet he is unique in human history, once again, in having to make such a shift. The question certainly deserves to be asked: how well has he succeeded at finding happiness?

b) the necessity of a moral component in social analysis

I have believed for several years now that an academic field should be dedicated to such queries. We currently have nothing in the curriculum of which they are the nucleus. History studies human events of the past. Political Science studies the theory and practice, past and present, of systems and institutions that direct human activity through laws (i.e., through force). Economics studies the behavior of markets—a project which may certainly predict human events on a grand scale with some accuracy, but which, in studying *only* markets, fails to measure (or even consider) the full measure of "humanity" or "happiness", either one. Psychology translates satisfaction into endorphins, and does so, of course, on an individual level. Philosophy allows the inquisitor to probe the meaning of abstractions without being chained to empirical terms; yet besides the troubling fact that current philosophy seldom does anything of the sort (and hence is moribund as a study independent of the sciences), the classical philosopher's tendency is to see things in universals, and so to overlook—quite deliberately—the critically peculiar elements of times and customs. The same objection might be raised against Theology; and, of course, that field throws an even smaller shadow over the contemporary campus than Philosophy.

It has been suggested to me that what I seek is Sociology, or some branch thereof. I think not. The methodology of the sociologist seems to hinge upon establishing a statistical baseline for whatever anomalous behavior or condition is being analyzed—median income for poverty, average marriage and divorce rates for familial dysfunction, average years of education for the population of incarcerated youth, and so forth. This approach necessarily divides the social house against itself. On the one hand, it invites ideologues to draw conclusions that represent those in the margins as victims; and on the other, it implies that those within the standard deviation do not themselves illustrate any sort of anomaly. The given society's numerical averages are those stable references against which we recognize instability.

What if entire societies, however, are suffering from a kind of collective neurosis compared to their own behavior of a generation earlier, or to a contemporary society's in a very different environment? Perhaps no society is ever perfectly stable and happy, just as no single person is ever so. Have we, then, no benchmarks from which to reckon relative health? The contemporary sociologist, it appears to me, is so deeply imbued with the notion that norms are practically arbitrary—virtual products of chance, ungrounded in any abiding principle—that he or she would scarcely even register ritual human sacrifice as pathological. This analyst, while forever "passing judgment" (in the popular sense of being his society's conscience), does so only behind the screen of statistics.

In contrast, the investigator I have in mind would openly "moralize" in some measure, and would do so with rigorous discipline. Mere rationality, after all, should be able to specify that the healthy society does not consume its members as a fire consumes wood. Without an enhancement of safety, individuals would have little motivation to form societies, in the first place. Should the group begin at some stage, therefore, to believe collectively that ritual slaughter of certain members increases the survival rate of the many, we ought to be able to understand the collective mind as suffering from a variety of paranoia or hysteria. Something is wrong here. It isn't wrong with this sub-class or that alienated minority, but with the entire social organism; and it isn't wrong because the victims appear shortchanged, for they may even compete to go under the high priest's knife. If a very high percentage of the surviving group remains fully convinced that life is now better—if the sacrificial victims themselves are content to die for the multitude, or if they bask in the honor of doing so—the illness is no less. On the contrary, such "stabilizing attitudes" make the problem more palpable than ever: for what attitude could be more "sick"?

Collective illness of this kind must be defined as objectively as possible, naturally, if we are ever to gauge the spirit of the times and predict with any accuracy what times await around the corner. What drives a society to embrace, say, a murderous irrationalism? What societies have done so in the past? What future trajectory do such societies tend to follow? How are changes in their environment (e.g., in kind and degree of technology or in pressure from rival societies) likely to affect that future? We cannot ask meaningful questions such as these if we cannot first identify a society that leaves human hecatombs in its wake as "interesting".

Other value judgments would similarly arise from rational assumptions. Truth allows understanding and collaboration; falsehood creates confusion and disorder. Even at the simplest levels, people are uncomfortable with patent deception. To be told that X isn't home and then glimpse his face in the window, to hear one's own witticism or insight claimed by another, or to be promised support on Friday only to find empty seats on Saturday can destroy friendships and feed enmities. When a society invests heavily in formal and persistent fraud, we should likewise detect a symptom of illness.

Again, I am by no means calling for a rain and hail of moral condemnation upon societies around the world that we, thanks to our own cultural conditioning, decide to target. I am observing, instead, the vital importance of objective moral judgment to predicting humanity's future on a vast scale. Certain patterns of behavior wear a society's members down over time, regardless of economic, technological, military, or other successes. The decline of societies suffering crises of mass hysteria or mass deception or mass despair is inevitable. Yet the social sciences that I see currently on the books will not allow us to make this calculation, since it requires assuming that all values are not relative to time and place. Hence these same sciences, as they stand, must prove inadequately predictive whenever they turn to the future.

I hasten to observe, as well, that the mainstream social sciences have failed miserably to hold aloof from sweeping value judgments, though their practitioners are quick to denounce the moral prejudice of methodology not their own. In several particular cases, these "professionals" have indeed shamefully discredited themselves. I think, for instance, of the Stanford Prison Experiment of 1971. Researchers at Stanford University, led by Professor Philip Zimbardo, designed their own mock-prison to document what sorts of atrocity would rise to the surface once ordinary human beings settled into "guard" and "inmate" roles. The specific motivation behind this "inquiry", though crucial to determining Zimbardo's prejudices, has not been made generally available. All participants were volunteers from the local campus community; and, while screened for physical fitness, they too were never questioned about any specifically political interest in the undertaking. Those chosen as inmates were "arrested" without explanation before friends or family and carted off to the artificial prison by a highly cooperative local police force. Though physical torture was not permitted, verbal abuse, sexual humiliation, sleep deprivation, disruption of toilet routine, and similar types of harassment were dished out so zealously that the intended two-week experiment was shut down after running less than half of the projected span.

In the first place, giving so little attention (exactly none, in fact) to the ideological predispositions of both experimenters and subjects hopelessly compromised the "findings" before they were ever "found", since the self-selected participants would quite likely have perceived their adventure as a chance to make a political statement. It was 1971. Formal authority was held in very low regard, especially around elite campuses. Students "role-playing" as guards could be expected to dose their performance amply with sadism, and students posing as prisoners to invite and mime agony with the same enthusiasm. Zimbardo himself claimed that the control he enjoyed over events corrupted his objectivity; might his purpose all along not have been to watch things get out of hand and then blame the situation? Arrest before one's peers by local police, furthermore, scarcely equates to being rounded up after an armed robbery (except, of course, in the mind of someone who has deemed "suspects" to be randomly selected bystanders: QED). There was, besides, no attempt made to approximate in the laboratory setting the kind, degree, and frequency of abuses alleged to have occurred at any particular prison. The "experiment", in short, was farcical, its self-fulfilling prophesy a fit monument to the subjectivity of all science that scorns moral truth as subjective.

Most human beings cannot resist admiration in certain circumstances and condemnation in others. To study the human animal closely yet forbid, as a measure of one's rigor, any admission of moral value judgments into the project is to invite being blindsided by one's own moral prejudices. The analyst is also a human. A contempt for the notion of moral axioms would in itself strongly indicate that a given analyst was importing far too much personal baggage into the laboratory setting.

c) the failure of previous academic predictions

Francis Fukuyama speculated that we had reached "the end of history" in 1978 (with an essay of that title), confident that the global triumph of Western political and economic institutions had accomplished all the major objectives of social evolution. Fukuyama's thesis might be glossed "the end of ideology", for he viewed great historical struggles precisely as the competition of alternative systems. Yet by the early years of the twenty-first century, the world had dissolved into turbid, often deadly ideological warfare. Religious fundamentalism vs. secular liberalism, theocratic socialism vs. democratic capitalism, the traditionalism of Arab Islamic states vs. the progressivism of Western technocracies... these and other formulas were proposed as defining the central conflict. One might well challenge all of them. In fact, the specific ideologies at issue may not be possible to define succinctly—not the least reason for which is that they were (and still are) constantly misidentified, whether for propagandistic ends or out of sheer ignorance. For instance, Islam *in abstractu* is supposed to overcome nationalist tendencies in favor of a global caliphate. The so-called "Arab Spring" that has set North Africa and the Levant afire, however, displays no impetus more powerfully than that of nationalism. While the politics of punishing the 9/11 attacks, furthermore, had a distinctly pro-democratic aroma at the time, they have produced in the United States a series of statist initiatives so aggressive that a radical realignment of the old Democratic/Republican divide may be taking shape around basic constitutional issues. The animus beneath this upheaval is entirely ideological, though its critics attempt to defame it as primitive tribalism of one kind or another.

Professor Fukuyama, in short, was so spectacularly wrong that his essay very nearly heralded the dawn of a new ultra-ideological era. A political scientist *cum* economist, he had projected that the new and free circulation of wealth in a global marketplace would replace Cold War rivalries with universal prosperity. Money speaks the same language to all cultures and political powers (we were to realize). Everyone would want a piece of the savory pie. Fukuyama had failed to foresee (among other things) what enormous strains on cultural values—on linguistic customs, religious practices, health habits, conduct between the sexes, and so forth—would be generated as companies roamed the planet in search of the cheapest labor force, and also mobilized labor forces from all over the planet to come and fill domestic niches cheaply. Economic competition, of course, feeds cultural tension; yet an assault upon one's culture, much more than upon one's wallet, leads one to grab a pitchfork or make Molotov cocktails.

Globalism had played havoc with the stability and conformity that human societies need to survive. Far from resolving the differences that have divided people for time out of mind, the movement identified by Fukuyama loaded the powder kegs and then struck the match. A "prophet" who ignores the importance of their past to human beings—who assumes that money can make everything right—is destined to end up looking a fool: *that* prophecy will not disappoint.

Albert Einstein once remarked that nuclear power could be an incredible blessing or an unimaginable curse upon the human race. As a prediction, this hedging of bets may yet come true by way of the latter alternative; but the former, though often extended to other technological innovations, is always doomed to contradiction. Technology will never bring paradise to earth. The reasons are embedded in basic human nature—which Mr. Einstein, like so many people of staggering intelligence, was poorly positioned to assess in all its disappointing folly.

Say that a novel form of energy is developed in such a fashion as to be readily renewable, cheaply produced, and environmentally harmless. Humans would be spared an incalculable amount of arduous labor. At first, they would rejoice to be thus liberated. Then the luxury of physical ease would become a necessity. Everybody would expect to have a bottle containing a genie—would demand to have one. Unlimited free energy would soon be guaranteed by a central authority, like clean water: it would be a right, not a privilege. As government monitors set about monopolizing the energy market, of course, their venture would be financed by tax money, not by private-sector purchasing (for nothing is truly free in this life). From one direction, then, "quality control" would be difficult to sustain, since a massive bureaucracy would respond to setbacks by increasing its own mass rather than promoting, firing, reorganizing, etc. This is how bureaucracies behave: it is a hard fact of human society. From another direction, the disappearance of the profit motive from the equation—of the chance to grow rich by improving the product— would cause the once-new technology to stagnate in the face accident and abrupt challenge, even if it were basically well maintained. Free energy would become a dependency—a kind of drug—and the inbred certainty of its perpetual and unrestricted presence would have two inevitable results: 1) it would be used more and ever more, creating discontent over such trivialities as delayed access (e.g., standing in line or waiting for "juice" to transfer); and 2) it would represent an ever-growing vulnerability (e.g., through terrorist attack or natural catastrophe) within the society that gorged upon its fuel.

Entrepreneurs would not likely vanish, even after the magical energy source was nationalized. They would apply their genius, rather, to introducing more and more toys to consume the boundless supply of animation. Things would be designed in the tens of thousands to draw upon "free motion"; and the specific purpose of these things, usually, would by no means address a niche that once demanded arduous but necessary physical effort. In fact, purpose would probably be almost indeterminable in some cases: the very essence of high-tech playthings is frivolous. Yet as society in general grew enamored of its gadgets, they would be viewed as "must haves". The paradise of affluence would be forever teetering, in individual cases, on the verge of an inferno of privation. A citizen who hadn't the latest robotic dog or cat paraded by his proud neighbor would not know an instant's peace until he could bridge the gap. This, too, is immutable human nature.

"Real life" examples of the moral degeneracy just described will leap to the mind of any thoughtful person over the age of forty (old enough, that is, to have already lived through several such transits). Ortega y Gasset attributed many of the qualities mentioned above to "mass man", while Aldous Huxley illustrated in more than one novel how material progress can proportionally drive spiritual regression. The author of the present essay poignantly remembers a first-grade assignment in *My Weekly Reader* that portrayed the late twentieth-century city as humming with monorails. Cars and their nightmarish chaos of traffic were to be gone in a few short decades. The change was lead-pipe cinch. If we hadn't all the necessary technology already, our rate of advance was yet such that we had every right to picture clean, fast, efficient, enjoyable travel throughout the metropolis of the future. Only a fool would think otherwise.

The fools, however, turned out to be wise in this instance (as in so many others), while wise men were made fools. Innovation in transport began to atrophy about the time that our central government invested in heavily car-bearing highways and attendant infrastructure. The metropolis of 1990 came and went without those glistening monorails shooting hither and yon: the cities of that era had been radically rebuilt to suit the automobile, and now one could not move through them except by automobile. Many citizens of the twenty-first century hate their commutes, and new technology obligingly promises cars that drive themselves—more of the same, that is, but tweaked to mitigate the misery of an existential trap without exit. Suburban residents also hate the impersonality of their neighborhoods, where widening roads have thrust houses farther and farther from each other and where each garage door automatically seals like a portcullis as soon as Milord or Milady returns from fighting daily dragons. Satellite dishes and the Internet are the proposed answer: a superabundance of artificial socializing, of voyeuristic neighborliness. The result isn't really happiness at all, let alone paradise—but its deception suffices to hold misery at arm's length on an average day.

The technologist does not understand the fragility of artifice. He or she fails to divine the true social needs of human beings. The Japanese, one hears, are even developing robotic sexual partners for lonely adults in the high-tech urban jungle. Such science-fictional scenarios fascinate, but they seem only half-prophetic. They open before us a great glowing abyss, but they do not intimate what kind of landing we should expect at the bottom.

As a third and final example of failed contemporary prophecy, the "progress in race relations" vein of visionarism reveals yet further blunders. HP is surrounded by progressive rhetoric, and his metaphors of history are steeped in progressive imagery. We could never fly before, but now we fly; we could never cure an ailing heart before, but now we do open-heart surgery. Why, therefore, should we not expect the persistent presence of racism in human history at last to dissolve before our time's spreading enlightenment? If it fails to do so, the cause can only be that certain segments of society linger in their Neolithic stupor. The Scopes trial publicized how fiercely such minds could resist the evidence of science, just as the Catholic Church's resistance to the Copernican Revolution had done. The battle over race was earnestly joined in the Fifties and Sixties of the previous century, and it has since been hard fought in various pockets of barbarism; but the march proceeds, and the legions will both swell in number and reach their destination, as surely as tomorrow's sun will rise.

This kind of forecast, with which Americans of my generation have grown up and grown old, has not necessary proved false—yet if true, then its fulfillment looks nothing like what we expected. Citizens of African descent have won election to our highest offices, they attend our children's schools and come to weekend sleep-overs, they buy houses where they wish, they eat at restaurants of their choosing... the days of Jim Crow appear to be mercifully distant. Why, then, are we now told so often that this is not the case? Within the same week in April 2014, US Attorney General Eric Holder fumed that critics of his unorthodox tenure in that office have attacked him because of his African genes, while high-profile baseball hero Henry Aaron charged that those who oppose President Obama's initiatives are merely "Klansmen in neckties and starched collars". To hear such figures speak, one would conclude that most progress in black/white relations has been illusory.

From an angle whence these denunciators would neither expect nor want confirmation, probably, it comes aplenty. This writer might mention the case of a certain local doctor who now avoids hiring black nurses or technicians. The reason? Because he has found repeatedly that they can become impossible either to correct or release: if disciplined or fired, they instantly file a racial discrimination grievance. A professional attempting to keep a small practice afloat cannot afford such risks for the sake of doing the right thing. Hence real discrimination occurs under the table, precisely because the menace of being bankrupted over manufactured instances of discrimination has grown fearful.

What has happened? Where did our progress go?

The rope that is throttling progress in this instance, of course, has many strands. I will trace but one. Racism, to invoke the platitude, has indeed always existed—and it has also, just as fluidly, morphed from one era to another. A devout New England Protestant would once have threatened to disinherit his son for asking to marry an Irish Catholic; now the *pater familias* wonders if the boy will find a Christian woman of any description amid a sea of "pagan college girls". Anglo settlers in the South or Southwest would have killed a man a hundred years ago for suggesting that a drop of Cherokee or Choctaw blood ran in their veins; their descendants now boast of those drops—or manufacture them—on certain applications or on the political trail. Once-prickly situations did not relax because the people involved were at last "sensitized to otherness"—more likely, just the opposite. They probably forgot about "otherness", that is, as their major socio-economic adversaries changed. Previous prejudices evaporated because everyone concerned had more pressing things to worry about. Such is the natural course of human events. Races in conflict hate one another bitterly, then generations pass and economies shift, then Romeo marries Juliet and Hatfield marries McCoy... and the new tribe emerging from these unions turns its collective dread upon a new rival.

One might speculate that the African/Caucasian situation is more complicated because physical differences are more pronounced. A Montague looks much the same as a Capulet—but the epidermis is a giveaway in America's most troubled racial divide. Yet history offers little support for this thesis. The original Celts were distinctly dark compared to the Scandinavians who invaded their shores; but now red hair is considered a signature of Irishness, and the stereotypical Scot has blond ringlets and fierce blue eyes.

What we failed to see (or one important thing, out of several) as we collectively prophesied progress in America's black/ white relations was the political utility of lingering division. Racial difference is now emphasized, in an official and codified manner, as it has been at no other point since the Jim Crow laws. To that extent, we are certainly backsliding. The formal, even academic justification of this "yellow star" approach is that it forces potential bigots to reflect explicitly and consciously upon the otherness of the person they are about to slight. Such "sensitization" is actually an open invitation to a revised—and deeply obnoxious—paternalism, where the White Man's Burden assumes the disguise of Aiding Victims of Prejudice. No honest, intelligent observer would dispute this... but honesty is in short supply where manipulation promises such profit. Advocates firmly anchored in the power structure are unshaken when confronted with their hypocrisy, since (like all Machiavellians) they are profound cynics, immune to any mirror's indictment. The goal is to divide and rule. Man as a political animal quickly finds this out, if he does not know it instinctively: i.e., that masses of people are more easily handled if they view themselves primarily as members of a group rather than as individuals.

The prophecy of racial harmony has proved overly optimistic, in short, because it viewed the problem merely as an educational challenge—a material volatility needing a material additive to become stable, like a bunch of chemicals in a beaker. The malice and sordid advantage of political calculation were never weighed. The assumption was simply that those who hate a certain race must listen to reason; the fatal omission was that the dispensers of reason might—for their own selfish interests—poison their therapeutic doses of enlightenment to be more provocative than informative.

d) the content of "erchomenology" as a discipline

The examples just offered have a lamentable disorder and are certainly not exhaustive of the possibilities. Yet they suffice to highlight a few of the more obvious reasons for why contemporary scholarship cannot reliably predict the next turn of society. To recapitulate:

- Human beings are not motivated simply by greed and self-interest, or at least not when "self" is narrowly defined. Many models in the social sciences appear to assume that cynicism of this kind is empirically sound. Economists, for instances, often seem to treat cultural and religious factors that stand in the way of profit as "playing hard to get" tactics, to be overcome by raising the amount of the bribe. Naturally, history offers many instances of individuals and entire peoples who "sold out" their cherished traditions for material profit. Even when *auri sacra fames* wins in such cases as these, however, it loses; for volatile emotions like a loathing of oneself, a resentment of the gift-bearing intruder, and a longing to purge guilt in some bloody act of penance may lurk dangerously just beneath the surface. The failure of our national policy-makers (let alone our rank-and-file electorate) to comprehend how emotions of the sort influence the Third World continues to lead the United States into situations of high risk.

- Our own cultural faith in technology has also created an almost invincible blind spot. Visionaries like Ray Kurzweil base all of their forecasts upon the exponential growth of our technological capacity. Yesterday, a man on the Moon: tomorrow, a colony settling a yet-undiscovered planet. Yesterday, a heart replacement: tomorrow, a life expectancy of 10,000 years. Such sanguine outlooks isolate a single characteristic of technological development without giving any thought to how changes will affect human beings. Will we want to visit a new planet, even if we can? Will we want to live longer once a virtual immortality lies at our feet... or will we, perhaps, long to die? Technology alters the values and attitudes of those beings whose lives it was made to improve. We cannot say what thoughts and feelings will stir within our great-grandchildren: Kurzweil, for one, believes that this unborn generation will be more artificial than biological (i.e., more robot than human). Any prophecy concerning how human life will be bettered by technology, therefore, must begin in an assessment of what is good. Insofar as mounting evidence suggests that we rapidly shift to accommodating our machines after those machines have initially accommodated us, is our glorious, golden future really more liberation than servitude? Might we be approaching the state of the Aztec maiden who is told that she will be infinitely happier once her heart is cut out?

•   When we attempt to study our human world directly (as in the issue of race relations), our disciplines often lurch from cynicism to utopianism. Racism, poverty, alcoholism, delinquency... all such ills are statistically objectified with implicit outrage, leading to the obvious conclusion that society must care more about its own. The objectivity here is quite slippery. What is racism? Is it "hate speech", or perhaps a lower employment rate? Can a Caucasian ever be a victim of racists? Are homosexuals such victims, as is increasingly claimed? And what is alcoholism, other than a chemical dependency? Is dependency on caffeine-laced drinks of the same order? Or since the brain can produce is own chemicals in response to proper stimuli, is pornography a dependency? Are Star Trek and James Bond movies? The game here seems to consist of taking the fundamentally unquantifiable—the human—and whimsically defining it into something susceptible to measure. What does this accomplish other than foregrounding issues and problems that the researcher, for purely subjective reasons, finds interesting? Is the result ever a workable solution to a problem; is not the whole process, more accurately, a symptom of a society that feels its humanity slipping away?

One would of course like to say that the disciplined forecaster of human events should know something about everything, since the recurrent failure in all of my examples is over-specialization. Yet any career academic will recognize in the word "interdisciplinary" a red flag warning of potential slovenliness. He who knows a little about much knows not much about anything. This commentator's Ph.D. was earned in a field called Comparative Literature, which has now (mercifully) vanished from the academic map. Though there ought to have been a wealth of material for the literary comparatist to study—though there awaited nothing less than a science of literary aesthetics, such as Northrop Frye hinted at in his wonderfully synthetic books—the very term "aesthetic" (along with its pompously ivory recasting, "universalist") became anathema in comparative circles. Comp Lit programs ground out feminist and neo-Marxist "theory" at break-neck speed, while annihilating the very possibility of a basic human attraction to a good yarn.

Yet another stab at an interdisciplinary discipline would therefore be dangerously exposed to yet another ideological hijacking. An ever-guiding principle in the field of "Erchomenology" (the study of things to come) would hence have to be a deliberate and systematic abstinence from ideology of any sort. This is easier said than done, to be sure. I have used the phrase "human nature" repeatedly in this essay, yet many a scholar would bluntly insist that human beings have no more than the nature of a highly developed primate: no altruism, no disinterested admiration of beauty, no intimations of immortality. It is precisely in acknowledging such fundamental differences, though, that the erchomenologist would demonstrate rigor. A model of urban collapse after a natural catastrophe—say, of Southern California's behavior after a 9.5 earthquake—might be developed using a Zola-like estimate of human nature, and another might assume in people a degree of redemptive "common humanity". Of course, both models should predicate their assumptions not upon whimsical inclination, but upon research into how human beings have behaved under similar conditions in the past. In the not unlikely event that responses differed (i.e., that no view of human nature managed to yield a fully reliable prediction), the researcher would then question *why* they differed. Was culture the decisive factor? Was technology?

Possessed of such information, a public policy-maker, a clergyman, and even an entrepreneur would be able to take productive steps (though "productive" might be understood very differently by all three). The erchomenologist would leave to each the interpretation of data based upon ideology: his or her function would merely be to furnish the most likely projection. While supposing that this projection itself might entirely avoid ideological bias would be naïve, time would eventually vindicate the better models. False prophets are eventually stoned and double-talking oracles eventually ignored. Only the truth lives to see the sun set.

Now, exactly what proportion of an "erchomenological" program of study should be history, what sociology, what economics, what psychology, and so forth does not really concern me here. It ought to do so, admittedly, if I were indeed proposing an academic discipline. My present purpose is not to attempt a wade through that morass, however, but simply to observe that predicting future events with some degree of accuracy should be possible if one had proper preparation. Today it is done extremely poorly by the people in academe who seem to be best prepared... so the magical formula, whatever it is, doesn't lie concealed in the vaults of any particular department. I may say now that the deep incursions of ideology into many departments is as much a source of failure as the over-specialization mentioned above. Scholars know too little beyond their area of expertise, and they assume far too much, at the same time, about how their special area connects to the broader world (the dilemma of the specialist described so well by Ortega y Gasset almost a century ago). For the academy, then, a more important requisite than merely dispensing interdisciplinary information might be securing a generous flow of information in any favored discipline, such that the warping effects of ideology cancel out. Where knowledge is concerned, gluttony is more healthy than selective spoon-feeding.

d) toward some initial predictions

I conclude with a demonstration: I shall place myself on prophecy's "hot seat".

Recall the conditions enumerated at this essay's outset that make of postmodern society a unique venue. Several factors related to those conditions have created a ticking time bomb.

1) The most technologically advanced societies are being flooded with Third World peoples largely ignorant of technology, and even more of the scientific principles that undergird it. These newly arrived residents learn to drive a car quickly enough and show up at the emergency room quite often, yet few of them understand anything about chemical reactions or bacteria. One vector, then, shows our high-tech lifestyle being financed ever more by uninformed consumers and managed ever more by elite technicians. The gap between the two was already widening as the internal combustion engine, for instance, became so computerized that a mechanically inclined teenager could no longer overhaul it in his father's garage. Now that the general populace throughout the West is absorbing hordes of immigrants whose parents once traveled by donkey-cart, the gap must grow chasmic.

2) The previous tendency is magnified and accelerated by birth rates. For whatever reason (and there are indeed many), members of the technocratic elite seldom reproduce at replacement levels throughout the Western world, while the immigrant blue-collar class produces very large families—too large, often, for the manual labor of a head-of-household to support in so sophisticated an economy. The one rapidly growing segment of society, then, not only brings little knowledge to bear upon its consumption of the high-tech lifestyle: it also has insufficient resources to partake of that lifestyle unassisted.

3) Education, the benign goddess who presides over the future of progressive societies and is expected to relieve the pressures identified above, is but a cold stone idol; for no amount of education can transform unskilled laborers of peasant, traditionalist stock into an army of prosperous technicians. This is far less due to the limits of classroom instruction or the number and ignorance of the students than to the nature of technology itself. Developing and maintaining machines is exorbitantly expensive. The financial benefit of mechanization to businesses rests solely upon the ability of said machines to eliminate human labor. That millions and millions of well-tutored young people might somehow find a gilded future in the world of robots is patently absurd. In other words, the very successes of technology would drive the creation of a highly exclusive elite even if the working class were not reproducing at four or five times the rate of the technocrats, and even if

the working class were not being supplemented by vast infusions of undereducated Third Worlders.

4) Medical technology, specifically, is allowing people of all classes to live longer. The emerging portrait of the last few paragraphs is thus still further shadowed around its most worrisome features by our twenty-first century ability to keep our huge populations from stabilizing through the natural intervention of illness and aging.

5) The high-tech Western society with its ever more non-Western force of manual labor is a democracy: this generality is true to some degree in every specific case. Thus we have people in families too large to reach an average standard of living, and whose job skills are unlikely to provide them a ticket into the technocratic elite, representing an ever larger percentage of the electorate.

6) At the same time, as observed earlier, technology has a way of turning luxury into necessity. Everyone in the United States has a "right" to indoor plumbing, to heating and cooling, to dish- and clothes-washers and driers, and now apparently to a cell phone and to health care. Even as a lower percentage of society is able to afford the newest gadgetry, the gadgetry is coming out faster and thicker. The transit from cordless phones to cell phones took years; now cells themselves are passé, a stigmatizing dinosaur in a generation of "smart" devices. Resentment therefore mounts as the person on the streets can afford less and less of the accelerated "more" appearing thanks to the exponential increment of high-tech skill.

7) To other strains in this pressure-cooker might be added the cost of that education which the child of the *paisano*, eager to break into the fast lane, has acquired through enormous loans. When the coveted degree leads back to sacking groceries, this hapless dupe is not only poorer than ever, but also the more resentful for now having a modicum of the savvy and competence demanded by his brave new world.

8) Up to a point, Western governments have been releasing little jets of pressure by giving our young grocery clerk a job in the public sector. The impoverished need their heating in winter, the underprivileged need their cell phones for job-hunting—and all of this distribution and quality-control needs loyal footsoldiers. Resentment is a potent element. Sifting through the people who loiter about this economy's dead ends and employing some of them to service the families remaining at those dead ends may keep the city from catching fire for a while… but it is not, of course, a long-term strategy. Even heaping astronomical taxes upon the technocracy (while, at the back end, giving the technocrats huge contracts to equip schools with "educational" playthings and hospitals with "life-saving" miracles) cannot keep the ship of state afloat indefinitely.

What kind of forecast could flow from such observations that would not involve gloom and doom? None that I can imagine… yet neither do I see one predestined, ineluctable outcome. I would stress at this point, then, that the erchomenologist's utility lies precisely in his being able to see likely outcomes, so that the alert might steer for lesser rather than greater disasters. After all, as Cicero gently rebukes his brother Quintus in the treatise, *On Divination*, what would be the point of knowing the future if you could do nothing about it—yet if you could do something about a dire prognostication, in what sense would it be prophecy? We human beings cannot really foresee much of anything; yet we can reckon probabilities fairly accurately, and, with a little will power, we can cause the future to lean in the direction of the better option.

One of the worst options for us postmodern Westerners would surely be to keep on as we're going. Eventually—and sooner rather than later—our economy will collapse; and I think this is as much because of the technological marketplace as because of the public sector's takeover of that marketplace. Most of us grasp the threat of a seventeen-trillion-dollar debt, and more than a few of us the danger of paying down that debt's interest merely by printing money. Few, though, seem to rate the "hyper-technologized" economy as one of the largest storm clouds. On the contrary, a further advance of technology is generally regarded by economic disciplinarians as the only way back to prosperity. I might put it this way: the distaste for freeloading and for financing freeloaders has never adequately been connected to agricultural values in the minds of policy-makers. People who grow their own food, or at least provide services to independent small farmers, understand the "work product" in an intimate way, learn neighborliness and charity in the routine struggle to survive, and can quickly assess a demagogue by the height of his soapbox. People who slave for a wage producing an item that they never fully see must always feel vaguely cheated and naggingly paranoid; for the company's wealth often seems inversely proportional to theirs, and the operators of the urban labyrinth that has left them absolutely wage-dependent fear only one thing from them—their sheer mass.

We must find a way to make and keep our work local—to index it narrowly to our community rather than to transform it into a faceless abstraction adrift like a "bitcoin" in planetary tides. From sacking groceries to running one's own grocery store hasn't traditionally been an unsatisfying career path—and the Internet seems unlikely to deliver tomatoes in a download any time soon. Today the obstacles to such an ambition (and they are formidable) stem primarily from oppressive codes and regulations that our great benign employer of the jobless—our government bureaucracy—has generated by the ton (cheered on, of course, by mega-businesses with deep pockets).

A lot of wild cards find their way into the deck if social unrest reaches unruly levels. Riots are a distinct possibility. In an equation that would strike many academics as inside-out, I believe violence to be more likely, not less, in urban areas with stricter laws concerning private ownership of guns. Here local police and the National Guard would be more apt to confront massive uprisings directly; and once shots were fired and fatalities incurred, the situation might well spiral out of control in a fashion that would tantalize any Hollywood filmmaker. Other regions of a nation as vast as the United States would remain relatively inert, both because of a better-armed citizenry and because of a more agriculturally based local economy amenable to weathering short-term storms. Beyond these quiet backwaters, one can well imagine racial/ethnic antagonisms being used by the politically savvy to stoke the fire artificially and create a popular demand for the central authority's intervention. For this sad truth must be acknowledged: if political forces existed that wished for some excuse to suspend elections and seize power, violent riots in the streets would come as a very welcome opportunity.

Another very unsavory, but all too likely, scenario is a pandemic. The influx of millions upon millions of people into industrialized societies throughout the world who have no science-based education primes a kind of Petri dish for a new influenza that resists all known treatments. Such ill-informed masses often misuse antibiotics, taking their pills infrequently due to cost or desisting from the treatment as soon as they feel better. The eventual result is a much stronger strain of the "bug". Mere travel is also a source of menace; for even the humblest workers like to visit the old folks back home once in a while, and air travel has become one of our new collective "rights", one might almost say. The indiscriminate mingling of people from all over the world within time spans of just a few hours is an excellent recipe for a pandemic. Yet another factor could be the virtually promiscuous sexual habits to which young immigrants are introduced in the West, as well as the abundant use of recreational dugs that sometimes involve needles.

Again, one must wonder if the democratic government of the near future would necessarily be terribly distraught to see its underemployed, resentful masses decimated or halved by a new plague. Might such a government, indeed, having gotten what mileage it needed out of "democracy" (i.e., election of a like-minded elite), actively elicit the scourge through required public inoculations, and then suspend elections indefinitely during the "crisis"?

I shall stray no farther down that dark corridor; for a word to the wise if sufficient, and I cannot stress enough the importance of preserving Erchomenology from the taint of rigid ideology. What people need to hear is not that their elected representatives are calculating Cesare Borgias capable of murdering them in their sleep. They need to know, rather, that a highly manipulable situation is evolving. They need to bring to their consideration of public affairs the understanding of a sober adult, not a gullible child; and they need to realize, thanks to that level of maturity, that the intent of our republic's founders was to give no representative or body of representatives *the chance* to go bad. Those apostles of progress who will instantly protest that several of the founders were slave owners, and hence morally discredited, only prove my point: i.e., that generally or apparently good men and women are yet capable of vile acts due to lapses in judgment. This must be a constant in our calculations.

If we desire not to be slaves again, then we must keep those who lead us in carefully legislated chains. That, I know, is far more of a homily than a prophecy. What will ultimately determine events to come, however, is exactly the moral character of their human participants. I would go so far as to say that Erchomenology must achieve three ends, of which we have already mentioned a training broader than the specialist's and an abstaining from ideological intransigence. The third must be this: an understanding acceptance that all human beings are an immensely complex mixture of good and evil spirits.

Four Wild Cards: Volatile Elements in Our High-Tech Future, as Magnified by Space Travel

*First published in **Praesidium** 14.4 (Fall 2014).*

Space Exploration: A Magnifying Glass Upon Our Own Time

In the previous issue of *Praesidium*, I suggested that the formal science of Erchomenology (the "study of things to come") might succeed as an academic discipline under certain conditions—none of which seems likely to meet with fulfillment, by the way. First, the erchomenologist would have to be exposed to a vast array of component disciplines, ranging from History and Economics to Psychology and Sociology. Second, his or her exposure to these disciplines would have to be purged of ideological presumption as much as possible (in itself perhaps the greatest stumbling block; for all of the four fields just mentioned by way of example suffer from heavy ideological colonization). The student would also need to be keenly aware of human nature—of its very existence (at which proposition the contemporary academy scoffs) and of its labyrinthine architecture. How might we ever accurately forecast the behavior of human beings if we lack a firm grasp of what it means to be human?

For reasons practical (e.g., the cost of so many years of study) as well as pathological (e.g., the egotistical joy of radical chic), this academic craft is unlikely to leave its hangar any time soon. Yet nothing restrains us amateur erchomenologists from honing our skills. Even if no one formally pays us for looking into a crystal ball, we may arrange our personal lives advantageously (through investments, stockpiling of necessities, choice of location to live in, etc.) after we have cultivated an informed sense of where the epochal ship is sailing. I believe a term—slightly inaccurate, maybe too optimistic—has already been invented for such endeavor: common sense.

All this metaphorical talk of aircraft and ships under sail has perhaps been suggested to me by the popular images surrounding space travel; for to most people, any discussion of the distant future invites visions of strange new planets and miraculous conveyances that easily take us to them. I confess openly that I am not an avid consumer of the science-fiction genre. This is by no means because I object to colorful fantasies as escapist and irresponsible; on the contrary, it's more a matter of my distaste for an extreme lack of creativity in the sci-fi realm where crucial elements of human nature are concerned. Of what few space epics have meteorically collided with my free time (and I have always managed to extricate myself from George Lucas in five minutes), none seems to have calculated to a remote proximity the likely effects of twenty-second century technology upon the human psyche. None, indeed, seems aware that any such calculation is needed. We human beings simply remain as we are now—or as we were in the Seventies or Eighties of some filmmaker. We don't even remain as we have always been; for the producers also appear to be blissfully ignorant of manners and morals a mere generation of two before their time. The imagination deficit balances perfectly with a deficit of historical and cultural knowledge.

I'm being a little unfair to Kubrick's *2001: A Space Odyssey* and the creators of the original *Alien* in making these remarks; and I freely admit that my confession about avoiding the genre disqualifies me from passing an objective judgment upon its contents. I realize that there are darker visions of the future whose default value for human nature is not a nursery-rhyme naïveté. "Future" does not always equal "progress" in Hollywood arithmetic, and "progress" does not always equal "return to adolescence": only almost always. The signature-line of the old *Star Trek*, "to boldly go where no man has gone before," mocks itself unwittingly by violating the grammatical code both of the immediate past and of the immediate future: first it splits an infinitive, and then it hoists a "sexist" formulation! No matter: we're still bound for Never-Never Land, where (it is implied) we shall find new selves as well as new playthings. Nothing will hamper us—nothing will drive us to self-restraint! We will boldly go wherever we feel like boldly going!

Perhaps no period in our culture was more contemptuous of its cultural heritage or more gullible about the technology congesting its future than those decades—from the late Sixties to the mid-Eighties—in which I fully matured. Yet one can scarcely maintain that *Avatar* or Hollywood's butchery of Asimov in *I, Robot* has shaken off the romantic dualism—the child's "good guy/bad guy" naïveté—of the latter twentieth century's intellectual stultification.

Allow me, then, to use a stereotype of the space adventure retrieved from my superficial sampling of popular culture as my "foil" in suggesting that our imminent adventure in space is likely to straitjacket us rather than to free us. We foresee heavenly new vistas with three moons low on a purple horizon; we foresee a Shangri-La with toadstools the size of redwoods; we foresee singing flowers whose petals are an edible chocolate and whose stamina smell of ambrosia. We do not foresee flipping over a card where the Jester tweaks us by the nose, or where Old Mortality beckons us with a boney finger. Our tendency to disregard our own nature in gauging the future is magnified when we daydream about space travel, because advanced technology lures us hubristically to suppose that a patch, a bypass, or an upgrade will become available for every problem we have ever known within an unspecified lapse of time. We will begin all over again in space. We will get everything right.

Of course, we will not. In fact, a realistic look at space travel reveals that it may well seduce us into preferring several disastrous solutions to current controversies. Being a "rugged individualist", and maybe even a "good person", could easily prove more liability than asset in a spaceship, and the strains that assail our common humanity can only multiply in an artificial environment surrounded by death. All things considered, space is a very strange choice of venue to go running away from oneself and looking for heaven's gate.

Here, then, are four volatile "wild cards" that are likely to change the make-believe game we play with the stars, once the hands are actually dealt and the bidding and betting start:

1) Sexual Habits

Space travel could transform human sexuality, or assist in transforming it, into something we would not now recognize as human. It could even annihilate our sexual identity utterly.

Naturally, duties and taboos in these matters have always differed from era to era and from culture to culture. Yet the differences generally orbited a nucleus of consensus throughout human history, and changes within a society's sexual habits used to take several generations. All that was before advanced technology became a major force in shaping attitudes. In my own lifetime, I have witnessed a very straight-laced North American social order dissolve with alarming rapidity (alarming simply for its runaway pace, whatever one might think of the change's vector) into a loose aggregate where the greatest sin appears to be regarding any behavior at all as impermissible. Many have indeed argued that the transformation was driven by the entertainment industry. I find this argument to be somewhat overplayed: movies were in fact quite rigorously censored until the mid-Sixties, and television was self-censoring while the Big Three dominated it. Technology appeared in other, more influential forms. The Pill, the exponentially increasing physical mobility of families, the easy access of teenagers to cars, and other such tech-related factors allowed the stigma of "misbehavior" to be evaded. Sexual pleasure had its way, and the rest of society—including, at last, TV and the movies—yielded to its advance like an edifice of ice submitted to a blazing sun.

The Hollywood spaceship rather quickly flew in formation with the "new morality" (as it was then called), to be sure. Every televised or filmed space adventure from those early years of opened floodgates seems to have had its shapely young cadets in tight-fitting futuristic leotards. To be fair, television remained comparatively tame. Any TV producer who had dared to unleash something like the futuristic soft-porn gamma-sludge of Jane Fonda's *Barbarella* upon prime time would have been sacked on the spot and blackballed from the industry. Yet if such "pimping" was generally more modest and gradual, even among movie-makers, it was also universal—as is quite understandable, from a marketing point of view. The genre attracted (and still attracts) a large proportion of adolescent male viewers, who naturally shared certain preoccupations.

Now let us consider the probable reality of sexual practices in the lives of intergalactic travelers. Will sexual adventures be free and on-demand wherever starships cruise (the obvious preference of the Seventies generation)? Will they be strictly forbidden except within narrowly observed parameters (reflecting the inclinations of a politically correct, sexual-harassment conscious Gen X audience)? Will sexual appetites be satisfied by a few minutes of virtual love-making on a computer (such as Ray Kurzweil seems to have in mind for us all)?

> [The original article carried three color photos at this juncture: one
> of the relatively decorous Lt. Uhuru in the yet-restrained Sixties
> *Star Trek* series, one showing Counselor Troi of the show's
> Seventies version from the waist up in very low-cut livery, and one
> full-length of the voluptuous Seven (Eighties version) wearing a
> uniform that might as well be slightly opaque shrink-wrap. The
> caption reads: *The **Star Trek** version of heavenly bodies. Although
> the blonde bombshell in the latest edition was most provocatively
> marketed (as in this photo), she was also scripted with a semi-
> robotic past and represented as having emotional impairment. In
> her, one glimpses the paradox of the sexual drive's self-
> annihilation."*]

In any work environment—but especially in one where inattention can be as massively fatal as deep space—we must suppose that these Hollywood romances would be severely curtailed. A small group of people critically dependent upon each other in tight quarters for years at a time cannot afford to become involved in love triangles or secret jealousies. A focus upon any interest, in fact, capable of competing with official duties would be actively discouraged. Sex—including the mere contemplation of the sex act, as through pornography—can become obsessive to the point that it acquires certain attributes of an addiction. Functional starships would not likely tolerate the presence of many such people in the engine room or on the bridge. A single one would be enough to create catastrophe.

Our hyper-efficient, tech-intensive, star-hopping descendants would therefore have to handle the "problem" of sex in one of a very few ways. These occur to me at the moment:

> a) Each crew member would be issued a robotic bedmate; the Japanese, I
> am told, are blazing a trail in this line of production.
> b) Pills or injections would be available to govern hormone levels so that
> the "urge" would never become a nuisance.
> c) People of the future would simply be neutered; their extended lives
> would render regeneration all but unnecessary, and such "replacements"
> as were required could be engineered to precise specifications in a
> laboratory setting.

None of these options, of course, is in the least romantic. Yet, ironically, our own age's celebration of sex as among life's purest sensual pleasures and comforts, like lemon meringue pie or a favorite wine, seems to lead inexorably to one or another of such termini. Once the pleasure is reified as an "it" (*la chose*, as the French say), it becomes susceptible to being discreetly bottled or packaged—in this case, via computer or robot. It is dehumanized. It must be so, because the human element—the involvement, the entanglement, the "love"—will threaten that efficiency upon which our futuristic society constantly relies. That this "greatest of life's pleasures" might thus become the most persistent and annoying of life's burdens is more than plausible. At least in the "starship" scenario, the transformation of sex into a major nuisance appears to me all but inevitable; for why endure the negligence of a chief engineer who lingers abed with his robo-geisha when a neutered dynamo of ability, himself more robot than person, might scarcely even need sleep itself, let alone recreation?

That depressing contemplative, Epicurus, observed long ago that all pleasures are succeeded by pains, and that the greatest pleasure is thus the absence of pain—the static serenity of a neutral *ataraxia*. This is ultimately the creed of a robotic world, humming right along and checking off its daily tasks. Sex runs the risk of inducing passion, and passion can inspire love, and love can generate no end of longing and worry. Great pains, one and all: the ship runs more smoothly without them.

Having mentioned incidentally both lemon meringue pie and Epicurus (who is wrongly but inextricably associated with fine dining), I should add that everything in this section might be extended from sex to eating. The pause from purposeful labor for the sake of time-wasteful eating at least twice every work-day introduces gross inefficiency into our spaceship world. People can also become fixated on their favorite food, and perhaps addicted to it. We should anticipate, therefore, that meals will be consumed in a matter of seconds from plastic wrappers, or else that something like a literal battery within the robo-human will be recharged during rest. This is not even to figure into our calculation the huge amount of onboard capacity redeemed from bulky storage.

The attitude that future societies will adopt toward sexual behavior will send ripples throughout other areas of personal bonding and commitment. One is challenged to imagine, for instance, what kind of world might evolve should "expressions of sexuality" be wholly "liberated" from child-bearing and -rearing. Indeed, what future adults would be produced where the very notion of childhood had become, perhaps, a merely clinical concern over growing the "best" child in a lab (as we grow the best tomatoes in a highly engineered hothouse)? What would life be like without the parent-child connection? What would people live for, or die for? We are only beginning to face such questions at this historical moment. By the time the Space Age brings their terms fully into focus, they will already have been answered.

I might share, in a final aside about hybrid beings, an observation that dissolves the most telling criticism of "alien visitor" advocacy: i.e., that no alien competent enough to fly to earth would permit his UFO to be seen against his will—and, if he willed exposure, he would have found a more direct and expressive way to declare himself. An alien UFO (if such things exist) would very probably be piloted by a robot or a bio-robotic hybrid: a creature-creation ageless and sexless, undisturbed by sexual appetite, unencumbered by children. As a deliberate manufacture, this intelligence would likely not have been programmed to handle the dizzying diversity of situations that evolve around planet Earth. A certain amount of ineptitude in his/its response, generated by a brain whose excessive "efficiency" cannot accommodate a chaotic degree of contingency, would be entirely understandable. It would even be something that we should expect.

2) Self-Defense

The manner in which the human being views him- or herself as an individual partaking of a social existence critically affects the formation of broader social units. Is this individual an individualist, or a cog in a machine? Some will surely be offended if I suggest that the right to self-defense—and the insistence on having means to avail oneself of that right effectively—are a measure of this psychic state. Unlike issues involving sexual behavior, questions of self-defense have elicited very strong responses from either polarity of opinion in our time, leaving little evidence of a middle ground or a gradual slide from one direction to the other. American citizens are "caving in" on sexual issues: on self-defense issues, they are "digging in". That is, they either believe with conviction in their right to use the deadly force of a handgun (say) in protecting their person from a brutal aggressor, or else they believe with equal conviction that this "right" is a barbarity. Of course, defenders of the latter option would not suppose themselves to be willfully surrendering their lives to The Collective as a fanatic would fling his body under a juggernaut. They argue, for instance, that a 911 call will bring expert help within the minute or so between the bedroom window's shattering and a dark figure's shaking out glass shards on the carpet; or else they so trust in the basic rationality of all humans that they imagine something like Chinua Achebe's "scientific robbers", who politely take everything at gunpoint and leave.

To say the least, this is a highly paradoxical attitude in people whose political ideology otherwise teaches them to view police as arrogant, mindless Nazis serving corrupt bourgeois paymasters. No doubt, the desire to be confident of one's safety is so strong that one will subconsciously embrace opinions contradictory to one's philosophy, all for the sake of a good night's sleep.

My intent is not to paint advocates of gun-ownership, in contrast, as rugged individualists. Yet it must surely be true that people who will actively resist physical assault tend to have a stronger sense of self (even when that sense is unwholesome) than do people whose reflexive response is the fetal position. Therefore, the eventual resolution of these self-defense issues in the coming years is bound to affect what sort of human we at last export to the rest of the galaxy. Reciprocally, as we contemplate sending humans off to colonize planets, the degree of freedom we allow them to protect their individual person against violent aggression will modify our views about such situations here on Earth.

The most popular space epics of our electronic age (going back to the radio days of Buck Rogers) have displayed a truly laughable predilection for a model of the cowboy's Colt .45 adapted to shoot death rays. The weapon is usually slung at the hip, and its owners apparently have to exhibit a certain amount of marksmanship if they are to neutralize their target. When I was an undergraduate, I recall a standing joke among my small circle of upstarts about the original *Star Trek*'s being a direct spin-off of *Bonanza*. Captain Kirk, clearly, was the patriarchal Ben Cartwright, and his elite entourage was the band of "sons" with widely differing characters and levels of maturity. The transporter beam provided hooves and horsepower to penetrate each new planet's Indian reservation or den of thieves. To say that Mr. Sulu was the Chinese cook Hop-Sing would certainly be a bridge too far (not to mention a magnet for "racism" accusations); but the *Enterprise* gang did, in fact, join Wyatt Earp at the OK Corral in one episode.

[Here the original article offers a photo of William Shatner's
Captain Kirk standing in the dusty street of a Western town after
some species of time-travel. He is surrounded by Spock, Chekhov,
McCoy, and Scott, all of them wearing sixguns with (for good
measure) holster straps tied. A marquis across the street reads
"saloon". The caption runs: *The **Enterprise**'s crew limbers up for a
gunfight at the OK Corral.*]

These absurdities spoke to the times, to be sure. Americans still viewed themselves as self-asserting individuals; and if they thought of space travel at all, they cast it in images of The Way West ("space: the final frontier" was a phrase also poured over each *Trek* episode's signature christening). The *Enterprise*, granted, had standing orders not to interfere in whatever planetary cultures it might encounter—as if the mere appearance of a starship would not permanently alter a primitive belief system. We Americans seem to have carried well into the twenty-first century the same naïve notion that we can beam our soldiers into alien settings, do a good deed, and beam away again without altering the cultural landscape. The pioneers didn't really think that their farms, which claimed only "unused" land, did the native peoples any harm, either.

So just how accurate is the *Bonanza* version of self-defense as we contemplate the future? Merely from a technical standpoint, it is of course ridiculous (and Luke Skywalker's comet-sword is so, *a fortiori*). The very essence of technology is to reduce reliance upon the individual user's skill.

Weapons of the future must be no less effective in the klutz's hands than in the black-belt shootist's. (Indeed, the Colt .45 was popularly dubbed the "equalizer" because, with one in hand, a man no longer had to be big and strong to stand his ground.) If star-travelers of the future have personal weapons at all, then, these must be virtually self-operating. Perhaps the user will flip down an eyepiece, which will read the point where he rivets his gaze for three seconds and then discharge a laser as he flicks his eyeball up to the red "fire" button. A child could do it. A child, for that matter, could pick off the galactic high command one by one if he were hiding under a tablecloth.

And herein lies the problem. One might formulate that the potential dangers of any defensive technology used abusively are directly proportional to its foreseen advantages. What happens if a child—or a psychopath—does indeed gain possession of the monocle-laser? How many stalwart peace-officers must be lost before the rampage ends? No doubt, human beings will always perceive a need for force; but a specific instrument of force, capable of being physically removed from its proper setting, becomes ever more troublesome as the technology of force becomes more sophisticated. The imaginative solution floated in *The Day the Earth Stood Still* (Robert Wise version) is that the biggest of ray-guns, manned by robots whose programming is tamper-proof, will cleanly, instantly annihilate any planet's inhabitants whose misbehavior rises to unacceptable levels. In other words, disarm every soft-tissued being permanently, and let a robot be judge, jury, and executioner.

This solution is naïve from several perspectives (e.g., anything that can be programmed can be reprogrammed); yet it credibly follows the vector of modern thinking on the subject. The probable twenty-second century answer to the question of force is apt to deal out irrevocable destruction upon its target once activated and to do so in an antiseptic, almost low-key manner (resulting in "ethnectomy", one might say: surgical removal of an entire people). Major political powers have been covertly playing with Extremely Low Frequency Waves (yielding the exquisite acronym, ELF Waves) for about two decades now. The idea is to bounce the waves off the stratosphere from immense transmitter-stations in such as way as to affect the global circulation of weather systems. Potentially, an adversary population could be flooded or starved into submission. China, Russia, and the US all have such stations. One must wonder just how much of our peculiar weather in recent years is owed to the "sighting in" of these wave-blasters—as our leaders, all the while, lecture us about the impact of our lifestyle upon climate.

Our leaders—the wise ones, the Mandarins, the central nervous ganglion, the brain: here we find the counterpoise to the rogue lunatic with a ray-gun. *Quis custodes custodiet?*—"Who will guard the guards?" If Starfleet Command is trusted to dispense force at the right time and in the right measure, then who will watch over Starfleet Command's understanding of the word "right"? And if the perceived solution is to deliver such decisions into the circuitry of a master-computer, how confident are we that an inhuman, inorganic data-processing machine—though it be the most elaborate thing of its kind ever created—can handle all possible contingencies as we would like? Or are we, precisely, trying to disarm and neutralize our "likes"—do we now (or will we soon) view our own humanity as inferior and dangerous?

The way that we address the issue of personal self-defense today, I repeat, must determine the answer to such broader questions tomorrow. If the individual is not worth defending, as a mere tiny appendage upon the vast body of a starship fleet—or if he will have been programmed to believe that the High Command is his safest, surest defense, even though the threat looms imminent—then the implied value of individual contributions to other aspects of life will diminish incalculably. A man alone who defends his life with his own resources regards himself as worth keeping around: the same man who waits for an impersonal data bank to deliver help has accepted that The Collective can and should deploy him as it chooses. The former writes poetry that only he could write, paints watercolors that only he could paint, conceives of a bridge that no one else would conceive of. The latter can be replicated in any lab where they assemble sophisticated robots.

3) Incidental Biochemical Changes

If the two previous wild cards lurking in our destiny's deck come quickly to the top after any shuffle—and are even the source of loud controversy these days—the next factor is indeed a mystery card. In particular cases, it has brought human begins to their graves without its presence ever having been suspected. No one really understood the durability and toxicity of nuclear fallout when the bombs that ended World War II were dropped: the scientists who worked on the Manhattan Project were themselves taken by surprise. No one divined the risks of working around asbestos before a sequence of untimely, painful deaths illustrated them years later. No one fully grasped the liabilities of pesticides until after many seasons of liberal use. No one thought that a connection between automobile exhaust and emphysema might evolve years after we had overhauled our cities to cater to car traffic. To this day, we cannot seem to obtain impartial, non-politicized assessments about the possible effects of such pollutants upon climate—but we readily believe, in the wake of so many other unpleasant surprises, that significant effects might exist. And so we race to embrace solar power, blissfully unaware (once again) that the "rare earth elements" used in coating solar panels create "cancer villages" (as they are locally known) in the Third World nations that permit such toxic substances to be mined; or at the very least, we lurch more insistently toward electronic sources of power, as if less visible forms of energy must be less malign.

A few short years ago, an urban legend circulated that homeowners through whose back yards ran large power lines were falling prey to cancer at unnatural rates. Similar claims were made about frequent cell-phone users and brain cancer. Studies have since dismissed these fears for the most part; yet persistent anecdotal evidence continues to unnerve many, and the role often played by "scientific studies" in covering up threats posed by hazardous by-products while this or that industry keeps on marketing its toxins has left us all rather cynical. Forewarned is not always forearmed, however. Whistle-blowing can itself become an industry: there is money to be made by convincing people that one commodity will shorten their lives if a "harmless" alternative can be hawked in its place.

And so the manipulation proceeds apace. I have made no secret in other publications of my own concern over our environment's being saturated around the clock with electromagnetic radiation—and I mean our home environment, even our kitchens and bedrooms. Of any relatively new technology, we should remember two commonplaces before perching it on our rib cage or sticking it in our mouths: 1) dangerous side-effects are almost always unforeseeable—we not only lack sufficient keenness of vision to look far down the road, but we also don't know which road to look down; and 2) the specialists on whose judgment we are increasingly forced to rely as technology grows ever more arcane can be bought or browbeaten by entities with conflicting interests. Our march into high-tech progress is inevitably a walk through a mine field.

With such anxiety astir even when we consider developments of the past few decades, how could we possibly predict what state our descendants will be in as they disembark upon an alien planet? All the many *Star Trek* generations manage to happen only upon planets with breathable, healthy oxygen, of course (and with inhabitants who speak English); but when our own air here on Earth has grown so undependable, what chance does our species have of breathing more freely on Zarkon? Since our real-life space traveler will almost certainly have to wear something like an aqua-lung and/or consume pills that neutralize atmospheric toxins, will his "success" in hostile surroundings not move bright minds to argue that it should be replicated here on Earth? Will we or our descendants, that is, not be popping more pills in the future as an alternative to demanding cleaner air?

Quite apart from any given planet's unique bacteria and poisons, what alterations would these space-pioneers have endured while in transit? We already know that astronauts must be elaborately protected from radiation once the earth's atmosphere no longer shields them, and also that something approaching terrestrial gravity must be generated in a space station if their bones are not to grow brittle. What other Band-aids must be applied to opening wounds? If these intrepid travelers are being dosed to reduce their sexual libido, what are the effects of being so dosed? If they absorb virtually all of their nourishment from pills and drinks, what are the long-term effects upon the human gut of relative inactivity? If they are negotiating the interstellar transit with the help of induced hibernation, what consequences does that state have later upon the waking organism? If they are given a drug just to get their night's sleep, how many such drugs can they take, night after night?

For space has no day and no night, in terrestrial terms. Circadian rhythms will go topsy-turvy. Even with adequate sleep, how will the crew react to having no real sunlight, perhaps year after year? What about the effects of existing in the same honeycomb of corridors for months on end, knowing all the while that instant death awaits just beyond the humming walls? Will the walls hum? One imagines that the craft's vast engines will create some background or other of steady noise. What psychological impact will this steady background have? What cost must be paid for never hearing a bird, never hearing complete silence, never hearing the same sounds within a variety of changing distances?

A certain amount of selective breeding—of genetic engineering—might precede the first long space ventures, and its justification could be primarily logistical. Size would clearly be a concern: smaller is better, on several counts. Hollywood will never recognize this, of course. Audiences like to "look up" to their epic heroes, so every generation of star-travelers that inherits the *Enterprise* seems taller and more strapping than the last. Sigourney Weaver, for that matter, is probably one of the tallest leading ladies in film history. Big bodies, however, consume more oxygen, more food, and more chair- and bunk-space. They are a distinct liability when vital resources are very precious. The so-called "grays" who, rumor has it, stalk from the UFOs visiting our deserts and pastures regularly are never reckoned at much over three feet. This much, at least, has the ring of truth.

To be sure, deliberately engineered biological change would not qualify as incidental—but it could certainly produce incidents, and a chemical like adrenaline might be implicated in these. In other words, it could ruffle feathers. (I am assuming that the smaller body's greater susceptibility to environmental stresses like extreme temperatures would pose few problems for technology, though in some sort of critical hardware failure the issue might arise.) The disparagement of short stature, especially in competitive situations requiring old-fashioned virtues like strength, appears to be instinctive in our species. If our future astronauts were dwarves, how might their marginal status among earthbound humans affect the attitude that they carried with them into space? Would they be generally viewed as an inferior race of lackeys—as trained dogs and dolphins are today by the military, perhaps, enjoying a "pet" status but not regarded as fully human? Would they therefore develop a compensatory kind of belligerence—a hair-trigger meant to reverse a dismissive first impression? Might not this acquired attribute jeopardize missions that demand tact? Or might our space dwarves, on the other hand, prove less than loyal servants to Mother Earth after she had bred them to be puny? Would they feel victimized, put upon? If asked to incubate the embryos of "normal" humans for transplantation onto new planets as colonists, would they balk at the task? Would they throw the babies out with the bathwater?

The problem is that we cannot know the problem—not before it appears starkly in our face, full-blown and perhaps lethal. This is true today, right now, in all of our relationships with sophisticated technology. Covering up symptoms with medication so that body and mind seem to continue plugging along for a while is one kind of risk: we almost always find, of course, that the day of reckoning has only been postponed. But what about problems that crop up too suddenly to be medicated—psychological problems, especially? In the tight quarters of a spaceship, an emotional eruption might ignite a catastrophic chain-reaction throughout the crew. One person says one word too many, or just the word that another person doesn't want to hear; a fight breaks out, other crewmen take sides… not a recipe for success.

We know stress all too well from our terrestrial routine of navigating rush hours, answering electronic prompts instantly, multi-tasking without ever having a free ten minutes all day to get up and stroll… in some ways, we have already created a spacecraft environment around ourselves. Many such perils involve not the positive activity—the presence—of a toxin or pollutant, but the negative activity—the absence—of a formerly routine circumstance taken too much for granted. The space traveler can prepare himself somewhat for the shock of entering a new and hostile environment… but how does he prepare himself for the realization that he will never again see his old home in recognizable form, even if he returns to Earth? How do *we* prepare ourselves for the same shock, as our cities devour the scenes where we grew up and the sites where our culture's history roots?

The very real threat of psychological stress, especially, is yet another indicator that big-time space travelers will be more robot than human. The depression and irrational resentment that are almost certain to assail any thoughtful human being in such a setting will obtain no hold upon the artificial intelligence. Yet such freedom from "a bad day" must come at a cost. Precisely because so many of advanced technology's drawbacks are unpredictable—precisely because the very nature of all this "miracle gear" is to thrust us into situations never known to anyone before—creativity will be essential for survival. Just how creative is a robot capable of being? The well-groomed, level-headed cyber-denizens of this warp-drive wonderland may find that they can live neither with us nor without us.

By that time, however, we may have come to resemble them so much that we, too, will no longer "suffer the anguish" of an active imagination. For as we make our own planet more alien to common humanity, disorientation and alienation will grow more frequent and intense; and as they do so, we will seek relief more keenly in whatever kind of "deprogramming" or "disengagement" liberates us from the torture.

[The original article featured the following caption below the photo therein described: *Marvin the Paranoid Android (of* **Hitchhiker's Guide to the Galaxy** *fame) demonstrates the inconvenience of* *personality in space travel, his makers having imprudently endowed him with human-like bouts of depression. "Life... hate it!"*]

4) Existential Panic

Several of the hypothetical situations above involving stress might be thought to represent panic. This would be a mistake, or at least a misunderstanding of how I intend the word. A space traveler nagged by insomnia, irritated that his attractive co-pilot is cold-shouldering him, and frustrated that he can't get away for a long walk might erupt into an irrational outburst. Behavior of such a sort could indeed be traced largely to various chemical imbalances, though we may like to think of it as the spontaneous overflow of powerful feeling. What I have in mind presently is much more on the order of an attitude, and almost a philosophy. It abides in suppressed form, this emotional transport, asserting itself with particular force at particular moments. Call it fear of the void, or perhaps *chasmophobia*. Certainly the view out any window of the spacecraft would be filled with vast black nothingness, the pinpricks of starlight only emphasizing the abyss in which they float. Like any phobia, this one could be controlled through will power much of the time; yet its spring would always be coiled, and a careless or overwrought emotional state indulged for an instant could suffice to unleash a kind of swoon—a vertigo of values in utter chaos.

Does the scenario seem melodramatic? Should we smile at the suggestion that seasoned pilots highly trained in the applied sciences would have constantly to fight down a creeping terror on the margin of their consciousness? I think not, considering how visible such a state is here on Planet Earth. Throughout my lifetime, I have often been struck by how many respected scientific minds lurch shamelessly into a degrading mysticism without apparent motivation, belying their proclaimed values and grasping at windblown straws. Carl Sagan was perhaps the most spectacular of these. His groundbreaking television documentary *Cosmos* was a kind of *De Rerum Natura* for the Seventies generation, meticulously detailing how matter has labored to create everything we see, and everything we can and will ever see. Yet the final segments of the serial inexplicably opted to revere in Hindu cosmology a source of truth as valid and profound, it seemed, as science. I do not mean to imply that belief in the Hindu system degrades an intelligent mind, but rather to observe that an exponent of the scientific worldview betrays his calling when—as a scientist—he retreats to such a system. For that matter, the Roman Epicurean Lucretius's lyrical hymn to Venus in the otherwise atheistic opus cited above belongs to the same category of betrayal. A materialist who presumes to advise us that all reality may be materially explained has no business jumping ship when the Mayan calendar or the stellar orientation of Stonehenge passes close by. If science can explain everything, then let it explain these curiosities, as well.

Why do such people do such things? Another, much more recent documentary on the Discovery Channel titled *The Pyramid Code* rightly calls into question how Egyptologists date and attribute function to the ancient pyramids. Indeed, the basic matter of how so many huge stones could have been moved for miles and then hefted high up has never been answered. Here as in the case of Stonehenge, the distinct possibility exists that electromagnetic radiation was tapped in a mysterious but highly effective manner. Anyone who attends the evidence is forced to conclude that ancient Egyptians were far more advanced than we moderns, with our arrogant assumption of history's having steadily scaled to our present lofty plateau of enlightenment, are willing to grant.

So be it: point taken, and very well made. Why, though, the need to conclude this series, too, by implying that ancient Egyptians and Mayan priests and various other shamanic cultures successfully read the book of history by studying the stars—that they were true "erchomenologists", in fact, and that the entire path of our species is mapped out deterministically in the Milky Way? Whose shamanic leaves were these filmmakers smoking?

According to Andrew Collins in *The Cygnus Mystery*, Sagan was smoking marihuana, as was Francis Crick when a vision of the yet undiscovered DNA double helix appeared to him. Collins's book chimes in, arguing that our distant alien progenitors must have embedded knowledge of themselves and the broader universe in our "junk DNA" which is released when we "get high". The insights Collins provides into the alignment of the most ancient human structures ever unearthed with significant stellar objects are welcome. Yet why, I repeat, the unmotivated odyssey to Lotos Land?

The frequency with which good scientific minds "defect" to fantastical, cultic beliefs is so pronounced that one cannot dismiss it as an aberration. One may even dare to propose that the defection happens not in spite of scientific training, but because of it. The empirical mind, having once boxed itself into a manner of viewing reality which allows no god to descend into the machine on any metaphysical contraption, appears to grow claustrophobic at some point (for the flip-side of void-phobia may well be its opposite: the abyss threatens because the box that preceded it squeezed). Perhaps, too, a kind of vanity is involved: perhaps the scientist, having found that his analysis never manages to solve the ultimate questions, would rather crown his work with irrationality than admit that he had never really taken the problem's full measurements. At any rate, this climactic thrill of the whirling dervish should not surprise us if it happens to break forth in a cosmic investigation's critical moments. And if we are trying to predict the probable course of our species' expansion into the stars, it should probably scare us.

The delirium I have described may seem more like ecstasy than panic (though panic, classically speaking, is a variety of ecstasy). In a Starfleet officer more pedestrian than Carl Sagan, however, it might indeed manifest as "the shakes". Popular representations of space travel, it appears to me, have fared miserably at visualizing the psychological impact of being very far— interminably far—from home in a cramped artificial environment surrounded by a vacuum at absolute zero and embarked on a mission to do… to do what? What could possibly justify such sacrifice, once one is actually paying it out with the prime of one's life? Yet I do not want to lead this imaginary drama back in the direction of chronic depression, for we have considered that. A pill and rest might do the trick on a bad day. No; once again, the psychic state I am struggling to represent would be steady. It would forever seek an answer, consciously or unconsciously, to the question, "Why?"

If human beings do not believe in a metaphysical system which ranks moral duty as the supreme motive of any mission (which explains, "Why this trip to Alpha Centauri?" for instance, with the answer, "To do good for other beings"), then drifting through the void may inspire them with some very weird ideas. The double helix or a code hidden in junk DNA will be the least of these. If I were myself writing a science-fiction story, it would seek a precedent at this point, not in the cave of an Inca shaman, but in the madness of Pizarro's lieutenant, Aguirre (powerfully portrayed in Werner Herzog's *Aguirre, The Wrath of God*). Leading his men deeper and deeper into the alien terrain of Amazonia until they all perish, Aguirre is driven by more than fantasies of gold. He imagines himself perched on a throne from which he will rule half the globe and siring an eternal dynasty upon his daughter (who has insanely been dragged along with the expedition). Once we fancy ourselves visited by little gray aliens acting as angels—once our fevered brains suppose that a force beyond good and evil has whispered a message empowering any elite ear that can hear it—then all the atrocities of hell may break loose. Why should a mind drunk on stars hesitate to vaporize one small planet's idiot population that refuses to get with the program?

Should such sick delirium be awaiting our descendants in deep space, then we really would be better off—morally better—sending robots. Our nightmarish twentieth century has graphically illustrated what a despotic leader is capable of who has staggering technical abilities to destroy and, in a panic over the godless universe's emptiness, elects himself to fill the vacant role. Whether this type is more Aguirre or more Klatu's robotic annihilator Gort, he isn't functionally human. So… so perhaps star-crazed ecstasy and robotic nullity are the same thing, and it will make no difference in the future whether the finger on the trigger is flesh or kryptonite.

[A photo appears in the original article at this point showing Herzog's lunatic conquistador facing his minions commandingly as he shakes a captive monkey in his fist. The caption reads: *Aguirre (Klaus Kinski) loses patience with one of an alien world's disrespectful inhabitants in his mad quest of gold and empire.*]

Conclusion: Our Future May Not Be Our Own

Perhaps my comments strike some as the alarmist pessimism of a typical enemy of progress. Sexual morals (these critics may protest) have always been somewhat fluent in modern societies, susceptible to sudden shifts as an economy or a mass-residential arrangement or a religious/ethnic factor changes. The parameters of self-defense are being hotly contested right now, and opposed advocates are clearly not awaiting any new direction from the Space Age to stake their claims. An equilibrium will emerge when certain disruptive elements settle down. We know, too, all about the lurking hazards of a highly artificial environment, even if we do not know the particular threat inherent in the latest artifice. A low-grade rasp of existential terror—or of "the jitters", at any rate—is fully audible in high-tech societies already, as well. Space travel should reduce rather than feed such anxiety. Give it time: we'll get everything right.

I doubt it. The very confidence inspired in us by our advanced lifestyle that every little problem can be solved, it seems to me, renders us impatient with small setbacks and traumatized by major disasters. In the back of many minds (and I speak for myself without apology) flits the constant suspicion that the gizmos and gadgetry ever less familiar to most of us—and yet ever more responsible for our basic survival—will malfunction without a trained technician within reach. No words are less welcome to the neurotic twenty-first citizen than, "Nothing could possibly go wrong"; for what these words imply is that the technicians themselves won't know where to begin when the whole system collapses.

If I have focused my lens upon distant planets, then, it was not to raise the specter of problems that do not now exist, but precisely to dramatize how several current problems whose existence we scarcely bother to notice may come clear as the clock runs forward. By that time, in fact, they will no longer be problems; for clarity is beholden to fixity, and a fixed condition is unlikely to be unstitched for examination by the dull authorities who "fixed" it. ("Where there is no solution, there is no problem," Russell Kirk once observed pithily.) I don't suppose the sanguine defenders of unbridled progress will disagree with me that Hollywood and popular culture have absurdly misrepresented our future in space. The onus thereupon shifts to them to demonstrate in what way my warnings have sounded a false alarm. Or is it not alarming to reflect that our great-great-grandchildren may be wholly unrecognizable to us; or though they may remain similar physically, that their habits may seem to us those of well-organized insects?

The same popular culture's recent saturation with "zombies" and "walking dead" suggests to me that, at a subliminal level, we already dread what may be coming. If we ought not to dread it, then why ought we not? Is it because, as Ray Kurzweil answered Bill Joy, the life of a robot isn't really so bad? Or is it because (and this is really another version of the same answer) we could not resist our own technological evolution if we wanted to—that we are hard-wired, as a species, to keep moving in one direction?

But this amounts to saying, contradictorily, that the nature of human nature is to change its foundations—whereas the truth, I believe, is paradoxical: i.e., the nature of human nature is to crave fundamental change without ever finding it. Our species will always want to be something superior to what it is, but it will only ever manage—thanks to this embedded and destructive discontent—to make itself less than its finest moment. In striving to become a race of constantly pleasured immortals who know no strife, we may at last make of ourselves a hive of neutered bees whose bloated queen lives forever on the collective's innumerable, endlessly replaced corpses.

For the exploration of space, like any other high-tech enterprise, will call for increasing centralization of control and diminishing tolerance of the eccentric: zombies, with their lock-step movements, would prove very efficient operatives on a space station. Parts must mesh: participants must be on the same page. Who would design a project to colonize Mars where two teams pursued radically different strategies without any effort at coordination? With so much expense invested in adventures so far away and having so many scarcely known variables, the only sane approach would be to achieve consensus among our most brilliant designers and prepare together for the most likely scenarios.

Personally, I am most worried by the possibility that this common-sense mechanization of effort will be taken as prescriptive of the path which earthbound humans should be following. I have striven to show that we are in fact following it already; but further success in a narrowly technical endeavor such as colonizing planets, far from warning us of undesirable cultural change, will be accepted by most as proof of the change's worthiness. In other words, we may end up allowing—or not allowing—individuals here among us to defend themselves with ray-guns based upon what we would allow a space explorer to do on Planet M-89. If we design a Martian outpost where colonists have robotic sexual partners because it seems to make sense "out there", then we will likely adopt the same lifestyle "down here" because it's obviously the "progressive" way to go. Technology dictates our culture nowadays: it does not ward off threats to that culture or create havens where culture may be infused. When the pioneers settled the West, they slowly but surely imported Eastern ways. Now our technological pioneers determine how we live by transmitting back to us their practices on the frontier.

I have grave misgivings about our ability to distinguish between what's needed on the galactic frontier, where robotic behavior is probably the securest means to the desired end, and what's fitting for civilized human beings. We very well may come to imitate our robots as zealously as youths once imitated their parents.

I do not want to live in that brave new world—and it's pretty clear that Captain Kirk, as little use as I had for his cowboy-in-tights act, didn't want to, either. Most of us, among the low-tech masses, are still attracted to space travel by its prospect of "elbow room": of opportunities, that is, to be creative individuals in a setting where our behavior will not be micromanaged. If I have demonstrated nothing else in this discussion, I hope that I have convinced the reader of the "galactic playground" paradigm's utter folly. Hollywood couldn't be more wrong. Space will become a scene of the most rigid regimentation should we succeed in probing it further. If our notion, therefore, is to recover somewhere in the night's billions of stars those freedoms and that human dignity which we have squandered here on earth, we are cruising at warp-speed toward a very bitter disappointment.

On Outlasting the Life Cycle of the Technology-Intensive Economy

*First published in **Praesidium** 16.3 (Summer 2016).*

I. Chaco Canyon: A Case Study

The prehistoric inhabitants of Chaco Canyon, in northwestern New Mexico, authored a technological breakthrough early in the second Christian millennium: irrigation. Called the Anasazi, these peaceful farmers must have observed the abundance of water that poured from the canyon's high cliffs during rare cloudbursts. They must have reasoned that trapping and channeling their area's most precious resource could advance them significantly in the struggle to survive. And so it did. They formed settlements so as to concentrate their efforts, worked together to spread water through their fields, and were eventually harvesting such surpluses that their central township—christened Pueblo Bonito by later explorers—housed huge storage rooms within its crescent-shaped, multi-storied outer structure. The finely wrought masonry of this desert Camelot, housing perhaps a thousand residents, would largely endure under shifting sands until excavation began about a century ago.

Chacoan civilization itself would prove far more fragile. In fact, despite evidence of extensive roads and watch towers suggesting a prosperous trade network, the whole complex arrangement had unraveled by 1200 A.D. Was it because the Chacoans' very prosperity had drawn depredation upon them from ruthless neighbors like the Aztecs? Did the stored grain attract rodents and other vermin that spread plague? Did the people, squeezed into uncomfortably close proximity by urbanization, take to fighting among themselves in competition for new honors and richer profits? Did a tyrannical political system exploit the masses of ever more specialized and dependent city-dwellers who would kiss whatever hand held the key to the granary?

Whatever the ultimate moral of the Chacoan tale's unknown dénouement may be, the ill-starred adventure is already in many ways a morality play about the human struggle. We develop technologies that allow us to reduce back-breaking, time-consuming labor; since these technologies require collaboration to create or operate, we form settlements; collaboration leads to specialization, since some people do some jobs particularly well—some of us became stonemasons or tribal runners rather than ditch-diggers or savvy planters; advanced settlements become scenes of grand spectacle and petty amusement as we allocate our increased leisure to more pleasant pursuits; the provision of luxury and amusement itself turns to gainful employ, producing a wide array of new specializations; a market economy emerges, perhaps based on barter

199

but pioneering the use of currency in more sophisticated examples; urban-dwelling specialists are at last wholly dependent upon sales or wages, since their ties to the land have been severed and the marketplace has disrupted the notion that crops are communally owned; social classes define themselves, their boundaries posed less by the logic of what the community most needs than by the relative popularity of labor's product; and so on, and so on.

The immensely complex evolution that I have squeezed above into one long sentence only crudely observes the sequence that I have traced. Many developments are concurrent, or else overlap in a way that sets the start of one well before the finish of another. My purpose is not to represent with precise accuracy a chain of events that a book would be hard pressed to lay out, but merely to show that a chain of sorts exists. Naturally, where you have a chain, you have links; and where you have links, you have the possibility of rupture. The "advance" to civilization can run off the tracks at any one of perhaps dozens of critical junctures. It is worthwhile listing a few of these, most of them already implicit in the Chaco mystery.

Geological or meteorological catastrophe can spoil everything. An earthquake, a volcanic eruption, a tsunami, or (as may very well have happened in the case of Chaco) a prolonged drought may effectively exterminate the political, economic, and social order within great walls, if not the walls themselves.

Epidemic disease may do the same. Archaeological evidence of such events is extremely hard to come by. The speculation that Pueblo Bonito, with its huge storage chambers and concentrated population, may have been the Petrie dish for some rodent-borne contagion is entirely my own; but we need hardly prove that people are more apt to sicken with transmissible illnesses when they live closer together, and especially when they also travel frequently to other communities (as in commercial activity).

Rich settlements make rich targets. Christy Turner's highly controversial book *Man Corn* (1999) proposed that the Anasazi were brutally dominated by the Aztecs, who may well have employed (according to Turner's reading of forensic evidence) ritual cannibalism as a means of terrorizing these merchant-farmers. Wars have winners and losers, and often only losers. Neither Athens nor Sparta would ever enjoy the same cultural dynamism and moral clarity after the Peloponnesian Wars as it had known before them; and we see more plainly on every gray morning of our twenty-first century that the two world wars of its predecessor have undermined all the nations of Western Europe.

We don't know the details of Anaszai religion, but the bowl-shaped kivas characterizing the entire region (including tiny outlier settlements) strongly suggest solar worship. The Great Kiva in Pueblo Bonito features a tunnel by which the priest would manage to appear abruptly in the center of the amphitheater, like the sun rising from the earth. Sometimes religious practices can be spliced into the political power structure in ways that stabilize the ruling elite but also demoralize the general populace. Whether or not the Aztecs cannibalized the Anasazi, their horrendous custom of eviscerating maidens on a vast scale would not seem to lay the foundation of a durable society. Certainly Islam managed to mold a robust political unit in a miraculously brief span out of various local systems trapped for centuries in a petty tribalism; but it has also suffered in our own time (and as far back as the dawning of the West's Industrial Revolution) from a political hardening of the arteries, and one challenged to describe any major Islamic state today as a vibrant civilization.

If religion can be the means of political oppression, it is but one such means. I cannot help but wonder how the rituals experienced in the Chaco Canyon's outlying kivas would have differed from those in Pueblo Bonito's Great Kiva. The sheer numbers involved in urban existence change everything. Crowds become more unruly and volatile. Control of their behavior is necessarily less a matter of appealing to an inherited sense of decorum (which usually works in a tribal setting) and much more a matter of sheer terror. With large settlements come brutal tyrants. Rural/agrarian populations do not elect fascist dictators: urban/industrial populations do. Yet the despot who rules the people only by trampling them under the hooves of his cavalry is not secure in his power, as Machiavelli's little book often reminds us; the best plan is to mingle brief, bloody episodes of punishment with other, longer episodes of largesse. In the absence of such statecraft, eras of strongmen merely succeed each other. Dense populations are readily manipulable. They can be formed into an army upon a promise of rich plunder or whipped into a rebellious fever over abuses suffered under a declining autocrat. When such tides of dominion become systematized (as, for instance, in the Chinese imperial dynasties), they can impose atrophy upon a civilization's creative vigor for generations, centuries, or perhaps millennia.

II. Urban vs. Rural: Health and Safety

The fragile links of any evolving civilization are so numerous that I believe they must call into question our progressive society's complacent truism about the superiority of the city to the farm. Any good citizen of the twenty-first century West will immediately protest that our medical technology gives us an inarguable and incalculable advantage. If the diseases and complaints from which humans suffered were uniform in kind and frequency throughout history (and pre-history), this would be sound reasoning; but such is not the case. Predominantly agrarian populations did not need clever strategies for fighting cancer because industrial wastes had not so polluted their diet that cancer constantly stalked them all. They did not require sophisticated protocols for handling heart disease because manual labor kept them fit and an unmechanized pace of life reduced their stress. Except for ritual purposes—and then often only for a select few—intoxicants and hallucinogens were rarely consumed. The relatively short lifespan of yesteryear's yeomen has a lot more to do with childbed fever (gravely affecting female life expectancy), poor hygiene leading to inflated infant mortality rates, and the daily use of large animals or heavy equipment in labor (jeopardizing the adult male demographic) than with anything inherently unwholesome about the farm. With a very few technological fixes and a small dose of education, the tombstones of country churchyards could have had considerably more generous dates on them.

The contemporary city, on the other hand, seems to immerse us in more poisons the more it "progresses". Its accommodation of our biological rhythms is so stinting that a permanent merger of human and robot is seriously being proposed for the near future ever more often. As long as we continue to concentrate tens of millions of people in population centers, furthermore, we will see mutant "superbugs" springing up faster than our laboratories can create antidotes. The ease and rapidity of modern transportation will ensure, besides, that any new contagion will spread within days from major cities to remote towns. These are not high-risk conditions that a little fresh knowledge and hardware might resolve; they are, on the contrary, the suffocating "bottleneck effect" of a way of life that looks distinctly suicidal as its logical consequences play out.

Surely, however, the contemporary urban lifestyle is far safer than life on the frontier, where predators human and animal ruthlessly preyed upon the poor plowman and the frail milkmaid. In the popular mind (with much encouragement from Hollywood), our pioneer-progenitors led a life fraught with sudden and mortal peril. Indian attack, molestation by wandering hoodlums, ambush by mountain lion and rattlesnake… survival on the frontier must have been no better than a day-to-day proposition. Yet this lurid portrait turns out to be highly melodramatized when one adds truthful historical detail. Tocqueville dutifully recorded the observation of American settlers that buffalo would permanently flee an entire region as soon as they heard a belled cow; and where the buffalo went, most of the semi-nomadic natives would follow. Mounted hooligans, where they existed, would also have found the odds stacked against them. Every member of a frontier household knew how to shoot; and with the first bay of the loyal family hound at the approach of something unknown, three or four hands around the cabin would have reached for rifles. If the stranger were a cougar or a black bear, the dog's bellow alone would probably have sent it scampering.

The closest replication of the "endangered homesteader" scenario would have appeared in border states during the Civil War, when jayhawkers and bushwhackers burned and plundered under the guise of military service. Often ununiformed, sometimes displaying distinct signs of what we would call sociopathic behavior, these itinerant partisans were in fact the product, not of living on the wilderness's edge, but of grinding an urban/industrial economy's demands against a rural/agrarian economy's. The former community (i.e., the Union) was generally better equipped to impose its will, and would continue to do so in more regular mounted actions against the Plains Indians after the war.

The most sanguinary Indian engagements, then, were likewise precipitated by urban interests hidden beyond the eastern horizon (specifically and especially, by an industrial hunger for mined metals and a commercial thirst for the trade opportunities created by transcontinental railroads). But for gold, the Trail of Tears and the Sand Creek Massacre would never have happened; but for the wickedly clever policy of selling homesteads in a checkerboard pattern along railway routes, there would likely never have been a Wounded Knee.

Today's metropolitan centers are indeed quite dangerous by almost any historical measure. As many as 50,000 Americans die in a given year simply from traffic accidents. Gang activity has achieved a lethality in many major cities that equals or surpasses a Saturday night in an old mining town's corridor of saloons and brothels. Inhabitants of trouble-spots like Jefferson, Missouri, tend to vote in favor of gun-control advocates, as if young gangsters might be disarmed by ink on a page; yet they sometimes claim to be just as fearful of the police who patrol their streets, even as they complain that patrols are too few. If a Comanche had visited your ranch under cover of darkness, he would have made straight for the horses in your corral; when bullets fly through an infant's bedroom in a marginal neighborhood as a drive-by shooter sprays an urban block, they have no particular target or objective. The Comanche was the lesser risk.

I will draw out this contrast no further. Anyone endowed with a sense of proportion and a moderate degree of historical awareness can carry its terms to other situations. My point, in any case, is not that life was necessarily better in a log cabin with a long rifle over the mantelpiece than it is in a Manhattan apartment or a Kansas City suburb; I suggest merely that the frontier option was not necessarily worse. Our lifestyle has certainly changed—but those who insist that it has unequivocally *improved* speak in narrow-minded ignorance.

III. Postmodernity's Unique Formula: Inhuman Producers and Dumbed-Down Consumers

Nevertheless, I acknowledge that my own skepticism of progress is not widely embraced, unless with the help of lubricating self-contradictions. Many policy-makers and rank-and-file denizens of the contemporary world will at once maintain that we should live closer to nature and *also* that our social, political, and cultural institutions should continue to "evolve" into some ever-elusive higher state. We are to rid our world of pollution by living in an Edenic simplicity while *also* abandoning natural notions of gender and reproduction and enhancing brain function with implanted microchips or nanobots. As we attempt to muddle our way into the future with maps whose polarities spin, something more is happening to us than a mere reprise of the Chacoan cycle (whatever that may have been). We are not now courting calamity just because our drinking water is carcinogenic or because the supervolcano upon which Yellowstone Park sits may erupt without warning. Our political problems do not reduce merely to the lust of powerful representatives for more power or to the lazy cowardice of electors who bestow it upon them. Our economic troubles extend beyond our desertion of the land to seek urban wages, and beyond the invincible fluctuation in free markets that carries wages up and down. Our security, even, is infinitely more complicated than keeping nuclear weapons away from megalomaniacs and fanatics. We are not a Pueblo Bonito whose kivas are built of steel and concrete. A watershed has been crossed. We have become a qualitatively different sort of human civilization, and the past offers us no clues about our destiny in the form of precedents.

The word "hypermodernity" is sometimes used to portray our state. It is probably no more likely that any human intelligence could accurately, fully imagine the sequence of causes behind our "hypermodern" dilemma than a flatworm could picture life in three dimensions. Giving attention first to our technological shift, though, is not completely arbitrary. After all, the machine is the efficient cause of our running out of wage-paying jobs as the entire economy has turned urban/industrial. The transformation wasn't supposed to work this way—and, of course, it didn't in North America as long as capitalist expansion could create new categories of manual labor along with new products. The train reduced jobs related to the production of horse-drawn carriages but provided new opportunities for surveyors, engineers, iron-workers, porters, and so forth. The automobile robbed many a train conductor and switchman of their employment (especially after World War II, with Congress's bought-and-paid-for blessing upon the interstate highway system) but ushered in millions of positions for assembly-line workers, gas station attendants, car salesmen, drillers, etc. In many such cases, the emergence of new product lines may indeed have created more jobs than were lost in the obsolescence of forerunner-products. This was because, while new items themselves reflected a more sophisticated level of technology, the essential means of producing them still called for clever, active hands—and lots of them.

An economic sound barrier was broken when innovation began to address the thing produced less than the means of producing it. Our cars have not inarguably improved over the past half-century (some would argue the opposite). What has changed is the assembly line, which is now entirely robotic at most points. Even the humble garage mechanic is enslaved to a computer; for the malfunctioning vehicle diagnoses itself when plugged into special software, and the mechanic (he who remains after six have been laid off) merely substitutes the ordered part when it arrives—using an automatic screwdriver. Our economy is now pledged to creating gadgetry that performs repetitive tasks much faster and more reliably than human beings ever could while also, in the long run, engineering huge savings in salaries not paid. For a while, we could sell ourselves (or the underclass, if we belonged to the socio-economic elite) on the notion that re-educated, more highly skilled laborers make better salaries and achieve a loftier standard of living. Yet eventually all could plainly see what only a fool wouldn't have guessed from the start: that the employment pyramid must narrow as we climb the vertical "time" axis—that better jobs become fewer, and that no amount of re-education can absorb all blue-collar lay-offs into white-collar hires.

To the extent that blue-collar, low-skilled labor still survives in the West, it has held off the machine by beating the costs of mechanization with rock-bottom wages. A robotic waitress costs more to construct, for the moment, than half a dozen flesh-and-blood waitresses cost to employ. (Yet order-by-computer "kiosks" on restaurant tables are already reducing the number of waiters and waitresses on staff to those strictly necessary for serving food.) In many industries, the so-called point of singularity looms, when artificial creations will recreate improved versions of themselves on a schedule that they have independently devised. Human employees will be needed neither to write the software nor to turn the screws (and, perhaps, will not be able to control the direction, scale, or tempo of reproduction).

Our grandchildren, if not our children, will not be citizens of Pueblo Bonito clamoring for grain after a drought; they will be stray dogs fit only to be expelled from city streets no longer made for footsteps, their one remaining freedom a choice of where to go in the wasteland. They will have no practical use, hence no job, hence no wage, hence no food... hence no chance of life. A few may fuse with their robotic creations in the manner whose anticipation elates Ray Kurzweil; but even Kurzweil has lately admitted that our multitudes will mostly be excluded from this hybridization. Tomorrow's world will have rendered mere humanity, and the vast majority of humans, obsolete.

An incalculable tally of human bodies, at some critical juncture, will have to be disposed of in the transition. The disposal might proceed through such relatively benign and scarcely noticeable means as sterilization; but in the end, a virtual extermination of the species will have taken place as surely as if nine out of every ten had been pushed off the Tarpeian Rock. There are too many of us already, and there will be far too many in an ultra-high-tech future. This is partly because the same technical advances responsible for AI (artificial intelligence) have also produced medical miracles significantly prolonging life and increasing populations. Urbanization has also contributed to our mushrooming numbers, inasmuch as more mating takes place where more mate-material is at hand. Then, too, the politics of the hypermodern "democracy" rely heavily upon immense, needy hordes of urban dwellers milling about the streets restlessly in search of work, always ready to riot and loot, and not remotely aware of the cruel endgame in which they are pawns. Western metropolitan centers are indeed flooding themselves with large-family, low-skilled Third World laborers drawn in by the magnet of social-welfare benefits. These masses create an invincible voting bloc that secures the power of the welfare state's engineers until such time as resources run out... at which point, a national emergency—food riots, race wars, or very likely a pandemic nursed along by the unscreened and indiscriminate mingling of the planet's people—will justify an indefinite suspension of elections. Checkmate.

Another wholly unique facet of our hypermodern dystopia: our own intellectual degradation at the historical moment when we most need to be curious, skeptical, and creative. This unprecedented moment (whose duration we can only guess at) stretches between the end of blue-collar factory labor and the absorption of virtually all jobs, blue- and white-collar alike, by the Machine. In such a tenuous span do we presently find ourselves. For the time being, yes, factory lay-offs are bussing tables, trucking merchandise, and mowing lawns—all of which jobs are mentally more dulling than challenging. For the time being, too, many of the laid-off who cannot find even menial work (and some who can, but not full-time) are surviving on the monthly largesse of their government. One way and another, enough money continues to circulate through the hands of consumers that a thriving market in frivolities persists—and why wouldn't it, when so many are in such need of an illusory escape? Unemployed mothers of three receive free smartphones with free WiFi from Uncle Sam (that ultimate sugar daddy). Underemployed college grads spend hours in their parents' den playing Mortal Kombat. Blue-collar twenty-somethings "between jobs" grow obese on Slurpees and Blasts as they putter about putting in applications at Dairy Queen and Taco Bueno. Draft Kings becomes a major industry. Vintage Kens and Barbies may fetch hundreds on eBay.

The chicken or the egg? Is the prospect of utter economic marginalization, however dimly brought into focus, so palpable that people flee to giddy diversion the way soldiers get roaring drunk before another post to the front line? Or is control of our economic future exiting our hands so quickly because, like children in the proverbial candy shop, we cannot hold onto our money? Probably both: the picture's haze is again insolubly dense. Some of its lines, nevertheless, are thick and clear. Pornography in its myriad forms is always an easy sell; so is sugar, and so is caffeine. Snake-oil pills that cure cancer or cut your weight in half, bracelets that reduce stress, cruises to the Blessed Isles, front-row seats at the ballgame or the fight, cars that shoot along like the *Enterprise*'s launch and speak in the rich tones of Robin Meade... there is much in these both of the escapist intoxicant and of the puerile seduction. Yet whether we are willfully medicating ourselves or blindly surrendering ourselves, no one who retains a hold upon objective judgment will claim that the process makes us smarter or more mature. Perhaps the very successes of our technology have reduced us to "spoiled brats" (as Ortega y Gasset recognized almost a century ago); perhaps we want more titillation and obsequy even as material means of support are dissolving around us because instant, servile attention is what an electronic upbringing has accustomed us to.

In our institutions of higher learning, no less, where the cream of the crop is supposed to be learning to take command of the ship, infantilism is courting derangement on one side and idiocy on the other. Speech codes, originally the Nanny State's crash course in basic manners no longer taught at home, have morphed until they impair open discussion of delicate issues. Students are encouraged, and even required, to curl up in a utopian womb where moral challenges never set their hearts to racing. So-called "trigger alerts" are issued to warn their eyes and ears away from "unpleasant" directions. An Anglo-Saxon coed who wants to be African for a day, a year, or the rest of her life must not be dissuaded; or if a young man wishes to become that coed for the same unspecified duration, he/she must not feel the discomfort of stares. "Ze" is the new gender-neutral pronoun enforced on many campuses. In hypermodern circumstances, we might redact Hamlet's "nothing's either good or bad, but thinking makes it so" to read, "All is good except the thoughts that make things thus-and-so."

Lunatic self-indulgence of this sort is unique in human history (unless one looks for it in individuals: the Suetonian portrait of Caligula might be a model). Of course, any society that embraces it wholesale is committing suicide. The human inhabitants of our baffling pocket in time have no significant contact with the sun, the rain, the seasons, the soil, or food and water in their immediate form as natural products. They—we—seem more akin to the fantasy-inducing machines we endlessly play on than to flesh-and-blood fauna. Our tastes and whims are increasingly dictated, indeed, by technology that was supposed to have served a fully human will. So far have we slipped down the path to self-annihilation that we contemplate with equanimity a future wherein a robotic shell absorbs us. Indeed, we are all but volunteering to be sucked up by H.G. Wells's mechanized, pitiless Martian invaders, our terror transformed to admiration. What else can we do—through what other mutation can we survive? For we understand circuitry a lot better than photosynthesis, and one may fairly say, obesity notwithstanding, that our craving for electricity far exceeds our hunger for calories.

IV. Self-Sufficiency: The Optimist's Turn From the Abyss

What is to save us from this descent into the lobster pot which will anesthetize us so slowly, so luxuriously, that we settle into a sleep with no awakening? Prophets of high-tech trajectory like *Wired* magazine's Bill Joy assure us that the ultimate triumph of AI is inevitable (the "resistance is futile" line so popular in bad sci-fi movies). More glib, less canny futurists like Marina Gorbis (whose book, *The Nature of the Future*, I chided in these pages a few months ago for intellectual dishonesty) seem to think that we will make our way simply by giving—or "gifting"—each other what we need! Technology is supposed to make this easier by expanding exponentially the community of eager donors. Alas, eBay has yet to read the Gorbis memo.

I am a minimalist by nature. When confronted with an immensely complex question or chore, I seek to simplify it by identifying the bare essentials or necessities. To survive, a human being needs water and food. Over the longer haul, he also needs shelter and clothing in most environments;

and shelter often includes some defensive provision, to which might be added offensive means of protecting oneself and one's dependents. (Though hungry humans only ever ask for food in Ms. Gorbis's universe, in mine they sometimes kill for it.) Nothing much else is truly indispensable: certainly not iPhones, televisions, computers, cars, sound systems, GPS's, and the host of other electronic gadgets whose steady contribution of EMR (electro-magnetic radiation) to our environment may indeed be quite unhealthy. The refrigerator is far and away the most useful of such devices: keeping a steady supply of ripening food in the field or salted away in the storehouse was one of the frontiersman's major challenges. I will repeat that my purpose here is not to glamorize the log cabin and the blazing hearth. The consequences of returning to those days, besides introducing unremittent hard labor, would be devastating to two millennia of more or less constantly flourishing literate culture.

We would do ourselves no harm at all, however, to redirect technology toward a refinement of the pioneer's rugged self-sufficiency. While we need not hew our houses from felled logs, we can design them to be so energy-efficient that little or no electricity will be required in most months to heat or cool their interior, and to be so invasion-proof that alarm systems and 911-responders will become rarities. While we need not find a mule to yoke to our plow, we can operate greenhouses year-round along glassed-in sections of currently wasted attic space. As for the refrigerator, though solar power is often a boondoggle purveyed by cynical politicians, a few solar panels could probably preserve our food resources electrically.

Very little of this, once built, would require a salary to sustain. The economic Armageddon of massive and permanent unemployment which looms in the rise of the machine would pass its blade over our heads and wreak havoc only upon the foolish giants of the Spoiled Child clan. We would build our houses and then stay in them, adapting and improving them as the years wore on. If the high-tech, human-hybrid oligarchy were already well on its way to colonizing Mars (in an interesting reversal of *War of the Worlds*), it would probably not even torment us "neo-frontiersmen" with building permits and revised property-tax assessments. We would stay in our little communities instead of pulling up stakes every time the plant closed or the payroll was cut. We would get to know each other as neighbors, finding a lost species of happiness in abiding friendships based on physical proximity and collaboration in the basic, vital tasks of living. For there would be, yes, a certain amount of Gorbis's generosity among fellow villagers—not Tweeting and Facebooking "friends" who volley clichés and selfies, but hard-working people who swap a bit of engineering skill for some gardening savvy. Elementary bartering would grow commonplace, as it has always been in well-knit communities. Since the settlement's denizens would know each other by sight, suspicious characters would stick out like a wolf among sheep, and locally grown vandals and pranksters would also be recognized by sharp eyes at some window. Crime would therefore be minimal. Responsibility would be taught to the young through daily exchanges—as opposed to being integrated into the "learning outcomes" of state-funded institutions; and regional schools, for that matter, would have autonomy over the content of lessons, perhaps accomplishing their work in actual homes along residential blocks after the fashion being pioneered now by home-schoolers.

The market economy would not disappear: it would simply lose its power of life and death over our future. Indeed, what would emerge would certainly resemble the vibrant free-enterprise zones that small American townships everywhere knew before mega-corporations captured our economic activity through the combined effects of Internet marketing, outsourcing, and the promoting of oppressive regulations that suffocate independent craftsmen. No longer crushed under the "convenience" of a vast sameness, individuals would flourish. Mama Giovanella could operate her Italian restaurant out of the first floor of her residence. Old Man Callahan could sell sports memorabilia and ancient signage from a collection in his garage. The Panopoulos brothers would make and repair furniture; Mme. Yvette would style hair, and give children a trim on slow days. Nobody would "make it big" in such a setting. Nobody would really need to. Americans lived this way from the landing at Plymouth Rock until the dictatorial ascent of OSHA, local health departments, zoning laws, the minimum wage, and all the other "protective" bureaucracies and strictures of Nanny State mandarinism.

When some tentacle of Government instead of a neighbor is first to your house upon a fire's breaking out or a brawl's developing in the front yard, then you might as well view yourself as a tenant and minion of Government. The high-tech, urban/suburban, wage-dependent society and economy created by capitalism's final stages has ironically reduced us to just such tenantry. "Eschato-capitalism" (as one might call it) is the antithesis of free enterprise. Through wage-dependency reaffirmed by paternalistic safety nets and guard rails, it keeps us looking to "the system" for our day's bread. That the nets and rails eventually form a chute to the slaughterhouse (or, better yet, to that Auschwitz-like Lobster Pot) is something we haven't the leisure to notice—or the energy to resist, if we should somehow notice it.

I am assuming, then, that our neo-pioneers have managed largely to escape taxation, regulation, and observation. They may have done so simply by accident, the way some Detroiters are growing food on empty lots that do not, after all, belong to them… but who cares now? As I suggested earlier, the dysfunctional hypermodern community may well be left by its elitist architects to dry up and blow away. At most, contraception and sterilization will be "charitably" dispensed to reduce the number of mouths needing food, diminish strain on the planet's resources, and spare an unborn generation the misery of entering this world. (Such initiatives are already beyond the preliminary stage: the abortion industry supplied a rhetoric of justification decades ago.) In contrast, roving paramilitary teams in jeeps mounted with machine guns that drive up and down decadent urban neighborhoods and spray whatever moves seem unlikely. A standard dystopian scenario of popular fiction has dissidents being hunted down through the spying of their own televisions (viz, *Nineteen Eighty-Four*) and, if successful in their evasion, banding together in some extra-urban wilderness (viz., *Fahrenheit 451*). The truth, as well documented in Priest and Arkin's *Top Secret America* (2011), is that our "keepers" are already inundated in so much information than they can neither share it nor even process it effectively. The inevitable result will be the consignment of triage to AI, of course—and will not the computerized brain be far too interested in genuine subversion to monitor "threshold resistance" closely?

So the neo-pioneer, whether he is such by design or by accident—whether a survivalist or just trying to survive—will have an opportunity to cling to his humanity and pass it along to his children. Why wouldn't he? The means to survive are as accessible as ever, the Lord God "maketh his sun to rise on the evil and on the good, and sendeth rain on the just and on the unjust." Who will deny us a little sun to grow beans and tomatoes or a little rain to water them? The landlords of the Enclosure period had their criminal reasons for wanting to see the Potato Famines starve out their Irish tenants, and Stalin had his vile reasons for wanting to starve millions of Ukrainians. The situation I describe, however, does not involve any land that Central Authority, whether for fair motives or foul, wishes otherwise to deploy or any riotous rabble that it must quell. On the contrary, the neo-pioneer is staying out of the way—and there is no better plan for living off the twenty-second century's grid than to stay out of the way.

Machines, always remember, see what they are made to see. A flashlight pointed into the darkness illumines everything before its ray—and nothing to either side. As long as we resist desiring that which the machine dangles before us and hence defining our values according to the machine's vision of the good life, we will remain incomprehensible to mechanized understanding. We will continue to be as imperceptible as a dog whistle is to a man or as the colors of a Van Gogh are to a dog. What machines we do make to ease our chores should stay offline, their information not available for harvest by any database. We must grasp that to be united (i.e., "brought together") is no longer to be unified (i.e., "made one"); it is, perhaps, the very opposite. Every germinating apple seed (as my own sophomoric efforts at cultivation have taught me) looks like every other, yet they are not clones. One individual survives and thrives, while another mysteriously perishes in the same circumstances. Nature has made us to be thus individualistic, some of us responding better to heat or to cold, some better to bacterial attack or injury. The "root" in all of us paleo-humans struggles to reach for nourishment: that much we all have in common. It is those of us (and I fear that this may prove to be the vast majority) inclined to draw in their root atrophically and to feed like parasites, instead from an artificial hand who face fusion with artifice, and so oblivion as human beings.

V. Running the Program: The Pessimist's Acknowledgment of Our Technological Thralldom

Then again, maybe nothing of what I just wrote is any less a pipedream than Marina Gorbis's high-tech socialism.

It cannot have escaped the careful reader that increased centralization (centripety) plays the villain's role in my forecasts, whereas devolution of power to bestow more choice upon the individual (centrifugy) is the hero. Though the technological revolution has empowered individuals to perform certain traditionally collaborative tasks all by themselves (e.g., a single occupant traveling a thousand miles in a car, two cell phone clients holding an intimate conversation from distant parts of the world), I do not see how any critically astute mind could fail to recognize the overall centripetal effects of advanced technology. (As noted earlier, all cars now have computers and cannot be repaired by one mechanic with a wrench; and we need not review all the ways in which cell-phone users are susceptible to eavesdropping and data-mining.)

What worries me about the ground of my foregoing optimism (not just in the previous section, but indeed in several previous articles of mine belonging to the past decade) is that I may have underestimated the power of centripety; or, to put it more precisely, I may have discounted the willingness of human authorities to let centripetal forces have the rein—to surrender major decisions to their inhuman servant-masters. Flesh-and-blood brains overwhelmed by the data-deluge generated from brains of circuitry may not necessarily restrain the latter just because the volume of "intake" is dizzying. Silicon brains may simply "run the program"—whatever program Artificial Intelligence may have written—upon legions of human beings in the margins, even though that program may woefully lack a basic degree of "humanity". Machines, after all, are never overwhelmed. When they need an unbudgeted amount of time to clear a work load, they indifferently surge into overtime without the least anxiety. Eventually, they will deal with every last "quantity" or "data point"—and will do so according to the design which they crafted to handle the first and second members of a sequence numbering in the billions.

To express my apprehension more explicitly, I would ask the following. If human authorities decide that all populations must be concentrated within designated areas, if certain independent communities should resist the edict, and if the problem were then delivered to a fully automated system to solve... then on what basis should we assume that the "final solution" would not involve locating every remote, wayward village or cabin with an armed drone and vaporizing it? Would Central Authority detect the moral atrocity at work in such a plan before its execution and push the "abort" button"? Why would we hope for such magnanimity, when the twentieth century—an age endowed with far less technical efficiency—left tens of millions of Russians and Chinese exterminated for no better reason than that they didn't conform to a centrally devised blueprint? I wrote that Stalin had reason to starve six million

Ukrainians… but, of course, he really didn't; or he seemed to have reason only to himself. Annihilating resistance so that survivors remain terrified is reason enough to such a mentality. It may have been the very reason responsible for Chaco Canyon's ruin, if Christy Turner was right about the Aztec role.

Once the human soul becomes inebriated upon immense power, it apparently doesn't require an inhuman brain's intercession to engage in inhuman acts.

We see all too clearly in the "People's Republic" of China today, unfortunately, that technology (American-developed technology, at that) is assisting a megalomaniac elite in monitoring the moves of each individual within that nation's almost innumerable mass. The ultimate objective is to read even facial expressions and body language, and to do so in the privacy of the home as well as in public spaces. Citizens will be rewarded or punished with reference to how well they "perform" on a scale of mindless, abject servility. It goes without saying that the entire process, in practice (i.e., beyond the software-writing stage), will necessarily be administered by Artificial Intelligence. A net such as this has so fine a mesh that one may no longer confidently trust in the ability of subtle, "under the radar" individuals to slip through. The prognosis for human society within these parameters is not at all good. Indeed, we might even be tempted to argue that a robot programmed with something like "basic humanity"—and whose benign programming was cleverly designed by a rogue genius to evade prying human technicians—could be the planet's best chance of not swarming with inhuman robots one day.

What a hope!

Besides such head-spinning paradoxes, it seems to me that we have few plays left on the board better than self-sufficiency, for all its vulnerability. As the sanguine ideas of my younger days wither under the sanguinary lessons of longer experience and closer observation, I have to conclude that all human communities of any size and location could well present targets to tomorrow's insatiably power-hungry despots… yet the Devil Brigade might still miss a spot here and there. In the meantime, perhaps a supervolcano's eruption or a meteorite's impact or a raging storm of solar flares or the reversal of Earth's magnetic polarities will punch a reset button: perhaps all the Mephistophelian high-tech engineering that hems us in will vanish, returning society generally (or those within it who survive) to the American frontier, if not the European Middle Ages.

There's another hope—and that one isn't very appealing, either. But it may, all the same, be the best of a small lot. Men and women of good will would do well to prepare themselves for accomplishing whatever good results it has to offer.

The Dark Elite

From a series of posts on my personal blogsite during October and November of 2017.

I. A Game Played for Fools: The Sham Conflict Between Big Business and Big Government

The first notion of which one must rid oneself in pondering the Dark Elite (i.e., the select few who *really* rule us) is that the corporate private sector and the political public sector have any significant degree of separation. They do not. There is no "industrial-political complex"—only a single corporate monstrosity whose tentacles extend into both public and private domains. Big business gives donations to politicians; then government passes laws favorable to the proliferation of mega-business activity. The activity produces or takes away jobs in this or that locale or sector while multiplying product. Prices rise on cutting-edge technology and lower for the obsolescent, the reduced-capacity, and the knock-off. Politicians represent all of these changes in a "narrative" (as it's now called) that best serves their bid to stay in power. They may elevate taxes on their profiteering business cronies while also sullying their name in public; but the tax hike is paid for by higher consumer prices, hidden deductions, and lucrative government contracts. Not since Richard Burton and Liz Taylor have two entities fought so openly while spending so much time in bed together off camera.

Computer-related industries and their offshoots have consistently posed the most obvious manifestation of this unholy marriage from my perch of observation (as an educator) for the past two decades. From a capitalist perspective, the wonderful thing about the digital revolution is a) that "old stuff" is utterly useless—a PC literally cannot negotiate today's Internet through a landline; and b) that stuff gets old very, very quickly. Obsolescence may now occur within a year, requiring the purchase of state-of-the-art gadgetry at premium cost. The Managerial State has been surprisingly slow to harvest the enormous propagandistic benefits offered by this technology; but we should note that such "benefits" are latent and always ready for exploitation, should our elected officials decide to take the next Orwellian step. The Obama IRS has shown a rare talent for the game; and senior officials appointed to the Department of Justice, the FBI, and other strong-arm bureaucracies by that administration continue to resist the exposure of their lairs to the sunlight. We know this crew popularly as the Deep State—which is not, however, the same thing as the Dark Elite. The former merely defends its careerist turf; the latter, I believe, intends to rule the world.

Now, the appendage of the State that we may call Security—which includes the FBI and the police and military generally, but is increasingly out of uniform and unequipped with firearms—has in fact begun to open wireless windows through which Big Brother may watch. Yet Security's vigilance, again, is not motivated by the partisan ends of preserving careers and impeding unsympathetic political movements. At least at the Dark Elite level, it compiles dossiers on everyone everywhere, and does so with no short-term objective in mind. We will attempt to unknot this loop of the nexus later. For the moment, we may be thankful that Security presently operates with an almost blatant and arrogant defiance of mega-business's elected, constantly legislating pimps and panders.

To speak more roundly… most politicians, to this day, continue to fund vast phone banks at their campaign headquarters and to travel about kissing babies and belting down hot dogs. They are apt to be digital imbeciles. Their forte, after all, is tugging at collegial elbows, passing notes under the table, and smuggling into bills indecipherable riders that award special privileges to their donors. They don't actually use the Internet themselves: they just advance legislation that makes everyone else use it. Medical records pile up in databases like stalled traffic during an LA rush hour, the NSA's backlog of unsifted data mounts at a faster rate than the national debt, and identity theft spreads across the Internet like a digital version of Ebola… but our lawmakers persist in delivering more and more of our daily lives to the Cloud. It's progress.

In my opinion, then, most politicians are not so much "members of the illuminati" as they are unwitting facilitators of an ambitious few. Their objective is to get rich—through contributions, perks, speaking fees, book deals, and (after retirement) consulting fees. Accusing them of participation in global conspiracy is, generally speaking, an undeserved compliment. In the stupidity of the short-sighted, they settle for a small fortune rather than angle for control of the world. The more narcissistic they are, the less fit their temperament for slyly manipulating our lives behind the scenes. Any true member of the Dark Elite would be delighted to preserve complete anonymity, or at least to be thought boring and negligible. A Bill Clinton, a Barack Obama, or a Donald Trump would wither under such negligence. Everyone must notice his entry into a room and concede him to be far and away the most important person in it. Vladimir Putin is perhaps the one top-tier politico on the global scene who also, in stunning paradox, has the ability to lower his profile and pass by scarcely noticed—unnoticed, that is, in proportion to the influence he truly exerts.

One more example: say that a politician demands "clean energy" of the industrial giants. The electorate, being almost totally ignorant of how power gets to wall sockets, picks up the chant. Our heroic "Mr. Smith" vows to take General Electric, Exxon Mobile, and the others to the woodshed if elected; and indeed, shortly after victory, he withdraws with the bad boys to a tightly sealed space. The energy-producers emerge gushing public penitence and love of Mother Nature on television commercials, and the Senator Smith has a new bulge in his pocket. In their suits of sackcloth, the corporations fling themselves into the creation of windmills and solar panels—with plenty of tax-funded incentives, grants, and deductions to ease the transition. The senator sees that certain districts associated with producing these dream-dynamos enjoy an employment boom... and the hefty profits of the corporations, in turn, translate into a steady trickle purling into his campaign coffers. The public sees windmills and, like Don Quixote, supposes that a magician is at work and has solved the energy crisis. It does not see the cancer villages in Africa and Southeast Asia that supply Rare Earth Elements for the solar panels... but then, it doesn't need to see those, and the complicit news media ensure invisibility.

By the way, the news media are never part of the Dark Elite; few of their captains, I venture to say, so much as penetrate its outer circle. Their contribution to the effort is *gratis*. They are useful idiots, perhaps more likely to end up getting shot than anyone else, eventually—but they lubricate the spread of a totalitarian "progress", in the meantime, with the adolescent utopian drivel of a coddled social class.

II. Recruitment into the "Security" System's Dark Vortex

I have erred in the previous paragraphs if I left the impression that I consider our career politicos and captains of industry a seamless unit. I realize that CEO's don't retire to enter politics and that, by the same token, politicians (few of whom have any business savvy today) seldom retire to enter private industry. In a way, such was exactly my point: neither needs to stray into the territory of the other, because either side is already doing the other's bidding.

Now that I am focusing my attention upon the sector that I call Security, however (meaning the high-ranking bureaucrats who "protect" us more than men and women wearing any sort of uniform), I find myself uncomfortable with advancing any sort of provenance. I don't really know where these people come from, as a rule. Are they military personnel? Sometimes... but if so, they have seldom smelled powder or seen blood before being entrusted with a nation's survival. This type usually seems to scale the ranks by discreetly guarding or purveying secrets and working effective "damage control" for incompetent but powerful superiors. The military record of Michael Hayden, former chief of NSA and the CIA, is essentially that of what used to be called an *aide de camp*—a well-connected, copiously decorated "yes man". Might another type have occupied elective office prior to penetrating the inner circle of watchdogs? Less often, I would guess... but more often than never. Leon Panetta began life on the national scene in the US House of Representatives before embarking upon a series of cabinet positions that led to his being CIA director. George H.W. Bush's career path was similar, his few years of service in World War II having been long past before he became a national figure.

These are men, in short (and in my logarithm, they show up as male without fail), who have served in the "armed forces" without being armed, never having to choose between bearing a moribund comrade along clumsily and saving the rest of the squad in a quick dash; or perhaps they have represented the "people's choice" at some point in some capacity, but without playing the demagogue or polarizing the public. They have shown themselves to be "team players"—trustworthy practitioners of the inside game even when it bends the rules ostensibly observed by others. They keep things quiet rather than stir things up. There's something, maybe, a little cold-blooded about them. They enjoy a kind of aloofness from the madding crowd. Whether ex-military or former legislators, they have displayed a particular talent for making the right people look good and for making the wrong facts go away. They know where the skeletons are hidden—and, in their capable hands, those closets have been dry-walled over and hung with dim portraits.

One may wonder if someone like Bill Gates might prove himself worthy of admission into the club from the private sector. Gates's attempted trespasses into education policy strongly imply that he wants to be a member—that he wants to market hardware and software on a vast scale, yes, but also that he considers himself worthy of directing society's course for decades to come. Without question, he holds the keys to a lot of doors; and his legendary acts of "hard ball" when Steve Jobs took him too far into his confidence may impress the Dark Elite more as salutary ruthlessness than as risky infidelity... or perhaps they suggest to us, rather, that one does not deserve trust in this club who cannot be ruthless, and that anyone who trusts too much deserves not to be trusted.

Nevertheless, a nerdy milquetoast like Bill Gates would never be admitted into the rarefied ranks of Security... would he? Why not? If federally mandating costly communications and information systems creates the ultimate bonanza for tech companies, doesn't their proliferation also create the ultimate opportunity for the nation's watchdogs to eavesdrop on everyone's every movement? Isn't that, indeed, the mother lode for a private innovator: an advanced surveillance and data-gathering network's being purchased by public-sector bureaucracies? And if you were the Eavesdropper in Chief, wouldn't you want Bill Gates on board—all the way on board, and as gung-ho as you about a perfect planet where wars no longer bubble up because trouble-makers are preemptively identified and subdued? Wouldn't Bill Gates or Steve Jobs be all in for that?

I am already anticipating the next step in my speculations—the "tech whiz" portal; so allow me to backtrack briefly into the deathly-discreet vaults of Security for a few more words. I cannot over-emphasize that these elite few do not dream of clearing out Times Square with tanks as the Chinese did Tiananmen Square. That's a Hollywood script, recycled and retreaded God-knows-how-many times since *Seven Days in May* screened in 1964. (Hollywood, by the way, is now as seamlessly joined to the news media as corporations are joined to politicians: more useful idiots, their Woodstock-era nightmares of men in uniform create a very successful diversion from the real threat.) Preserving the myth of a fully armed, booted, and helmeted military probably assists Security in funneling money to its "black ops" programs, to be sure. The American voter is generally willing to be taxed more if he thinks he's financing new submarines and jet fighters. He is also completely oblivious to how much of this money disappears down the hole of off-budget projects.

But no, Security's vision of domination has no battlefields and no heroes. The planet will be made ready for her "great leap forward", rather, by handling obstacles with sanitary efficiency: by dazing armed militants with sound waves, by mollifying dissidents through the education system (delivered via home computer), by thinning out burdensome social elements with sterilants in the yearly flu vaccine, and by disgracing spirited opponents with *faux* mafia pay-offs uploaded to their bank accounts. While this portion of the Dark Elite is the more sinister for being the less disruptive of daily routines, its solutions are perhaps more permanent than a nuclear holocaust; for extermination of one's adversaries only postpones the power struggle for another generation, but the Orwellian integration of adversaries into the mainstream makes society forget how to say "no".

III. The Role of High Tech in Creating Dark Princes

The Dark Elite's security (read "enforcement") branch, then, is quintessentially high-tech. That's why the exposure of our nation's power grid to the threat of Electro-Magnetic Pulses is so worrisome: because, I mean, our rulers are far too sophisticated to have allowed such a vulnerability to take them by surprise. If our civilization risks such catastrophic collapse, it is because our "guardians" have decided to preserve collapse as a "pacifying" option. Should our numbers and demands become inconvenient, ninety percent of us may have to be culled so that the remnant may grow strong and straight.

Bill Gates, Steve Jobs, Elon Musk... Werner von Braun, Karl Heisenberg, Ferdinand Porsche... Andrei Sakharov, Aleksandr Prokhorov, Sergei Korolev... from where does the Dark Elite draw the genius that ultimately drives the progressivist vision? It has been said *ad infinitum* that capitalism causes genius to rise to the top like cream because our economic system so handsomely rewards innovation. Yet this argument, let it be repeated ever so lyrically, often suffers contradiction in practice. The names offered just above, in fact, show that a totalitarian regime can exploit its best brains at least as well as a free society. Indeed, the Soviets could make life very nice for their top-tier minds, pooling them together in idyllic communities abounding in all the existential comforts so woefully deficient elsewhere in the nation. These privileged few might not be allowed to leave their Shangri-La, or not for long... but within its confines, they were treated as princes. Capitalism doesn't necessarily make the going so smooth for its most brilliant citizens. There have been all too many cases, unfortunately, of revolutionary patents being bought up and buried by producers who want to keep the chain of manufacture and consumption moving just the way it presently moves.

If the Dark Elite, then, were seeking the best of the best to create a "brainwash ray" (say) or an assassin's bullet that could travel one hundred miles disguised as a happy little bee, recruitment would not necessarily target private industry that extended tentacles into such areas. There's actually a long history of the government's raiding academe for its magicians and alchemists: e.g., Robert Oppenheimer and Einstein himself. The "private industry" connection might have the advantage of turning up people who had already forged ties with influential figures in government—such as Gates; but the academic connection promises the equal or superior advantage of mentalities nourished in a progressive/utopian political atmosphere, such that a recruiter's well-delivered pitch for a one-world government with energies focused on interplanetary exploration would likely fall on sympathetic ears.

Let's not forget, either, that money makes the scientific world go round, however idealistic its ivory-impregnated air… and the Dark Elite can offer its prospects virtually unlimited funding. The private-sector wizard, in contrast, has to produce something at the end of the day that appeals to the plodding intelligence of John Q. Consumer. The case of Elon Musk is in fact quite instructive here: though ostensibly a producer of futuristic vehicles marketed to the general public, Musk would never stay afloat without immense infusions of government subsidy.

Nevertheless, as they have been at every stage of this discussion, the lines can get very blurry if we grope with too much persistence for a clear distinction between public and private—between Werner von Braun and Henry Ford. Sometimes the arcane fiddling of white coats working in the labs of Security can create a private-sector growth industry, as has happened so often with the space program.

Or take "climate change" and its impact on the energy industry. Wind and solar power have so far proved impractical boondoggles, profitable to a select few only because politicians engineer subsidies for certain corporations (whose execs invariably counter with generous donations). Yet something really innovative might come along, such as tapping into coastal wave energy, that Security would wish to exploit in a covert way. And, indeed, are we very, very sure that Security has not manufactured "climate change" (i.e., irregular weather patterns, which is what most citizens understand by the term) from its quiver of top-secret arrows? We know that programs to weaponize weather systems have been dithering about in Earth's stratosphere at least since the advent of HAARP in the early Nineties (though the Department of Defense only acknowledged the endeavor ten years later to say that it had been discontinued: most reassuring!). Wouldn't Defense be quite capable of creating destructive weather patterns just to gin up popular support for a "save the climate" governmental intrusion into the private sector, which in turn would generate more tax dollars and more abysmal bureaucracies for the development of more "mass-control tech"? To those who say, "No, our public servants wouldn't do such things," I would ask, "Please tell me why not. Are you going to use a word like 'conscience' or 'legality'?"

Academe, I think, probably remains the favored hunting ground for locating the miracle-workers who will transform our Dark Elite into the gods they already imagine themselves to be.

IV. Other Back Doors to the Inner Sanctum

It would be easier (especially for someone sitting on the sidelines) to say who the Dark Elite are *not* than who they are. They are not "mainstream media" and "fake news". Though our Fourth Estate has indeed assumed much too aggressive a role in shaping public policy, and though its sympathies overwhelmingly veer in the direction of creating a highly centralized utopia, none of this group, it seems to me, can credibly be visualized as pulling the strings of puppets on the national stage. At most, the owner of a communications empire—preferably one who has made his broadcast domain part of a vast conglomerate—might be a member of some covert Star Chamber; but this person's vast wealth and his influence over other sectors of the economy (as opposed to his specific achievements in propagandizing) would supply the ticket for admission. The people who directly persuade us, before their microphones or cameras, to take comfort in the emerging totalitarian state are not among that state's architects. In the phrase supposedly used by Lenin, they are "useful idiots" who champion the abrogation of our freedoms because they identify egotistically with the cause of creating a brave new world.

Still less are Hollywood's movers and shakers suitable collaborators for an enterprise that aspires to rule the world. Again, unless a major film producer also has his finger in several other entrepreneurial pots, his job is essentially meretricious, no matter how much lucre it spills into his bank account: that is, he is as much a slave to public taste as an engineer of public opinion.

I do not here dismiss the driving forces of leftist propaganda as a menace of negligible proportions. On the contrary, most of my almost daily anguish as a citizen and political commentator is aroused by constant assaults upon truth launched through "educational" institutions and "information" media; and these efforts at sabotage, in our time, are without question or exception the work of progressive crusaders. The only ghost of a principle might be argued to flit through such crusades is the systematic adjusting of reality to accommodate a "better world". (Yet are not principles supposed to precede and direct action rather than mop up after every whimsical act with impromptu rationalization?)

To me, in short, the unprincipled Left is indeed a fearful adversary of stability, maturity, responsibility, culture, and peace. Why, then, would I not include its chief architects among the Dark Elite? Does it matter, really, that the self-righteous progressive views his higher truth as something the world has never seen before, and which only he (and an elite few like him) can see with rare, superior vision—whereas the rightist regards that high truth as something delivered to the world in the hoary remoteness of antiquity, and since forgotten by increasingly decadent generations? Is such a line between two types of lunacy worth drawing?

I think it is, to this extent: the leftist is preoccupied by selling the new order-in-becoming, exploiting all means of communication with his formidable manipulative skills; the rightist, sensing that the grand old orthodoxy has been revealed and ignored, busies himself more with means of material domination. Ultimately, the distinction for which I grope may prove irrelevant. Brainwashing can tame multitudes as efficiently as the Bomb (probably more so, if taming is desired rather than annihilating). I can well imagine that master-manipulators of information would meet and form common cause with developers of Space Age weaponry at some point: the same drone that eavesdrops over the walls of a secret rendezvous may also launch a high-precision missile (or a death-ray) at those walls. Yet because of their preeminent interest in tampering with communication, agencies of the Left strike me both as more visible to the public and as less likely to be conversant in technologies of direct force. I would imagine them apt for exploitation, in their turn, by more covert entities that have their fingers poised imminently over red buttons.

Hence, as far as established political parties go, I shall perhaps not create too much surprise by suggesting that Republicans seem more credible source material for twenty-first century *illuminati* than Democrats. At the risk of over-stressing the point, I see significant psychological differences in these prospective recruits. With their superior appeal to "the masses" (which rarely translates into real benefit for ordinary people), Democrats are more conscious of "image". They enjoy applause and live for celebrity. Once they discover how much loot is also to be harvested in the corridors of power, their heads are more readily turned away from the hidden heart of the magnetic force field. They would rather bask on a Caribbean island in a lobbyist's company than explore the underground vaults of NSA's new megaplex in Utah. Among this latter type, one is more likely to find Republicans. They have cut their professional teeth in boardrooms and back rooms. They know how to dress, how to be discreet, and how to blend into the wallpaper when necessary. The hard part for them is being flamboyant enough to get elected, in the first place, as the electorate grows more YouTube-addicted.

This is not to imply that politicos of any stripe are very likely to sit on the Board of the New Knights Templar. As with publishers and film producers, politicians would almost certainly require connection with some other avenue of power to receive the initiation: banking and finance, energy production, and defense contracting are three of the private-sector ties that our elite-eligible may have formed before entering public office. But these avenues are little traveled now. Most congressmen come to DC by way of the bar and the bench. In other words, they know how to design and manipulate legalese to reach a desired objective through a squid-like ink screen. While this can be a useful survival skill, it doesn't get you to the top of the food chain. Honestly, I doubt that most of our elected representatives have any idea where the greatest power ultimately resides, any more than a little pilot fish carries around a full mental image of the shark's jaws under which he comfortably feeds.

Many have proposed George Soros as a prototype for the Goldfinger-like character who darkly subverts the mechanisms of nations as if he were toying with pawns on a chessboard. My initial reaction is to concur—perhaps because the world of high finance is so alien to me. (Tacitus writes, *omne ignotum pro magnifico est*: a very free translation might be, "We like to imagine that all the boxes we can't find are in the closet we can't open.") On the other hand, Soros is very visible, and a characteristic of our kind of shady figure might almost run thus: you can be sure X is *not* one if you're convinced he is. Soros's money, besides, has not been spent with particular efficiency. He has unlimited amounts of it to meddle in other nations' affairs, but the horses he backs come croppers far more often than they visit the victory circle. He also has no apparent connection with high tech: and this, I believe, is an indispensable quality in our Shadow King.

I like bankers as prospects... but they need to have a mine of pixie dust somewhere in their portfolio. William Gheen once wrote me (in defense of his support for Donald Trump) that Ted Cruz was disqualified in the struggle to "drain the swamp" because his wife Heidi had worked for Goldman-Sachs. The suspicious, however, are not those who engage in pursuing material profit; they are those invested in materially engineering the future of our species for the "betterment of all concerned".

V. The Emerging Profile

So who are the Dark Elite, now that we've considered who they are not? Let us review.

1) They are likely to appear in the intersection of several rings of influence and power. A politician with strong ties to the defense or energy-production industry, a career intelligence officer with an academic background and a family fortune, and investment mogul who also owns several radio stations and production studios... such characters are not necessarily prime suspects, but they deserve to make the "suspect" list.

2) They should possess some significant awareness of and involvement in advanced technology. They needn't be Bill Gates or Werner von Braun... but they should be on intimate terms with people of that caliber. A mere billionaire subversive without any plan for society's technical overhaul isn't much of a threat these days.

3) They are discreet: they keep a low profile. A demagogic firebrand or charismatic exhibitionist might well be useful to them, but would never be admitted to their inner circle. This criterion alone eliminates several public figures who have obviously been seduced by applause, adoration, and the vision of a mighty throne.

To these three criteria might be added a commitment to the enterprise which turns it into a virtual family affair. Perhaps there is something of the hostage-taking motive involved; that is, perhaps those figures are most trusted whose wives and children will tumble down catastrophically in the event of betrayal. I have heard it said by an insider that politicians, *tout court*, are not trusted because they "come and go". Membership in the Dark Elite lasts for a lifetime, and preferably for several generations. It isn't an ideology so much as an ethos, apparently.

Dick Cheney's name often surfaces in discussions. A political gamesman of savvy demeanor and great poise who contentedly played second fiddle for eight years to a president very much his intellectual inferior, Cheney also had strong ties to Big Oil; and, for good measure, his wife was a career federal bureaucrat and his daughter a wannabe politico. I always found the Cheneys to have good manners, and even charm... which was sufficient to make me nervous. Yet the Vice President's accusers (who have charged him with everything up to and including the murder of 3,000 Americans on 9/11) could never hang a better motive around his neck than that he wanted to sell more oil. Members of the Dark Elite would not be so retrograde and paltry: they have plans to save the world from itself, not to multiply their dividend income. If I were to find that Cheney had some sort of connection with transformative technology, I might consider boarding the "conspiracy" ship. As things stand, I am incredulous. I think my fellow birddogs in these matters (e.g., Steven Greer), tending to have a progressive worldview themselves, are too quick to ascribe "caveman" lusts to their adversaries. They fail to realize that the enemy they seek is probably one who shares their ideology at an abstract level.

Now, the Bushes have created a political dynasty, they enjoy extensive ties with mega-business, they have fearfully chummy relationships with utopians on the other side of the political aisle, and George H.W. was once head of the CIA (where he might have been introduced to all kinds of "dark ops" programs). The same electorate that considered Ted Cruz too close to Goldman-Sachs in 2016 would have nothing whatever to do with Jeb Bush... so the suspicion of that family appears to be pretty widespread. Almost too widespread. Maybe Cheney is the better bet, after all.

Or the professorial Newt Gingrich. What I "like" about Newt's credentials is that they bespeak a genuine affection for utopian projects. An "idea" man who always has something new on the drawing board, Gingrich often shows a commitment to transforming society which could easily adapt itself to transformative technology. His Catholic conversion has put him in touch with a certain "shepherd leading the sheep" mentality in that faith which has conduced to secret "philanthropic" organizations for centuries (and also rendered Catholicism traditionally suspect to the self-determining American electorate); while his daughter, an active political commentator, appears to the manner born.

But as Donald Rumsfeld so correctly observed, we don't know what we don't know. My suggested candidates above are probably disqualified by the unpromising fact that someone as far on the outside as I can finger them.

VI. The Role of High Tech in the Hidden Throne Room

As I conclude these remarks, I find that one observation leaps immediately to the fore. I wrote in the beginning section that we must deprogram ourselves from viewing multinational corporations and Nanny State politicians as adversaries, for in fact they are two sides of the same coin (and a counterfeit coin, at that). In the same way, we must no longer automatically view a utopian progressive building a staircase to heaven as the opposite of a dogmatic neo-Bourbonist awaiting the return of a rightful king. For what were Stalin and Mao, if not the most despotic kings imaginable exploiting their society's long acclimatization to emperors? The progressive is always waiting for a master, whom he calls Beloved Leader. On the coin's other hollow-ringing side, the ultra-conservative who wants God's ways (as understood by him) to intrude into the management of the body politic produces, in his Richelieu or his Metternich, little more than a Stalin or a Mao clad in holy garb—perhaps yet hampered by a few abiding moral scruples.

I submit that this is a deeply relevant paradox in unmasking the Dark Elite. I strongly suspect, in other words, that people with misguided religious convictions may possess all of the qualities essential for participation in such a covert enterprise. They would likely be discreet, fiercely faithful, tirelessly industrious, and steeled against second thoughts by utter conviction. They would be modern Crusaders; and what would make them distinctly modern would be an understanding of advanced technology of the practical variety such as the Space Program generates, or even of the somber variety such as the Department of Defense generates. They wouldn't be designing video games. They might be invested in delivering the Internet's instant knowledge via an earbud… but they would be aware, as frivolous people are not, of the potential to filter the Internet's content and distill coy suggestions into everyone's ear.

I find the profile of the person I have just imagined not unsympathetic, I freely admit. Democracy seems to be entering a self-destructive stage (as Vladimir Putin's advisor Aleksandr Dugin argues, rather incoherently but not without reason). People are expected to arbitrate issues at the ballot box about which highly trained experts disagree—and never has an electorate been more impatient with training itself in our nation's history. More and more voters, as well, are claiming their right to a bigger and bigger portion of somebody else's income, while it grows increasingly obvious that all the wallets of the next two or three generations cannot fund the host of stridently registered claims. Infatuation, irresponsibility, selfishness, and outright stupidity characterize the choices made in the broadest and most consequential plebiscites. Wouldn't we be better off if some Beloved Leader—some Anointed One—would step in and do God's work? I can see how men and women of good will might answer that question affirmatively.

If you worship the God of Goodness, yet you forget that good ways are only so when freely chosen by thoughtful individuals, you may indeed be tempted to do away with the "folly" of democratic elections—with their susceptibility to trend and their cult of personality. The good is the good; and since people will not reliably select it, it must be selected for them. They must be saved from themselves, the silly children—the bloody fools, some of whom may have to die until the remaining accept that they are silly children. You, as God's agent, will see that the hard lesson is taught.

There's not a paper's thinness of difference, I repeat, between this line of reasoning and that of the utopian ideologue: hence the strange affinity that has evolved between the radical Left and radical Islam, the one boisterously atheist and the other fanatically pious. Even so are there sincere but self-deluded Christians in the United States who would cheerfully adopt a know-nothing attitude as a paternalistic government oversaw and overheard whatever passed in every kitchen, bathroom, and bedroom to "protect" us; and there are those of this same group, as well, who would dutifully undertake the "protecting".

I don't mean end my rambles in the assertion that the Dark Elite are a gang of religious fanatics… or perhaps I do. I will accept that characterization of my conclusion if you, in turn, will accept that devotion to the ever-recessive image of a manmade utopia is also a religion—or a cult, to be precise. Our covert Chosen Ones may feel that they are bringing about the eternal life of the soul by fostering a world where downloads may enter an indefinite number of corporeal residences… or they may feel that they are elevating humankind to new evolutionary heights by merging the biological with the robotic. The former idea is Catholic physicist Frank Tipler's, the latter charismatic secularist Ray Kurzweil's. Either one of these two would be quite comfortable in a room where the enlightened engineering of humanity's future by a select, fully initiated few was under discussion.

In my restless thoughts, I keep returning to the Phoenix Lights, an inexplicable display of aeronautic prowess viewed by hundreds and filmed by dozens. Either extraterrestrial craft were aloft that spring evening in 1997, or else our government has developed technology capable of what any civilian Physics professor would call impossible. Either way, we have been lied to on a scale that sets our dull world wholly adrift from the futuristic reality known to the Elite. Yet these same "protectors" have overlooked the little matter of securing our power grid against EMP's… or have they, really? That, I would insist, is a moral impossibility. If we live thus exposed to almost complete annihilation, it can only be because the Dark Elite have already decided that they wish to hold such a trump card in their hand. Perhaps an America of ten percent its present population would be much easier to feed and defend, equipped as she would be with apocalyptic technology; perhaps the Elite have decided that her deadwood simply needs to be pruned.

This subject terrifies me, frankly. Our world is not perfectible, and attempts to force perfection upon it by its human occupants invariably bring Hell a little closer. Our free society was intended to give individuals a chance to work out their soul's salvation or to squander their mortal time upon things that perish, as they prefer: it was to have been a place where people may learn from failure or simply fail and fail some more. Should the "illumined ones" among us decide to outlaw failure, our grand experiment in freedom will have failed catastrophically.

Postscript: Unexplained, Perhaps Inexplicable... But Definitely Concealed

Dr. Steven Greer has made at least one Netflix documentary previous to *Unacknowledged*. That's how I know that the man has suffered greatly—and suspiciously—for his probes into the UFO controversy. Having been warned off with varying degrees of subtlety for some time, he and his initial group of investigators were beset by a curious outbreak of cancer as contagious, apparently, as the flu, and a lot more deadly. (One recalls Aleksandr Litvinenko's radioactive cup of tea administered by a couple of Putin flunkies.) Greer survived; his wife and many of his colleagues did not.

James Woolsey, former head of the CIA, had on one occasion in his chief-of-spies capacity manifested such an active interest in tracking down the actors and the script behind America's massive, off-budget, quasi-military R&D operations that he privately summoned Greer to brief him on certain issues—privately and bizarrely, since Greer is a medical doctor who has immersed himself in "ufology" only as a concerned citizen. Woolsey was obviously convinced that more accredited sources were not giving him the true low-down. Later on, Greer was apparently told by a Clintonista of very high rank that the nation's forty-second president would not risk prying into the Roswell/Area 51 files because his personal security—Secret Service and all— wouldn't suffice to keep him alive beyond the first few weeks of snooping.

Unacknowledged is packed with declassified documents that support Greer's outlandish (or should I say "otherworldly"?) claims in surprisingly graphic detail. A few insiders with high security clearances also share enough of their experiences on camera that a coherent picture emerges... or perhaps two-thirds coherent. The assertion is resonant and sustained that extraterrestrial visitors to Planet Earth are a reality, and also that some imponderably covert branch of our government has been reverse-engineering alien technology for its own undisclosed ends. One would like to suppose that these ends would be defensive, and that the extreme secrecy enveloping them would also be related to our nation's preservation....

But here the picture grows hazy. The documentary floated several motives for the obsessive, sometimes ruthless suppression of information about UFO's by "men in black". One is that an elite band of corporatist megalomaniacs wants to deprive the world of unlimited, virtually free energy resources so that fossil fuels may still be marketed at whopping costs. Another applies the same kind of conspiratorial thinking to the arms industry. Yet another would have these neo-illuminati planning to stage an alien invasion with reverse-engineered craft so that the planet might be persuaded to create a single vast alliance—with the U.S. its leader, and the insiders leading the leaders.

Where there are too many motives, there's no motive at all—and it's desperately important that we figure out precisely who in our employ is lying to us, and why. Speculative "Tousle-Haired Rebel vs. Gray-Flannel Father" melodramas fished out of ancient Hollywood scripts and old George McGovern speeches neither bring clarity nor enhance credibility.

The quasi-political spin that concludes Greer's documentary greatly disturbs me. I've seen this movie too often, where imperialist generals and mad scientists coalesce behind Dick Cheney to take over the world. To be sure, I can believe—all too easily—that our government is behind the macabre livestock mutilations performed with laser technology that have filled back pages of local newspapers for decades now. The objective, supposedly, is to insinuate into the popular imagination the image of a pitiless extraterrestrial surgeon pulling critters apart as an entomologist might dismember a butterfly, thus bringing to simmer a highly "usable" panic in preparation for a later boil-over. Abductions of humans by this weird race of dissectionists (claims one of Greer's interviewees) have likewise been funded by some insolubly intricate disbursement of our tax dollars. I confess that I can visualize only too readily our unchecked civil servants acting like sociopathic adolescents in the chem lab. It's what they do. In contrast, such activities simply don't fit the profile of an ET, who would surely have mastered the rudiments of anatomy before traveling across the galaxy—or would at least have developed less intrusive ways of analyzing a new world's fauna.

Let us assume that government activity such as whatever's happening in Area 51 has indeed created technology capable of maneuvers that no professor of Physics at any public university would consider currently possible. We may even bypass the supporting claim that this technology has been parasitized from visiting aliens: let's say that the "black budget" has financed anti-gravity vehicles by assembling a new generation of Werner von Brauns. We know that these vehicles exist, because hundreds of residents in Phoenix (just to name one locale) saw them on March 13, 1997. These witnesses included then-Governor Fife Symington (who was visibly shaken before ridiculing the event a couple of days later on orders—as he would later disclose—from unnamed higher authorities). As I insisted in the essay above, a nation that can author such futuristic physics cannot possibly have left its power grid unsecured out of mere oversight: one might as easily imagine a nuclear sub sinking because the last sailor off the conning tower forgot to close the hatch. Likewise, whatever energy permits large craft to defy gravity and zoom away suddenly like a lightning bolt should more than suffice to crush ISIS and free up our grain for the dinner table rather than the gas tank. Yet our interests—yours and mine—are obviously not a high priority in the grand vision.

That being the case, I should like to know exactly what the vision is. Do they—our government, our Dark Elite—simply not care if we live or die, or is Step 8 of the Plan to remove most of us, deliberately and permanently?

This is a life-and-death question, both for us as individual American citizens and for what remains of our democratic republic. How does Dr. Greer advance our understanding at the climactic moment, however? What is he alleging of the Dark Elite, based on his vast experience of it? That Dick Cheney is really Darth Vader? That Hillary Clinton or Jimmy Kimmel could be the Theseus who guides us out of this lethal labyrinth? Does he think that alien captives were being held in the Twin Towers and had to be vaporized— or was 9/11 all about starting a war of diversion because Congress was about to undertake an investigation into UFO's? And, Dr. Greer... are you truly, sincerely maintaining that China is an innocent bystander being drawn into confrontation with us to lure our eye off the ball, and that the threat posed by Kim Jong Un is the latest act in a harmless sideshow?

There's a lot in Greer's presentation that needs to be seriously considered; but the hit-and-run montages of faces and events without any narrative comment, just when one hopes for a deeper explanation, is beyond confusing, beyond disingenuous: it's sordidly manipulative. One doesn't defeat disinformation with more disinformation. We require undramatized, factual testimony in these matters. Dribbling subliminal, politicized messages into the brief will only make fair-minded people run the other way in the uncomfortable feeling that they are being played, yet again.

I heartily second the motion of anyone who proposes that we sound a much louder alert about our covert government than about visiting aliens. The Extra-Terrestrials, if they exist, are plainly not as much a threat to freedom as our mendacious Big Brother. Yet infusing that cry of alarm with political ideology which vilifies one side of the aisle while excusing the other will not inspire greater vigilance. It will, on the contrary, induce more of the agenda-driven, messianic progressivism that has created a dangerous Dark Elite, to begin with. The fusion of immense power with dense secrecy always threatens a free society, no matter what motives guide the invisible engineers.